Asia and the Pacific

Issues of Educational Policy, Curriculum and Practice

Editors

Donald C. Wilson
Faculty of Education
The University of British Columbia, Canada

David L. Grossman
Consortium for Teaching Asia and the Pacific in the Schools
East-West Center, United States of America

Kerry J. Kennedy
Curriculum Development Centre
Canberra, Australia

The publication of this book was made possible by a grant from the Public Participation Program, Canadian International Development Agency, Government of Canada, and with institutional support from the Faculty of Education, The University of British Columbia, the East-West Center, Hawaii, and the Australian Government's Curriculum Development Centre, Canberra

Detselig Enterprises Limited
Calgary, Alberta, Canada

Asia and the Pacific

**Issues of Educational Policy,
Curriculum and Practice**

Editors

Donald C. Wilson
The University of British Columbia, Canada

David L. Grossman
East-West Center, United States of America

Kerry J. Kennedy
Curriculum Development Centre, Canberra, Australia

Canadian Cataloguing in Publication Data

Main entry under title:
Asia and the Pacific

Based on a conference held June 1988 in Vancouver, B.C.
ISBN 1-55059-008-1

1. Education – Asia – Congresses. 2. Education – Pacific Area – Congresses. 3. Asia – Study and teaching – Congresses. 4. Pacific Area – Study and teaching – Congresses.
I. Wilson, Donald C. (Donald Cathcart), 1938-
II. Grossman, David L. III. Kennedy, Kerry J.
LA1052.A85 1989   370'.95   C89-091643-8

© 1990 by Detselig Enterprises Ltd.
P.O. Box G 399
Calgary, Alberta, Canada T3A 2G3

All rights reserved. No part of this book may be reproduced in any form or by any means without permission in writing from the publisher.

Printed in Canada   SAN 115-0324   ISBN 1-55059-008-1

Contents

Preface *Jan L. Tucker,* Florida International
University, United States of America v

Introduction: Education and the Emergent Pacific.
Donald C. Wilson, University of British Columbia, Canada 1

Section One: Policy Issues

1 Canada and the Pacific Era. *B.T. Pflanz,* Department
of External Affairs, Canada 9

2 British Columbia Pacific Rim Initiatives. *John W. Crawford,*
British Columbia Ministry of Education, Canada 17

3 Education for Development and Beyond: A Korean Perspective.
Bom Mo Chung, Hallym University, Republic of Korea 21

4 Education and Social Change in the Philippines: A National
Illusion. *Sr. M. Bellarmine Bernas,* O.S.B., St.
Scholastica's College, The Philippines 33

5 The Changing Human Dimensions of the Pacific Rim: Education
for the Future. *Terry McGee,* University of British
Columbia, Canada 43

Commentary on Section One. *Kerry J. Kennedy,* Curriculum
Development Centre, Australia 57

Section Two: Curriculum Issues

6 Images and Interests in the Pacific: A Framework for
Teaching and Analysing International Affairs. *Steven L.
Lamy,* University of Southern California, United States of America . 61

7 Islands in Between: Some Social Studies Curriculum Development
Problems for Pacific Island Countries. *Konai Helu Thaman,*
University of the South Pacific, Fiji 77

8 Schooling and Citizenship in Malaysia. *Thunguvala
Marimuthu,* University of Malaya, Malaysia 91

9 Making Asian Women Visible in Curriculum. *Machiko Matsui,
Yuanxi Ma* and *Catherine Cornbleth,* State University
of New York at Buffalo, United States of America 99

10 Education for the Twenty-first Century: A Japanese Perspective.
Akio Nakajima, Kumon Institute of Education, Japan 109

11 The Evolution and Direction of South Korean Social Studies
Curriculum since 1945. *Se Ho Shin,* Korean Educational
Institute, Republic of Korea 115

12 Curriculum Reform and Teaching Materials Development in China. *Wu Yongxing* and *Wan Dalin,* Curriculum and Teaching Materials Research Institute, People's Republic of China 125

13 Exploring Pacific Issues through Small-group Cooperative Learning. *Don Northey,* University of British Columbia, Canada 131

14 Mapping Asia and the Pacific. *Angus M. Gunn,* University of British Columbia, Canada 139

Commentary on Section Two. *David L. Grossman,* East-West Center, United States of America 145

Section Three: Classroom Activities

15 Living in Japan. *Mary Hammond Bernson,* University of Washington, United States of America 149

16 Mental Maps of the Pacific. *David Dufty,* University of Sydney, Australia, and *Theodore Rodgers,* University of Hawaii, United States of America 153

17 The Yin and Yang of the Asia-Pacific Region. *Charles Hou,* Burnaby North Secondary School, Canada 157

18 Teaching about Pacific Island Microstates. *Margaret A. Laughlin* and *I. Grace Bell,* University of Wisconsin – Green Bay, United States of America 161

19 Brainstorming about China: An Introductory Activity. *Marilou Madden,* Douglas, Alaska, United States of America 169

20 What's in a Name? *Elaine Magnusson,* Seattle, Washington, United States of America 171

21 Comparing the Status of Women in Pacific Nations Today. *Gayle Y. Thieman,* Fairbanks North Star Borough School District, Alaska, United States of America 175

22 Visual Images of the Pacific Rim. *Virginia S. Wilson* and *James A. Little,* North Carolina School of Science and Mathematics, United States of America 179

23 Creating a Product for the Pacific Rim Market. *Tuckie Yirclott,* Stanford University, United States of America 183

24 There's Someone at the Door! *Susan Soux,* Canadian Red Cross Society, Canada 187

Commentary on Section Three. *Rick Beardsley,* British Columbia Teachers' Federation, Canada 193

Final Commentary 197

Preface

Jan L. Tucker
Florida International University, United States of America

The Pacific century has already begun. The top ten banks in the world are located in Japan. Japan's 1988 per capita gross national product of $23,358 was the highest in the world, surpassing the United States for the second straight year. Delegations from 154 of the world's nations paid homage to the late Emperor Hirohito, by far the largest global representation ever to attend the funeral of a head of state. The four Asian 'tigers' – South Korea, Taiwan, Hong Kong and Singapore – have led the world in economic growth rates, and are increasingly looked to as role models by other developing nations such as Mexico. The eyes of the entire world were riveted upon the student occupation of Tiananmen Square in Beijing during those fateful weeks in April and May of 1989. Mikhail Gorbachev has announced the intention of the Soviet Union to become a major player in the Pacific Rim.

A recent report of the RAND Corporation, located in Santa Monica, California, confirms that economic and military power will continue to shift to the Asia-Pacific region – and predicts that this change will have a dramatic global geopolitical effect. Already, the North American nations are feeling this impact. For example, the amount of trade the United States conducts with nations in Asia and the Pacific now exceeds its total trade with Western European nations? Wealth and population within the United States are being geographically redistributed to the West Coast. Investments in North American assets by buyers from Hong Kong and Japan have increased by leaps and bounds. The United States and Japan have agreed to jointly develop the FSX fighter plane. More than 150 colleges and universities in the United States are planning to establish a presence in Japan. These few examples vividly illustrate that the center of gravity of world affairs in North America is shifting towards Asia and the Pacific.

The issues of educational policy, curriculum and practice that arise from this major geopolitical shift are numerous, varied and complicated. From a perch in North America, where we have been accustomed to a Eurocentric approach to almost anything we can think of in the schools, the geopolitical shift to Asia and the Pacific challenges almost everything in view.

An initial list of questions from the standpoint of the United States might include: Can we come to grips with the fact that Japan, as the first non-Western nation to industrialize, is leading the world's economies into the twenty-first century? Can the West, where industrialization and democracy have been equated and where our early successes frequently have lulled us into a smug sense of superiority, overcome the colonial, patronizing and racist attitudes that often have prevailed in our relations with Asian nations. Do we have a choice? To what degree has the economic success story of Japan and other East Asian economies contributed to the worldwide decline of Communism as an ideology of the future, especially in the eyes of developing nations? What can history teach us? For example, Japan's crushing naval victory over Russia in 1904 led to the development of anti-colonial, nationalistic movements throughout Asia. Will its recent economic success have a similar influence upon its Asian neighbors?

The upcoming Pacific century will make such questions more important as we attempt to align our contradictory past into a workable congruence with our future. Of course, each Pacific nation has its own list of questions. How will Japan, for example, with its legacy of World War II aggression, convince its Asian neighbors of the beneficence of their new trading approach? Can China, with its 4,000-year tradition of authoritarian government and being the Middle Kingdom, provide the political freedoms necessary to participate fully in the economic benefits promised by the Pacific century? Can the Philippines and Indonesia develop sufficient national strength to participate as equal partners in the Pacific century? Can Australia and New Zealand remain as bastions of the Anglo-Saxon tradition and still be successful in the Pacific century? Will modern transportation and communication render obsolete the traditional functions of the Pacific Islands as economic and cultural exchange stations? And what is the role of Latin America in the Pacific century, and will the United States insist on being a power broker in this new relationship between Latin and Asian nations?

These questions and others will require us as educators to rethink the traditional questions of curriculum and context. Can social studies education which tends toward a static view of the world be able to deal with the dynamics of global change as reflected in the rapid emergence of Asia and the Pacific in world affairs? Business as usual is not adequate.

As the global village becomes a reality, educators in all nations need to ask, refine and redefine what they think are the major questions. Initially, the questions will be determined by our own national and cultural perspective. Through international dialogue we should gain a broader perspective and acquire a greater confidence that we are asking better questions. Guided by this cosmopolitan temperament, educational responses and solutions should evolve into higher standards of expectation and performance. Educators in all nations can begin to 'think globally while acting locally'. Persistence and patience are prior conditions for progress in this field. But beginnings are important. Thus, the regular series of international conferences on social studies education initiated by the United States National Council for the Social Studies and held first in Vancouver in 1988 on the Pacific Rim and continued in Miami in 1991 with a focus on the Caribbean – and this book on Asia and the Pacific, spawned by the Vancouver conference – are very important first steps.

Jan L. Tucker is Professor of Education and Director of the Global Awareness Program, Florida International University, Miami, Florida 33199, USA. He is a past president of the United States National Council for the Social Studies, was co-chair of the steering committee for the first international social studies conference held in Vancouver in June 1988, and is co-chair for the second international conference which will be held in Miami in June 1991.

Introduction

Education and the Emergent Pacific

Donald C. Wilson
The University of British Columbia, Canada

New areas of study always raise important questions for educators. A focus on the Pacific region is no exception. Its growth in global politics, its expanded trade links with the rest of the world, and the increased cultural influences through migration of Pacific peoples provide a context for new directions in social studies education. How educators interpret the emergent Pacific is a matter worthy of consideration.

This book addresses the emergence of the Pacific from the viewpoints of educators from ten Pacific nations. It is based on addresses and workshops from the first International Social Studies Conference with a focus on the Pacific Rim which was held in Vancouver in June 1988. It is intended to generate awareness of the diversity of concerns and respect for the efforts of educators and policy-makers addressing changes that speak to internationalization. The ensuing discussions encourage the reader to interpret the 'newness of the Pacific' in thoughtful ways.

The Immediate Concern

An immediate concern of educators is being knowledgeable about a new area of study. The Vancouver conference was an opportunity for over one thousand registrants to learn more about the significance of the Pacific and to exchange views with educators from sixteen nations. Presentations and workshops provided relevant knowledge about the history of Asian civilizations and their contemporary economic developments, sensitivity to cultural diversity, and awareness of social inequalities in an increasingly interdependent world. Becoming knowledgeable about the emergent Pacific encouraged educators to establish a position of professional commitment.

Introducing a new area of study into an established and already crowded curriculum always raises questions concerning the availability of resources, the development of teaching ideas and the organization of teaching topics. But other questions coinciding with teaching must also be considered. How will the change be infused into existing school courses? Is the area of study mandated or voluntary? And, most important, what will the students learn from studying the new topics?

Institutes, such as the Keizai Koho Center of Japan, and government programs, such as the Pacific Rim Education Initiatives of the British Columbia Ministry of Education and the Asian studies efforts of the Australian government, provide teachers with travel experience, language competencies and curriculum development opportunities to improve the teaching of Asia and the Pacific. In addition, publishers are preparing new textbooks, maps and visual materials for teaching the Pacific. These are important instructional contributions for today's students who, as citizens of the Pacific Century, will benefit from our efforts in teaching.

The Reflective Stance

Beyond the practical concerns of teaching a new area of study are questions addressing the nature of new school programs. Questions about conception and approach seek to clarify the emphasis and organization of content. Is the intention for teaching the Pacific to: introduce a new 'area study'?; provide a historical account of Asian civilizations?; establish a regional geography or a economics course?; foster the development of a global perspective?; or illuminate how Asia and the Pacific is a manifestation of internationalization? Moreover, should curriculum be organized according to social science disciplines, interdisciplinary themes, or contemporary issues? These are tough questions because answers are rooted in our beliefs and values about what is significant in the teaching of social studies. They also determine the lens through which a deeper understanding and appreciation of the Pacific is fostered.

Questions about the nature of curriculum are also questions of language. For the words selected to describe and define what is emphasized in classrooms underlie each approach to teaching. For example, using the term 'Pacific region' to refer to all countries that border the Pacific Ocean does not appear educationally appropriate. Nor does it seem useful to use 'Pacific Rim'. As an economic term it leaves out the cultural dimension of the Pacific, omits Latin America and irritates Pacific Island peoples. Those living in Vancouver, Hong Kong, Singapore, Los Angeles or Sydney, each located on the Rim, view the Pacific differently from students in Honolulu living in the Pacific Basin. And 'Pacific Rim' does not address the educational concerns of the relationship between the developed and developing countries of the Pacific. One's viewpoint of what is important often differs because of location, interest and sense of connection. Travel and study experiences quickly reveal how historical context, cultural values and economic trends create a different sense of what is educationally significant. Such differences can shape our thinking about what ought to constitute school programs.

Collectively, however, our efforts to forge various definitions of 'what to teach' highlights our desire as professionals to understand the diversity and interactive nature of the Pacific. The term 'Asia and the Pacific', as used in this book, is one way of defining what is significant to teach. It recognizes the need for professional awareness of the economics and cultural dynamics among the highly developed countries of North America, Australasia and the Asian countries that border the Pacific, with the developing nations of Asia and the Pacific Islands.

A Broader Outlook

The book also challenges those beliefs and values that guide our teaching of the Pacific. A reading of the book can raise three questions: What are the different concerns and perspectives of the Pacific? What are the underlying reasons for these differences? And how can such understanding give new direction to international education? Discussion of these questions can create a new agenda for social studies education – one that will provide new directions, new metaphors and new structures that will allow educators to help young people enter the next century.

Two issues stand out in dealing with development of a broader outlook. First, North Americans involved in curriculum development need to be aware of new liaisons between what is selected as important for teaching and the national goals and policies of one's respective country. Linking education to national policies is not a new position for Asian countries. Concerns for establishing social programs, ensuring ethnic stability and training for information-oriented society are all central to nation-building efforts in Asian countries.

In North America and Australia, national policies are increasingly promoted by business interests and increased immigration of Asian peoples. Many policy analysts contend that a new constituency of government officials is increasingly seeking directions to serve national interests in a rapidly changing world. Focusing on the Pacific highlights the global economic and political momentum increasingly termed 'internationalization'. What becomes significant about these rapid changes is that education is being considered as a tool for nations to ensure their place in an increasingly interdependent world. Such developments raise questions concerning who should be involved in deciding what schools are to teach and the implications of basing social studies programs on the pragmatic values of an increasingly information-oriented society. There is need for educators to be involved in these changes, to be aware of a changing political process and to be reflective of the significance of curricular decisions made by those outside education.

Second, a broader outlook calls into question many of the premises and values upon which international education is based. North Americans and Australians, with a predominantly 'Eurocentric' worldview, have a strong record of promoting greater understanding of other cultures and people. This tradition is important because it allows a sharing of experiences and exchange of ideas. These experiences now need to be placed in a world context that is changing who we are and how we relate with one another. Discussions at international meetings, as evident during the interactive sessions at the Vancouver conference, are one way to broaden horizons.

Yet, there is growing division among educators about how to address changing world conditions. Some North Americans interpret new world relationships as a need to look inward and establish a stronger sense of national identity. Others want to look outward to create a new sense of global interdependence. Although both arguments are convincing, social studies provides the opportunity to bring to classrooms a dynamic and not static world view of the lives of people. And it requires developing programs that are rooted in new ideas. Robert Reisch contends in his book, *Tales of a New America*, that new myths and metaphors are necessary to deal with the political reality of a rapidly changing global community.

Setting the Agenda

Often books that follow a conference become simply a record of its proceedings. Through selected articles this book captures the spirit of the one hundred papers and workshops given at the Vancouver conference. *Asia and the Pacific: Issues of Educational Policy, Curriculum and Practice* selectively focuses on the instructional and conceptual aspects of teaching as well as the political context for addressing change. It represents a statement about how the emergent Pacific is a representation of changing world conditions. Its purpose is to promote discussion that will encourage social studies educators to become involved in creating new agendas for educational change. First, articles in the book clarify changing political and economic conditions and resulting national policies. Second, articles focus on educational developments and issues shaping the development of school programs and suggest a pedagogy for addressing cultural and political diversity. Portraying the range of concerns and interests of educators, the book facilitates discussion about opportunities and possibilities for social education. Such future-orientated efforts acknowledge the importance of the political process in bringing about educational change.

The book is divided into three related sections. Each section addresses an aspect of education from the viewpoint of a number of educators from around the Rim. A commentary summarizes each section, while concluding comments highlight the significance of the book for new directions in education.

The first section addresses policy considerations for greater educational emphasis on Asia and the Pacific. The opening article illustrates the importance of the political, economic and cultural connections of Asia and the Pacific for Canada, a nation so dependent on world trade links. This viewpoint could also be that of an American or Australian government representative concerned with the dynamics of the Pacific. Two articles portray an Asian outlook on national educational policies based on the efforts and aspirations of the Philippines as a 'developing' country, and on the rapid growth of the newly industrialized economy of South Korea. The concluding article describes the characteristics of the vast Pacific and the human dimensions arising from internationalization.

The second section focuses on selected issues of curriculum and instruction associated with the emergent Pacific. Authors stress the need to have studies of Asia and the Pacific introduced into school programs. Their articles recognize the need to use different worldviews for analysing trade and security issues of the Pacific, portray efforts of Asian and Pacific Island countries to reform national curricula, and call for the study of Asian women to provide a more balanced view of the contemporary nature of Asia in North American school programs. Other authors advocate the pedagogical advantages of cooperative learning for the teaching of themes and issues associated with a globally linked society, and the need to develop a more accurate visual image of the Pacific through improved map projections.

Collectively the articles call for a rethinking of the educational significance of Asia and the Pacific. They reflect the need to see Asia and the Pacific through a new lens that captures the vitality of Asian countries as they shape the direction of a changing world.

The third section of the book features ten teaching activities from the many workshops given at the Vancouver conference. These have been selected to illustrate what is possible for teaching the dynamic and interdependent nature of Asia and the Pacific in elementary and secondary classrooms.

A First Step

Asia and the Pacific: Issues of Educational Policy, Curriculum and Practice is the first comprehensive book to identify educational issues associated with the emergence of the Pacific. Its conception grew from the experience of an international conference. Its preparation was a truly Trans-Pacific venture in which planning was conducted in Hawaii, the editorial work and disk preparation in Australia and the printing and distribution in Canada. Communication of such collaborative efforts was supported by facsimile, courier and E-mail.

The articles represent the collective efforts of educators from many parts of the Pacific addressing issues of national policy, curriculum development and classroom practice. They illustrate the possibilities for social studies teaching as the next century approaches. In this way they serve as a catalyst for educational change.

Donald C. Wilson teaches social studies and curriculum studies in the Faculty of Education, The University of British Columbia, Vancouver, Canada V6T 1Z5. He has been involved in various international curriculum projects and was conference program chair and co-chair of the steering committee for the first international social studies conference which was held in Vancouver in June 1988.

Section One
Policy Issues

1

Canada and the Pacific Era

B.T. Pflanz
Department of External Affairs, Canada

I have been asked to provide a Canadian perspective on developments in the Pacific, and their importance to, and impact on, Canada. The topic is broad, and I will necessarily have to confine my remarks to certain phenomena across the Pacific which have become the focus in recent years of much of the world's attention, including our own. There is no doubt whatever that Pacific Rim affairs have assumed greater and greater importance to us, as they have to most nations.

Let me begin with a thumbnail sketch of our own social history. From our beginnings we have been profoundly affected by migration, as have all in the Americas. Our native peoples came, thousands of years ago, over the bridge from Asia. In more recent times, and until the 1970s, the population of Canada was derived from our small natural growth, augmented by immigration, primarily from the countries of Europe. Having been settled in colonial times by people from England and France, we quite naturally developed a trans-Atlantic focus, which was strengthened during this century with our active involvement in the European theatres during World Wars I and II. Apart from the mature trading relationship which evolved with the United States, the European markets were the prime targets for our exports, and at the same time the prime source of our immigrants.

On the political and security fronts, we maintained constitutional links with the British Crown until the beginning of this decade, and we are a member of the Western alliance. During the 120 years of Canada's existence as a nation, I believe I can safely say that Canadians from St John's, Newfoundland, to Victoria on Vancouver Island have looked eastward to the British Isles and Europe from where their forebears had come.

While we did receive immigrants from China and Japan and other nations of Asia, their numbers were not significant during our first century of nationhood. In fact we actively discriminated against Asian immigrants in our immigration policy until after World War II. Had we had the ability to divine the future, and been less narrow in our world view, we may have taken a different course and created a larger population base with strong family and cultural links with Asia. It would have served us well in meeting the twenty-first century.

We are now faced with a phenomenon for which not only Canada but also other Western nations were ill-prepared: the rapid rise towards ascendancy of the Asia-Pacific region.

For Western countries, including Canada, the Asia-Pacific region had for centuries been widely considered as a great enigma: as beyond comprehension, as utterly fascinating, but ultimately unimportant. The peoples of the region were described as 'inscrutable' and with terms of derision based on ignorance and tinged with a little fear. Eurocentrism had a firm hold on our minds, typified by the British author Rudyard Kipling who stated that 'East is East, and West is West, and never the twain shall meet'. The wisdom of Kipling's day has been overturned. East *has* met West, and progressively on its own terms, especially in the last decade.

The shape of the next century has in small part been illuminated in a few demographic and economic projections. What is it the futurists tell us?

Today 58 percent of the world's population lives in Asia.

By the year 2000, 70 percent of all humanity will live there.

There will then be four billion Asians or almost as many people as currently live on this planet.

By the year 2000 Asia will produce 50 percent of the world's goods and services.

All the major Asia-Pacific countries will have higher economic growth rates than all OECD member countries for the next 20 years.

Today five of the top fifteen exporting countries in the world are in Asia: Japan, China, Korea, Taiwan and Hong Kong. Only Japan made that list in the 1970s.

By the year 2000 the economies of Asia will be more diversified than those of Europe and the USA.

Most dominant, by far, in Asia will be Japan.

Japan has become the largest source of capital in the world, greater even than the Middle East at the height of the oil crisis. In five years, Japan has become the greatest creditor country in the world, replacing the USA, now the largest debtor. The top twenty-one financial institutions in the world are *all* Japanese. By 2000 overseas investment holdings by Japanese will exceed one trillion US dollars. The yen will increasingly replace the dollar in international trading.

Japan is now the largest source of aid to the third world, 20 percent higher than that of the second donor, the United States, and just 20 years ago, Japan was the second largest borrower from the World Bank.

By 2000 Japan will be a recognized world leader in process technology and one of the world's largest investors in pure research.

By 2000, in the face of protectionism in the Western world, Asia will be more economically integrated. Japan, India and China will be the leading nations.

By 2000, China will increase its trade at least tenfold. By 2000, India will have another 250 million in its middle class – another USA in less than 20 years. Japan, Hong Kong, Taiwan and Korea each have about 40 percent of their exports going to the USA, and each is intent on reducing this dependence. The objective is to increase sales to other Asian countries.

The newly industrialized countries of Asia, the so-called NICs, are expanding their manufacturing with the assistance of the higher yen and Japanese investment, moving into the production of such items as automobiles, consumer electronics and computers. As Japan moves on to higher levels of technology, the NICs will occupy the vacated areas, creating and developing their own products and increasingly competing with their mentor, Japan.

This regional economic drama has been characterized by mutually reinforcing growth, along with a growth in regional confidence and a developing appreciation of a common interest. Hard work and competitiveness, emphasizing long-term gain – traditional Asian values – are the rules of the game, the only game in town, during what some observers are calling the Pacific Era or the Pacific Century.

What does this all mean for Canada?

I will quote the words of our Secretary of State for External Affairs, who in November 1986 stated here in Vancouver that, 'We recognize, as national policy, that our future prosperity is tied to the Pacific'.

Canada has more economic interests in Asia than any member of NATO or any of the Western countries, except the USA. Our trade with Asia and the Pacific exceeds that with Europe. In 1987, countries of Asia and the Pacific purchased 11 percent of our exports, as against 9 percent by Europe.

Japan is Canada's second largest trading partner after the USA – larger than the UK, France and West Germany combined. Three-quarters of our exports to Japan come from Western Canada. Japanese portfolio investment in Canada exceeds $35 billion. Canadians are increasingly dependent upon Japanese companies for employment; our exchange rate and interest rates are influenced by capital flows to and from Japan.

Developing countries in Asia and the Pacific are receiving the largest percentage of Canada's bilateral aid: over 40 percent of the total. A large and rapidly growing share of this aid is for human resource development, especially in our programs with China, the ASEAN countries and the countries of the South Pacific.

Canada, like all countries, derives growth and prosperity from its people and the results of their effort. The philosophy of growth, inherent in our system, includes growth in our population base. We have a large absorptive capacity for growth in human capital which is carefully managed, through our immigration program. Asia-Pacific is now the *major* source of new Canadians. Currently nearly 50 percent of our immigration comes from the region. And according to trends which have developed over the past decade, this proportion will increase.

The established pattern for many new arrivals, after they have settled and become established, is to sponsor family members to join them in Canada. There is, therefore, the capacity to experience exponential growth. However, our levels of immigration at any given time are designed to reflect our ability, at that same time, to ensure that those who are admitted have the best opportunities to obtain work and become productive Canadians.

Already the cultural mosaic here has been altered with the community of over 100,000 who have come to Canada from Indo-China since 1975. Many of their youth are now marrying and producing a new generation of Canadians with roots in Vietnam, Laos and Kampuchea – similarly with the communities of people who have come from China, Hong Kong, the Philippines, India, Korea, and so on. We are rapidly increasing the proportion of our population which will influence the orientation of Canadian culture and society in a way not dissimilar to the influence of European civilization in the past. The basis for strengthening our human and cultural ties with Asia is being firmly established.

The area in which Canada needs to make the greatest strides in its relations with the Asia-Pacific region is that which may be generally described as human contact. By this I mean the broad range of activities which bring people together – international students, tourism, cultural relations, visits at all levels, academic exchanges, media reporting and relations, international meetings and conferences, such as this one, and bilateral associations like the Friends of Thailand Society just established here in Vancouver to build personal, professional and social networks between Canada and Thailand.

The flagship of our new focus is the Asia Pacific Foundation located here in Vancouver. The Foundation, created four years ago this month, has a fourfold mandate – to develop Canadian interest *vis-a-vis* the region in cultural, academic, business and public affairs, with the fundamental objective of nourishing a greater sense of mutual awareness and understanding between Canada and Asia-Pacific. I hope you will have the opportunity of meeting members of the Foundation participating in this Conference. I will place you in their capable hands for further elaboration of their work.

I do wish, however, to expand for a moment on some specific aspects of what I called 'human contacts'. Let me just note in passing that Canada now receives over 300,000 tourists annually from Japan, an increase of 30 percent over each of the two preceding years. Canadians also, in greater numbers, are choosing the countries of East and Southeast Asia and the South Pacific as vacation travel destinations.

But of even greater significance is the development of numerous student exchanges which create a cross-cultural bonding of more lasting value on both sides. We now have about 1,200 Canadian students seriously studying Japanese, and other Asian language teaching is beginning to take hold, although I will admit, however, that we have some way to go to match the intensity with which Australia is pursuing Asian language training.

Also, in the field of education, a Canadian university, Concordia in Montreal, will break new ground by being the first university in the Western world to establish an extension of its campus in the People's Republic of China. This landmark event is the result of a five-year agreement signed in 1987 between Concordia and the Nanjing Institute of Technology.

In order to attract more students from Southeast Asia to Canada we will soon open the doors of an educational counselling service to be located in the region. Concurrently, the Canadian International Development Agency is looking into increasing and streamlining its scholarship program within the framework of existing agreements to assist in human resource development in selected Asia-Pacific countries.

Canada is taking further initiatives in the field of cultural relations. We are presently preparing the way for bilateral arrangements with two countries which should, over time, greatly add to the exposure of Canadian cultural expression in Asia and the Pacific. Earlier this year Radio Canada International initiated programming transmitted to Asia.

My own Department has, during the last few years, devoted a larger piece of the financial pie to supporting Canadian cultural activity in the region. Included in this spending are Canadian studies programs, for Pacific Rim academics, designed to increase knowledge and understanding of Canada.

You may be interested to know that academics from Pacific Rim universities are funded to spend a month or so in Canada to gather information and materials so they can develop and teach a new course about Canada when they return to their own country or to publish an article about Canada in their own language.

I would be remiss if I did not mention the thirteen-week series called *Pacific Encounters*, produced by the Canadian Broadcasting Corporation. This program is being heard coast to coast at the present time on Sunday mornings, and is designed to give Canadians a glimpse of Asia. I can tell you from personal experience that it is original, exciting and provocative.

The CBC aims to increase the Asia-Pacific content of its national and local programming. Next week its local program directors from throughout Canada will meet in Toronto and discuss how they can help prepare Canadians for their changing country and their country's changing role in a changing world.

While I have spoken mainly of initiatives undertaken by the Federal Government and its agencies, it is important to give equal prominence to the efforts of our provinces in building bridges across the Pacific. Over the last decade a number of Canadian provinces have been engaged in opening their own offices in Asian capitals, not to compete with Canada's international objectives but rather to complement and reinforce them.

There is bilateral activity pursued at the municipal level with 'twinning' and 'sister city' arrangements struck between urban centres. And similarly between schools, and even school classes.

I wish to make special mention of a program called the Pacific Rim Education Initiatives, being undertaken by the Ministry of Education, Province of British Columbia – your provincial hosts. Because of its location, BC, as it is popularly known, is in the forefront of Canadian provinces with a keen eye towards our Pacific neighbors.

The Education Initiatives program is multi-dimensional in nature:

revision of the school curriculum to expand the study of Asia-Pacific countries;

a student exchange program funded at $500,000 in 1988 and the same amount in 1989;

an initiative fund to encourage innovative projects;

a scholarship fund to enable 10 BC students annually to study in one of nine Asian countries;

teacher study tours of Pacific Rim countries, funded at $1 million annually in 1988 and 1989;

and other elements about which you will undoubtedly hear during the course of this conference.

The Federal Government has made a strong commitment to the Asia-Pacific region. This has been reflected in policy statements, Prime Ministerial visits and ministerial travel, and through a redirection of our efforts towards the Pacific. More resources have been transferred to support our initiatives in the region. Country strategies have been developed for Japan, China, and India; trade and investment action for Korea, Hong Kong and ASEAN have been put in place.

We will need to build new avenues for cooperation in science and technology.

We will need to engage in political dialogue with a broad cross-section of groups in the region:

to promote the peace and stability needed for development and growth; and

to ensure that Asians take into account Canadian views, capabilities and interests.

All Canadians will need to increase their awareness and understanding of Asia if we are to be part of the Pacific Century.

We will need to tap all the resources at our disposal, including the expertise of this assembled group.

Ladies and Gentlemen, these are some of the ways that Canada is positioning itself for the Pacific Era. It is for us an exciting and rewarding process, as all learning and development should be. It is my *personal* pleasure to have been a witness to it through my association with the Canadian Foreign Service and the three assignments I have enjoyed in Tokyo, Seoul and Manila. As a representative of the public sector in Canada I can assure you that we are vigorously pursuing the policies of the government to maximize our understanding of, and relations with, the Asia-Pacific region.

In the Department of External Affairs we are continually developing a core of enthusiastic specialists in Pacific affairs. In the private sector we see the Pacific challenge being taken up country wide. In your role as educators, you too have the same challenge before you – to prepare our youth for the Pacific Century.

To the Conference participants who have come from abroad – I urge you to take back the message that Canada and Canadians want to know you and your countries just as we wish you to know us. I am confident in our future together which may well be called, in years to come, the era of the Great Pacific community.

Beno T. Pflanz is the Director, Asia and Pacific Programs Division, Department of External Affairs, Ottawa, Canada. This paper was the opening address at the International Conference on Social Studies – Focus on the Pacific Rim, held at the University of British Columbia in June 1988.

2

British Columbia Pacific Rim Initiatives

John W. Crawford
British Columbia Ministry of Education, Canada

In 1987 the Province of British Columbia introduced a number of educational initiatives designed to address the growing importance of the Asia-Pacific region. The decision to implement these initiatives was based upon the trends articulated by Mr. Pflanz in the preceding article.

In the fall of 1987, the British Columbia Government announced a major educational initiative, 'designed to prepare BC citizens for trade and cultural opportunities with the Pacific Rim'. In a news release education was identified as critical: 'Our ability to compete in Pacific Rim trade will demand a growing number of graduates from our schools who understand and appreciate the language and cultures of that area of the world'.

The Minister of Education for British Columbia (the Hon. Anthony Brummet) describes the Pacific Rim education initiatives as a 'bold new educational step for British Columbia, a step designed to broaden our view of Asia-Pacific nations, provide new opportunities and ensure that our students are competitive in a changing world. Asia-Pacific education is rooted very much in the present and at the same time is moving resolutely towards the future of our economic and cultural life. These are the elements of a vibrant education system that will prepare our young people for the 21st century'.

To this end the Ministry of Education introduced thirteen short-, mid- and long-term initiatives.

Four immediate projects were started in 1987. A Pacific Rim Initiatives Fund was established to encourage schools to develop innovative projects in languages, cultural awareness, curriculum enhancement and teacher in-service training. For example, one project has two British Columbia high schools working cooperatively to produce audio, video and photo 'postcards' about their community which they will then send to selected schools in Japan, Hong Kong and Thailand. Over the two-year operational period of this early Pacific Rim initiative, the fund distributed a total of $875,000 Canadian to schools throughout the province.

Another of the immediate projects was the establishment of a Pacific Rim Scholarship Program. Initially 10 scholarships were provided for grade 12 graduates to spend one year of study in an Asia-Pacific country. Japan, China, Thailand and Singapore were selected as the 1988 host countries. In 1989-90 the number of scholarships will increase to 19.

A Student Exchange Program and Teacher Study Tour Program completed the early initiatives. Over $1 million Canadian was invested in student travel over the first two years. Annual funding has been established for the Student Exchange Program and will be maintained at $1 million Canadian per year. Approximately 300 teachers took advantage of the Teacher Study Tour Program in the summer of 1988. Glenn Wall, Assistant Deputy Minister of Education (Policy, Planning and Independent Education) for British Columbia and the official responsible for the Pacific Rim Initiatives Program, commented on the first year's Teacher Study Program:

> This Summer's Teacher Study Programs saw teachers travelling to every Pacific Rim country, establishing new sister school 'twins', networking connections, homestays, exchanges, and schools visits from elementary to university levels. A variety of projects were reported, covering most of the curriculum areas of history, geography, science, ESL, consumer education, art, textiles, cooking, business education and sports.

Funding for teacher travel has been increased to a total of $1 million Canadian annually.

The Ministry of Education has compiled the details of the short-term initiatives on a computerized database. Information on teacher travel is organized by country/city/project title/applicable grade levels/subject areas/type of resource/travel agency analysis. The student travel base is simpler, organized by country/city/experiences/homestays/agency. The database also includes twinning profiles of British Columbia schools and schools of Pacific Rim countries wishing to establish regular and long-term relationships.

The mid-term initiatives include the expansion of Asia-Pacific studies in British Columbia schools in several curriculum areas. Business Education is being revised with a greater emphasis on the Asia-Pacific region. Teaching 'modules' are being produced which constitute complete teaching packages. They include detailed lesson plans and are supplemented with written case studies and selected video tapes on appropriate Pacific Rim countries. The first module on cross-culture communications prepares students for the differences encountered during face-to-face interaction with Asians.

The core British Columbia Social Studies curriculum in grades 4 to 11 is being used as the basis for improved availability of resources that focus on the Pacific Rim. Teacher resource books are being produced which include detailed lessons on selected Pacific Rim topics already in the prescribed Social Studies curriculum. These books will be supplemented with background information on Pacific Rim countries, custom-designed wall maps and atlases, and teacher-orientation videos.

A completely revised economics course for grade 12 students is being prepared, again with a focus on the Pacific Rim. Although the course is grounded in traditional micro and macro economic theory, case studies and examples to explain course content are drawn from Pacific Rim countries.

The final two mid-term initiatives concentrate on Asian languages training. A Teacher Training Language Program provides practising and new teachers with summer school training in Asia-Pacific languages, and Japanese and Mandarin will be expanded in British Columbia schools. Second-language student enrolment projections in British Columbia schools are increasing well beyond the original expectation of 20 percent annual growth.

Long-term initiatives tend to be logical extensions of those initiatives already introduced. As detailed, Pacific Rim student scholarships, student travel and teacher travel will be maintained on an annual basis. Curriculum development will expand Pacific Rim content into language arts, fine arts, and senior elective courses by the early 1990s. Eventually, students throughout British Columbia may have the option of taking intensive second-language courses in Asia-Pacific languages.

Several new initiatives are on the drawing board. British Columbia is investigating the possibility of accrediting existing international schools in Hong Kong, Malaysia, Thailand and Brunei Darussalam to teach the British Columbia curriculum with British Columbia teachers on one- or two-year assignments. International scholarships will provide the opportunity for 10 British Columbia secondary students to attend one of these British Columbia-accredited international schools.

These initiatives are extensive, representing short- and long-term planning and consequently are not without difficulties. One of the first issues addressed was the definition of the term 'Pacific Rim'. All countries with a Pacific coast could be designated as Pacific Rim nations but for the purposes of curriculum development the region was divided into four major geographic regions: Asia-Pacific (East Central Asia), Southeast Asia, other Pacific, the United States and Latin America (Coastal Pacific). These regions include many nations and so a two-tier priority system was established under each region. Countries of first priority are those within each region with which Canada and British Columbia have the strongest historic ties, and existing or potential economic ties. Countries in the second tier are those with which ties are not so strong and therefore could be dealt with at a later date.

As the initiatives are implemented new concerns arise. Curriculum overload is a worry of classroom teachers. The degree of new knowledge required by the teaching profession makes implementation of new curriculum materials a major task. Despite these concerns the Pacific Rim Educational Initiatives introduced by the Ministry of Education for the Province of British Columbia are an endorsement of the importance of the Pacific region. They represent positive action in fulfilling Mr Pflanz's call for progress in expanding 'human contact' with the Asia-Pacific region. As Mr Wall from the Ministry of Education concludes, 'We are looking forward to a long-term commitment, expansion and deepening of Pacific Rim activities as this program moves forward'. Ultimately, the next generation of British Columbians should have a clear understanding of the economic, social and political importance of the Pacific

Rim region.

References

Brummet, A. (1987). *Pacific Rim Education Initiatives*. British Columbia Ministry of Education.

Wall, G. (1988, December). *Pacific Rim Education Initiatives update*. British Columbia Ministry of Education. 1-2.

John W. Crawford is Coordinator – Pacific Rim Education Initiatives, Curriculum Development Branch, Ministry of Education, Province of British Columbia, Victoria, BC, Canada V8V 2M4.

3

Education for Development and Beyond: A Korean Perspective

Bom Mo Chung
Hallym University, Republic of South Korea

The Republic of Korea, till thirty years ago, was an underdeveloped country, economically at least, characterized by historical mass poverty with a per capita GNP of less than $5. It now ranks as one of the 'newly industrialized countries', and the per capita GNP is expected to shoot up to $4,000 by the end of 1988. This is a phenomenal growth.

It is generally asserted that during the period of a development spurt, there are clashes between the traditional and development mentalities and the need for a gradual displacement of the former by the latter. The traditional mentalities are represented by fatalism, conservatism, mysticism, particularism, etc., whereas the development mentalities are characterized by a sense of efficacy and renovation, achievement motivation, entrepreneurship, rationalism, universalism, etc.

'Development education', namely education geared towards the need for national development, which, though often holistically defined, in practice means mostly economic development, is called upon, among other things, to aid in the task of such reorientation from the traditional negativistic and passivistic to the needed positivistic and activistic mentalities.

However, when a country reaches a stage of development where it has solved the problem of basic poverty, nationally and individually, like South Korea around the year 1980 when its per capita GNP hit around $2,000, voices become gradually louder in all sectors of society, clamoring for reorientation. It is as if a person whose imminent hunger has been fed now comes to see the world in a broader perspective and to realize that the continuing adherence to past development orientations would not quite serve either the pursuit of the quality of life or the needs for future development. The necessary reorientation in this turn is from development mentalities to what may be called 'post-development mentalities'. To the extent that this is true, education at this juncture also needs reorientation. Five dimensions of such reorientation are discussed below.

From Economism to Holism

The will to get rich 'first of all', the preoccupation with the economic wealth and means, was quite an understandable prime motive in the early stage of South Korean development. Historical mass poverty is decidedly a human woe and a social ill to get over and done with. Furthermore, as many theorists argue, many underdeveloped countries suffer, for some reason, from the very lack of such will and motives for wealth. Therefore, it was a necessary preoccupation that sustained the long struggle for economic growth. People had to come to believe, as a phrase in a popular Korean song says, that 'to get rich or poor is not a matter of fate after all'.

But whether such one-sided preoccupation with the economic – economism – can still serve as a 'profitable' motive has come to be questioned on two grounds.

On one ground, there is a realization that unilateral economism does not quite promise the quality of life one has aspired to. Rather it has led us to environmental pollution, both physical and mental. The dictum of Schumacher, that the zeal of development has 'built a system of production that ravishes nature and a type of society that mutilates man', now regretfully applies to the South Korean scene too. Forcibly people realize that better life is not to breathe polluted air and drink polluted water, nor is it to live in a society infested with increasing crimes, juvenile delinquency, divorce, deepening gaps between social groups, and vacuum of values that have been brought upon us by the social climate of one-sided economic avarice.

People have also come to understand, with or without the teachings of saints and sages, that the good life lies somewhere beyond material gains, in certain political, social and cultural conditions in addition to the economic – that is, in certain 'holistic conditions' – and also that certain political, social and cultural aspirations cannot be quelched by material abundance. The desire for political participation, for example, cannot be subdued but rather further abetted by the growing GNP, which, sadly, many political leaders do not recognize. Such a realization calls for a holistic approach to social and personal affairs.

On the other ground, the nature of high-technology information society forces us to be holistic rather than narrowly economic if we want to develop further economically. If the biggest asset in the 'first wave' *agricultural* society was land and the greatest asset in the 'second wave' *industrial* society was capital, the strongest asset in the 'third wave' *information* society is, it is often said, knowledge, the brain. We can include in the work of the brain not only intellectual, but also artistic and ethical achievements.

One ton of a aluminum sells at $3,000 in the form of window sash, and it sells at one million dollars in the form of a jet airliner. The difference comes from the different intellectual achievement applied. A silk scarf in one country sells at $10 and a similar silk scarf sells at $100 or $200 in another country. The difference comes from the different artistic designs and tastes involved. A pair of sports shoes of a company sells at $10, and the same quality pair sells at $50 under another company brand. The difference comes from the occupational ethics, such as honesty and dependability, another company has built over the years. We are entering a world where more and more the investment in intellectual, artistic and ethical enterprises pays off the best, which again means a need for a holistic approach.

There are many educational implications of the general social reorientation from economic centeredness to the holistic approach to social and personal affairs. A few points are discussed below.

The ideas and the practices of 'manpower' education may have to be replaced once again by a more holistic approach. The economic slant in education took the form of manpower education, meaning that the purpose of education was to train the manpower forecasted as needed in speculated future industries. To begin with, though the claims of manpower education were very cogent, the actual methods for manpower forecast were never precise enough for us to rely comfortably upon them in educational planning. Furthermore, as some theorists argue, we do not yet know precisely beyond common sense what human traits we foster in education really contribute to economic productivity – knowledge, skills, creativity, industry, honesty, sense of efficacy, perseverance, ... or most probably some concert of these?

We may propose a thesis that as we enter deeper and further into a high-technology information society, the idea of manpower with specific sets of traits gradually merges into a concept of a more richly developed person, in which the general intellectual, artistic and ethical traits play more and more important roles.

This signifies three things among others. First, it means that investment in education in general becomes more and more crucial in the future, as is evidenced by the recent 'brain wars' and 'education wars' among the nations. A nation has to get ready for ever-increasing needs for educational investment. Secondly, it means going back to the old notion of the 'whole person', the holistic conception of man in education, a renovated interest in the well-rounded personality. Thirdly, it means again going back to the educational adage of 'going beyond rote memory'. More and more, the future development in the high-tech and information society depends on critical thinking, creativity and renovation. Educators are called upon to make more than a lip-service to education for the whole person and to education for higher mental processes.

From Short-term to Long-term Perspectives

Secondly, it is also understandable that, at the initial stage of development, there is a will not only to get rich as soon as possible but to get rich as quickly as possible. Mass poverty with a long history is so abhorrent that the sooner we get rid of it the better. Thus a short-sighted philosophy of 'as quickly as possible' has come to sway our way of thinking and doing. We prided ourselves on 10, 12, 14 percent of annual GNP growth, regardless of whether or not it created fragility in the economic structure itself.

Everything had to be done quickly. Construction of buildings, highways and subways had to be done much more quickly than planned, often with a result that these structures soon began to leak and erode. One also had to get recognition and promotion quickly in the bureaucratic ladder of the company, often at the sacrifice of one's own health, of one's relations with colleagues, and even of long-term interests of the company itself.

No doubt there is a virtue in the philosophy of 'the sooner the better' in that it makes one mobilize one's full capacity to get the work done quickly. But its excess brews a really destructive psychology in many respects. It encourages impetuosity and rashness in thinking. It relates itself to coarseness and crudeness in products. It calls for waste of resources and capricious change of policies. It even encourages deception, fraudulence and crimes that act on the spur of the moment.

There are things that can be hurried and there are things that cannot be hurried. Not to hurry things that could be hurried is laziness. But to hurry things that should not be hurried is rashness. Cementing needs time for hardening. Wine needs time for fermentation. Trees need thirty to fifty years to become timber. Man needs twenty to thirty years to become grown up. In such cases, you simply have to *'Eile mit Weile'*, or else 'haste with waste'.

Many things are causally or correlationally interrelated in a temporal as well as a spatial network. To move one is also to move others in the network. A Hindu concept, *karma*, which means historical causation between events that may be years, decades or centuries apart, should be a lesson here, If we realize that what we do now casts a long light or a shadow to the next decade or even to the ensuing centuries, we certainly cannot act rashly.

What we need is a long-term perspective in which we plant seedlings now in order to let our children and grandchildren have beautiful fifty-year-old timber, even if we ourselves would not have the fortune and the glory; just as a French winemaker who barrels fermented wine and puts a label on one barrel 'To be opened 100 years later' and on another 'To be opened 200 years later'.

In respect to education, we have to come to a fuller realization of 'the principle of time-lag' – that the social effect of education now can only be felt twenty to thirty years later. The social effect of elementary education now can be felt only when children become adults and will continue to be felt for fifty to sixty years more, good or bad, until they die.

This clearly self-evident fact is very often forgotten and many politicians and policy-makers inadvertently try to exploit education for contemporary and short-term political, economic and social purposes. This is foolish. Education neither remains passively exploited nor unhurt without harmful side-effects. It is also foolish if one does not feel the urgency of educational investment right now because of the far-off distance between education today and its social effect tomorrow. Literally, the proper stage of education is not society but history. We can even say that education does not have social value but only historical value. To educate is to build historical *karma* rather than to exploit socially.

If we take a long-term perspective, we try to meet various social changes and demands not only through a 'variable' mode but also through a 'constant' mode. That is, we try to meet different diseases now and then with different therapeutic measures, but we also try to meet all possible onslaughts of varied diseases by continuously building a 'constant' called health. Adjustment to changes is necessary, but building what is inherently necessary is also essential. In arithmetic, one may change the use of computing aids from abacuses to computers. But improvement in teaching for thinking, imagination and creativity is a constant need. The best and surest measure to meet the vicissitudes of social changes may as well be unchanging effort to build essential constants.

From Instrumental to Intrinsic Values

Long harassed by poverty, one had to get out of poverty not only as soon as possible but also 'by any means' and 'at any cost'.

Therefore, in the process of economic development, only economic wealth was the end and everything else became means to that end. Thus education, science, administration, politics, art, morality and even religion were now looked upon as means and instruments to economic development. Education was more a matter of 'manpower' education than 'whole-person' education. Concepts like development politics, development administration, development ethics and development value-orientations came to be freely in vogue. It was even argued that the tenets of some religion are 'developmental', while those of some other religion are 'un-developmental'.

Such an instrumental way of thinking gets so widely spread that love, friendship and filial devotion also come to be looked upon as means to wealth and success, and gets further extended as to see man, others and oneself too as mere means, at which point the value system stands completely upside down. Surely the joys, the tastes, the meanings and the values of living reside in the very acts of loving, mingling, serving, caring, learning, knowing, singing and playing – yet wealth was to be a means to these acts.

Every thing or act has both instrumental or extrinsic value and expressive or intrinsic value. Eating food gives you strength to work but eating itself is a joy. Playing tennis is instrumental to building health and to resolving stress, but it is also in itself fun. Studying mathematics will let you pass the entrance examination to a prestigious university, but it is in itself interesting, fascinating, profoundly elegant. To a real entrepreneur, so it is said, the beauty of an enterprise lies not necessarily in the wealth it brings but more in the process of total involvement and in the exhilaration of success itself. We have to see both in every thing and act not only its ensuing extrinsic value but also its current intrinsic value. But we have tended so far in a zeal for development to see everything one-sidedly in terms of its instrumental value.

Suppose a high school student studies mathematics solely because of a college entrance examination, with no interest and insight at all into mathematics' elegance? His life at the moment lacks in 'current' meanings and intrinsic values. At the moment he only has postponed 'moratory' values which are not in the present scene of life. In college, if he again sees no current value in college study itself but only its moratory instrumental value for a job, he would find current life intrinsically meaningless. The often mentioned ailment in modern society of meaninglessness, valuelessness, aimlessness may really have its roots in modern man's habit of looking for extrinsic values only.

Compare our student with another high school student who studies mathematics because it is intrinsically fascinating, delightfully enchanting, ecstatically captivating. Who then lives with fuller meaning? Who is 'happier'? And who would become a greater mathematician after all? The answers are obvious.

If we are one-sidedly intent on achieving some end and see all others merely as means, we would not come to attain that end itself easily either. Some years ago, a secretary from the Nobel Prize Office came to Korea and held an interview. He said, 'The Republic of Korea has achieved miraculous economic achievement. Koreans may soon like to get a Nobel prize in science too. But the quickest way to a Nobel prize is to forget about the Nobel prize entirely and just produce many scientists who are fascinated and enchanted by science'. Truth welcomes those who come to it with childlike innocence and curiosity rather than those who look for it with a calculation of use.

Unethicalness that would easily result from extreme instrumentalism is at once clear in its insistence on 'by any means' and 'at any cost'. To love and to be a friend with an external end is of course loathsome. To make money through unethical means is abhorrent. To be kind to make a sale is deceptive.

The first educational significance of the reorientation of values from the instrumental to the intrinsic is that education now has to make students realize and appreciate intrinsic tastes, charms, interests, meanings and values in a variety of life and cultural activities, and have occasions to immerse and commit themselves in them, be it mathematics or physics, literature or social studies, arts or sports. Before these become 'for the purpose of' entrance to college, promotion of science or national development and glory, they should be seen by students as fascinating human and cultural acts in themselves.

The second significance is that the acts of educating and of learning themselves have intrinsic value regardless of their assumed ends and uses. Perhaps we have to stop the unilateral thinking that education, and therefore learning too, is 'for' something else – for national development, for cultural transmission and renovation, for national integration or for personal advancement, and so forth.

We know that some educational philosophers like John Dewey and R. S.

Peters in effect asserted that education does not need external aims because education of man itself has inherent values. We should take this assertion as a warning against the occasional practice of wronging education for some political, economic or social ends. We should also take it as a plea to see intrinsic values and joys in teaching and learning itself. What we need is the spirit of Confucius, the famous Chinese sage, who, when he opened the first sentence of his famous *Analects*, perhaps the most influential classic in Sino-culture, said, 'Is it not delightful to learn and to relearn at times?'. He also said in his *Analects*, 'Learn without being satiated and teach others without being wearied'. It is also the ecstasy of Archimedes when he shouted '*Eureka!*', that is, 'I've found it!', at his sudden insight into the principle of buoyancy.

From Centralization to Decentralization

The fourth necessary dimension of social redirection is from centralization to decentralization.

Historical mass poverty is like an enemy camp that is extremely hard to attack and conquer. In order to drive it out, you need to attack it with a concentrated effort of economic power, political power, manpower and cultural power, all concerted and ordered in a wartime military fashion. People long molested by poverty also feel that they could relinquish their rights to freedom and autonomy for some time if it is necessary to drive poverty out. The time for development, some theorists have even argued, calls for 'strong leadership'.

Therefore successive five-year economic development plans in Korea have been drawn, administered, controlled and coordinated by the bureaucracy of centralized power. The inclination to centralization got spread to other areas of administration and gave rise to 'bureaucratic authoritarianism' and created a general social climate where centralization and concentration of political, administrative and economic power came to be the rule, with the attendant habit of heteronomy rather than autonomy, and dependency on authority rather than spontaneity.

However, as the problem of intolerable basic poverty has been solved and people have now come to concern themselves with 'the quality of life', and as society accelerates its speed of change and diversification, we face a different situation where the system of centralization and the habit of heteronomy no longer serve a purpose and gradually become socially dysfunctional.

As society changes with accelerating rapidity and involves greater dimensions, complexities and diversities, what Alvin Toffler called the 'decision load' of the society, that is, the total amount of decisions to be made in all sectors of the society, increases at a geometric progression. And Korean society has rapidly multiplied in recent years both its speed of change and its sheer magnitude, complexity and diversity in all sectors.

A centralized system can cope with augmenting decision loads up to a certain point, beyond which, however, the system breaks down as it is forced to make decisions on a greater number of more complex, more diversified and more specialized problems, at a faster speed to meet more changing, varied and specific conditions. Beyond that point the centralized system now comes to be more liable to make decisions that are inappropriate, ignorant of the real situations, too rash, too late, decisions that have detrimental side-effects and decisions that are to be later abolished only to repeat the same inadvertent decision-making process.

Beyond that point, therefore, the increasing decision loads have to be reallocated and redistributed to appropriate positions and persons in the total system. This, of course, means a gradual but inevitable change in direction towards greater decentralization, greater autonomy and greater participation.

More important than such practical needs for decentralization is the principle that the greater autonomy and participation enabled by greater decentralization is itself an essential quality of human life and a substantive step forward to democracy. That is, the experience of participation, autonomy and spontaneity in decision-making is the essential quality of life through which man feels himself to be a human being. It is also the mainspring of creativity, a sense of responsibility, and a healthy sense of community as well as of individuality.

The gradual transition from centralization to decentralization is also a requirement in educational policy-making, educational administration and school management. Here, too, the range of autonomy has to be broadened in the operation of elementary, secondary and higher centralized systems. Educational administration in South Korea has been a highly centralized system being a part of highly centralized 'development' administration. South Korean education, however, has meanwhile grown tremendously in its sheer quantity and in its diversity. In 1970, the middle school enrolment ratio was about 55 percent and it is now in 1988 nearly 100 percent, and that of the high school has grown from 30 percent to 85 percent. The college population has grown from 160,000 to nearly one and a half million. The decision loads within education that must have accordingly grown obviously cannot be taken up and administered by the continuing central bureaucracy without risking inappropriate, inadvertent and ignorant decisions.

Education in the classroom, on the other hand, needs to face squarely the needs to develop in students abilities of decision-making, capacities of autonomy, joys of spontaneity and austerities of responsibility by providing them with appropriate opportunities for autonomy and participation in individual and collective decision-making processes. Long habituated to a system of centralized political and bureaucratic authoritarianism, students as well as teachers themselves now need a rather soul-searching process of coming to a renewed grip of what freedom, autonomy and democracy mean.

From Meritocracy to Egalitarianism

The fifth and last dimension of social redirection to be mentioned here is that of meritocracy versus egalitarianism.

Development processes involve a host of problems to solve and tasks to be done. Therefore those who are able and competent get rewards and positions of eminence ahead of others. A meritocratic and achievement-oriented social climate is thus created.

On the one hand, this means that present-day South Korean society has been 'modernized' to an extent when compared with the ascription-oriented traditional society, where one's social status and rewards were determined largely by the family, class or caste one belonged to rather than by one's own capabilities and achievements. There is, however, another side to be considered – the problem of meritocracy versus egalitarianism.

Man must have been born with a paradox within himself. He wants, at the same time, to be the same as others as well as different from others. 'I want to get richer than others with my own hands', he says. 'Why bother?' says he on the other hand. 'Why you only? I want to get rich too', says he on another occasion. Someone else says, 'What's wrong with me wanting to have my child educated in the best aristocratic school at my own choice and expense?'. And another says, 'Why your child only? Why not build a school system where everybody can be, and should be, educated well?'.

Probably with every social policy there are two positions: the libertarian meritocratic assertion, 'according to one's will and ability' and the egalitarian assertion, 'all together', and the two are in constant synthesis as well as tension. This also may be the reason that there are almost always in a democratic political system two political parties, one representing libertarian conservatism and the other egalitarian progressivism.

In reality, however, there cannot be a purely meritocratic society. If it existed, it would be an animal kingdom in a jungle where the strong always preys on the weak. Nor can there be a purely egalitarian society. If there were one, it would be a 'distopia' where things are all gray, monotonous and tasteless. A real society forms itself in some balance, harmony and synthesis between the two. Nevertheless, as the meritocratic mentality becomes strong and overpowering, regulated and reinforced by development processes as it has been in South Korea recently, it is bound to cause a number of dysfunctions. This makes us believe that at this stage of the game what we now need is a more egalitarian consideration in the mix of the two.

We know, for example, that extreme meritocracy breeds short-sightedness, a short-term perspective, because one has to get the recognition of one's merits and capabilities as fast as possible. And in order to show one's merits, one quite often has to over-charge, over-act, over-manipulate and overexaggerate. One of the assets of the Japanese style of management compared with the American style is, we are told, that it places less emphasis on the merit system for rewards and promotion than on the seniority system, allowing employees to think in terms of long-term interests of the company.

Excessive meritocracy of necessity encourages a number of social inequalities and gaps. Unbalanced, and to many people unfair, distribution of wealth and consequent income gap are already a topic of frequent discussions. An unjustifiably arrogant sense of elitism, of 'chosen people', on the part of the privileged creates social gaps that are cacophonous to necessary social integration and stability.

Might it be that the three famous words of the French revolution – liberty, equality and fraternity – are not a simple linear listing of good concepts but a triad where fraternity should act as the coordinating principle of the other two that are liable to conflict with each other?

In this regard, there is a problem that requires in-depth thinking. That is, what is the origin of inequality in abilities? The meritocratic position rationalizes, 'If a person is poor, it is because he is not able. It is his fault'. Again, if a high school graduate fails an entrance examination to a college, it is his fault, because of his poor ability. But the problem cannot be set aside that simply. We shall not go into a discussion whether the origin of inequality is hereditary or environmental, or is in the individual or in the social structure. Suffice it to say here that it may be basically an educational problem.

In regard to education in this respect, first of all we have to recall that historically institutionalized school education started with an education of the ruling class both in the West and in the East. For the ordinary and the ruled there was either no school at all or a different 'track' of schooling. From the start, school education was aristocratic rather than egalitarian, thereby contributing to inequalizing rather than equalizing abilities. We probably should reflect on our modern educational system and its policies and administrative practices and determine whether or not we still keep remnants of the past consciously or unconsciously. There is plenty of evidence that we still do, widening the gaps in many instances.

Frequent assertions of some educational thinkers that we have to 'de-school' education, that education is really for the perpetuation of the establishment, that children of the poor are really educated to be poor again, etc., need at least thoughtful examination, if not total acceptance.

More serious, however, is the very likelihood that the typical instruction system in the school is a crucial factor in inequalizing the abilities of students. That is, consciously or unconsciously it teaches some students well and makes them able, while it teaches some students poorly and makes them relatively less able. Thus it brands some as able and some others as unable and drives them out to the society. The mechanism involved is as follows. In every learning process in any subject, a bit of deficient learning is bound to occur. Anybody, a genius or a dullard, makes a failure now and then, and is clumsy, immature and uncouth. This is so in learning to play tennis or the piano, or in learning mathematics. The learning process, when bared to its skeleton, is a chain of four elements: learning, trying, failing and correcting. If you learn only and do not have a chance to try, then succeed or fail and correct, your learning is severely curtailed and even truncated, so that learning deficiencies go unnoticed and uncorrected to become the cause of another, greater deficiency in subsequent learning. Thus deficiencies get cumulated. The deficient become more deficient and the able become abler, widening the inequality of abilities among students.

It is, then, only through a powerful instructional system that teaches each and every student in the classroom to a level of A's, to the required level of mastery and excellence, that education comes to 'educate' rather than to 'classify' students.

Can and shall we in the future envisage an education as powerful as this so that the whole premise of human inequality as well as of meritocracy versus egalitarianism will be examined anew?

I have offered you a story from the Republic of Korea. But I hope it has some general significance for other countries.

Every country, I believe, needs a similar periodic reexamination of the premises as well as the consequences of social and educational policies, which, of course, should be helpful to the country itself. But also countries obviously learn from each other's self-reexamination. The South can learn from the experience of the East and West. The East can learn from the West and the South. And, especially, the West can and should learn from the East and South, with or without the recent prophetic observations that the 'Pacific Century' is coming near and that the next turn of 'the rise of great powers' is in the East.

One thing that all countries on the globe share is that they are all approaching the 'future', that is, they are going to share many futuristic problems such as environmental pollution and depletion, ecological disturbance and mental pathologies. Futuristic problems are not a monopoly of the post-industrial developed countries. They are in nature global. Underdeveloped and developing countries may have to tackle them now, or 'sooner or later'. In this respect, developed countries which have been more responsible for creating futuristic problems and which are more 'within' and 'nearer to' the future should feel more responsible for coming out with a model of futuristic reorientation with which we shall chart the viable course of the uncertain future. Had we, in South Korea, incorporated the concerns with such futuristic problems right from the beginning of our development plans, we could have saved ourselves from unnecessary wastes and blunders.

Bom Mo Chung is a professor of education at Hallym University, Chuncheon, Kangwondo, Korea.

4

Education and Social Change in the Philippines: A National Illusion

Sr. M. Bellarmine Bernas, O.S.B.
St. Scholastica's College, The Philippines

In the 1950s the novelist James Michener wrote:

There is only one sensible way to think of the Pacific Ocean today. It is the highway between Asia and America and whether we wish it or not, from now on there will be immense traffic along that highway. If we know what we want, if we have patience and determination, but if above all we have understanding, we may be sure that the traffic will be peaceful, consisting of tractors and students and medical missionaries, and bolts of cloth. But if we are not intelligent or if we cannot cultivate understanding in Asia, then the traffic will be armed planes, battleships, submarines, and death. In either alternative we may be absolutely certain that from now on the Pacific traffic will be a two-way affair. I can foresee that day . . . when the passage of goods and people and ideas across the Pacific will be of greater importance to America than a similar exchange across the Atlantic.

Today, three decades after those words had been written, you and I are honored by the invitation to join, as it were, the traffic on this highway. I congratulate the organizers of this Conference for the attempt to span our several worlds and in the name of peace to invite us to exchange the richness of our varied backgrounds, perspectives, expertise and experience towards the vision and the building of a better world.

I have been asked to speak on issues concerning education from the vantage point of an educator from the Philippines. Allow me, in the Asian tradition, to begin with an allegory.

Once upon a time, it is said from out of the great Pacific Ocean there emerged a beautiful and mysterious island which no one could explain. It was a strange island, almost perfect in its symmetry, its foliage green like the color of emeralds, its edges disappearing into the sea as gently as a poem. It was a big island. Yet, from afar, one could not see how vast it was. For right in its middle sat such a huge mountain that almost the whole island seemed to disappear beneath it. From afar, the mountain was overwhelming and overpowering in its magnificence, looking like a glass cathedral against the sky. And the cathedral assumed the shape of multi-leveled platforms very much like pyramids with their tops cut off.

Upon even nearer view, one saw that the island was inhabited by strange creatures, their most unique feature being that after some time of moving around the island they grew wings on their heels and their heads were almost always looking up. Young children learned soon to grow buds on their heels and tilt their heads upward too.

For on that island, everyone assumed that there was nowhere else to go but up. If you just stayed at the base of the mountain there was danger that, some day, the sea might just come and eat you up. So everyone on that island moved around so that they could grow wings on their heels. The more you moved around, the stronger grew your wings. The stronger your wings, the higher you would fly up the mountain.

Every child and adult on that island knew by heart the tales of wondrous things to be found on each level of the many-leveled mountain. There were tales of orchards where the fruits of trees were made of silver and gold and fountains from where gushed waters of eternal youth. And so everyone on that island kept his head tilted upwards and exercised his legs so that he could grow wings on his heels.

The strange thing is that of those who flew upwards no one ever came back to tell the truth about what they saw on the mountain's many levels.

The truth was that the tales were not really true. There were really very few orchards with gold and silver fruit and very few fountains of eternal youth. At each level, sad to say, the newcomers only saw that other creatures had gotten to those few orchards and those few fountains ahead of them. And there was so little left for those who had just come.

It was really tragic that at the very top of the mountain, the few orchards had been surrounded by tall, gray walls and the gold and silver fruit had all been gathered, put into crates, and flown away to other islands by those who had lived there for many, many years, most of them, strangers themselves, who had come from other climes.

And so, at every platform of the multi-leveled mountain, one found thousands of creatures with broken wings and, worse than that, with broken wills. They had tilted their heads for so long upwards that they could not will them any other way. They had over-exercised their legs, moving around till their wings were tattered and torn.

And really worst of all, the fragments of their wings were gathered by the garbage collector and ground into bits of glass. These bits of glass were poured down the mountainsides, to which they stuck with salt from the sea.

And so, when anyone below looked up at the mountain, they thought they saw diamonds glistening in the sun. They never knew that the mountainsides glittered with the pain of broken dreams.

The terrain I have just described is the terrain of my country, the multi-leveled mountain representing the stratified social and economic landscape where the majority of my people live out their aspirations for the good life, often in the midst of poverty and oppressive structures. The wings on the heels of those strange creatures represent the value my people put on education as the only way to rise above their present state of poverty and powerlessness and to obtain for themselves and for their children the blessings of the good life.

In the same way that the creatures living on that island could not understand why after all their efforts to grow wings and to fly to the higher levels of the mountain they could still not get the gold and silver fruit of the trees, many of us, trapped in the romanticism with which we have been taught to look at the relationship between schooling and society, cannot understand the futility of our efforts to use schooling to narrow the gap between the rich and the poor and thus through education to achieve a more egalitarian society.

The Romantic View of Education

I shall now discuss at length two beliefs that proceed from this romantic view of education, prevailing as they do in countries like mine where scarce resources are in the hands of a few. In my paper, I shall attempt to show how the Philippine experience negates these beliefs and how, listening to the sounds of history, we perhaps ought to draw the veils aside and adapt a new and different perspective in looking at the function of education and its relation to equity and development.

These beliefs are:

the belief that education increases the social mobility of individuals and that therefore democratization of access to schooling will narrow the gap between the rich and the poor;

the belief that schools produce knowledgeable and skilled individuals and that therefore the expansion of the educational system will lead to the development of a nation.

I should like to present these two beliefs within the social context of the Philippine educational system, hoping that you may discern from this similar patterns in other developing nations. Specifically, I shall touch on the following: historical background, the school selection process, schools as allocators of roles in society, and the present paradox, the expansion of the educational system and income distribution.

I shall continue by sharing with you what I see to be the implications of all these for educators and policy-makers.

The Philippine Educational System

I shall begin with a brief description of the Philippine educational system.

Formal schooling in the Philippines is divided into three main levels: elementary, secondary and tertiary. Schools are either owned by the government or by private individuals or by corporations. State or public schools are supported by funds from the national or local governments. The resources of private schools are greatly determined by the capacity of their students to pay for their schooling.

Perhaps the most significant observation one can make of the Philippine educational system is the dominant role that private schools have played and continue to play, especially at the tertiary level. Present statistics show that although only 5.7 percent of the student population in the elementary level go to private schools, a little over 40 percent in the secondary level attend private schools, and more that 80 percent at the tertiary level go to private schools, colleges and universities.

This unique situation, in which tertiary education is mainly in the hands of private enterprise, has its roots in the history of Spanish and American colonization of the Philippines.

In the 400 years of Spanish colonial rule, in order to maintain a feudal economy no effort was made by the colonial government to provide massive schooling for the Filipinos. Elementary and secondary schools were few and found mainly in the large population centers. Although there were a few schools for higher learning (for example, the University of Santo Tomas which was founded in 1611) these were established mainly for the *illustrados* or the elite.

At the turn of the century when the Spaniards ceded the Philippines to the Americans, the new colonizers introduced the public school system for a different reason: a literate and skilled population would be necessary to introduce a democratic form of government and a capitalist economy. A shipload of American teachers were brought into the country to form the core of teachers who would staff the new elementary and secondary schools. The greater number of Filipinos, whose forebears had been deprived of formal schooling for the previous four centuries, seized the opportunity to avail of the services of the expanding elementary and secondary school systems. Thus, after several decades, there were to be large cohorts of high school graduates who wanted to study further and obtain college degrees.

Since the government could not absorb all these students in the few existing private and state tertiary institutions, many enterprising businessmen seized the opportunity to establish colleges and universities. These schools were managed for profit just like any commercial enterprise. Rich families, too, diverted their investments by founding private colleges and universities and managing them as profit-earning stock corporations. Some of these large private universities appeared in the list of the top 1,000 corporations of the country.

In addition, many sectarian schools which had been founded originally for elementary and secondary education were pressured by parents of students to open college departments so that their children could pursue higher studies at less cost in the same locality.

All these swelled the number of private institutions of higher learning. Thus while in 1941 there were only eight universities and 84 colleges in the Philippines, twenty years later the number had risen to 36 universities and 559 colleges. Presently, there are 785 tertiary institutions all over the country.

This dominant role of private schools in the Philippines education system greatly affects the social selection process for entrance and survival in schools.

The School Selection Process

Who gets into schools and who benefits from schooling depend on many factors. These factors may seem at first to be determined largely by internal school policies but are in fact predetermined by the characteristics of the society served by the school. In the Philippines, one strong determinant of the school selection process for entrance and continuance in schools is the socioeconomic status of the students and their families.

In the same way that we have rich and upper middle class families living in mansions and plush villages while the majority of our people live in poverty and substandard conditions, our educational system is studded with pockets of excellence exhibited by a few high-quality institutions amidst thousands of substandard schools. Through a selection process, students are funneled to these schools mainly through the capacity to pay for the cost of schooling and the possession of social capital to survive schooling.

Despite the efforts of the Department of Education, Culture and Sports to exercise control over tuition fees among private schools, great disparities in tuition rates exist among them. Entrance to quality private schools is determined in most cases by the capacity of students to pay the required tuition fees and incidental costs of schooling.

The scholastic standing of a student is another determinant for entrance to quality private schools and public schools of equal standing. Unfortunately the capacity of a student to pass entrance examinations is not determined merely by his/her intellectual capacity. In many cases this is also related to his/her socioeconomic status. At the elementary level, for example, entrance examinations are geared to measure characteristics of applicants which are related to language habits, reading readiness and social skills and behavior which are generally fostered by homes which can provide exposure to books and media, adequate nutrition and rich leisure activities. Or it is normally taken for granted that applicants to first grade in quality schools have been to one or two years of pre-schooling in some private nursery school or kindergarten. The social selection process has started already at the lowest rung of the educational ladder.

Among the high schools which try to maintain high standards, the school selection process through entrance examination takes on another variable. While the Department of Education, Culture and Sports requires six years of instruction for completion of elementary school, some private schools maintain a seventh grade plus pre-schooling of one to two years. Some high schools require that applicants complete a seventh grade or that they demonstrate through their scores in a battery of achievement tests that they can perform according to the norms set by the schools. Thus an applicant from a private school with seven to nine years of schooling has a distinct advantage over most graduates from the public elementary schools who have had only six years of instruction. This added advantage of having more adequate preparation to enter high school is carried on as the student moves on to the college level.

Entrance to the tertiary level is first of all regulated by the National College Entrance Examination (NCEE). Introduced in 1973, this national examination, which all students should take prior to admission to any college academic course, stipulates general cut-off points for admission to college and specific cut-off points for various professional courses – medicine, nursing, education, law, etc. Students who do not reach the prescribed cut-off scores may only take vocational and technical courses. Once again, the less affluent student loses out to the one with more years of elementary schooling and who has had access to a better quality of high school education.

Even in the state institutions which are highly subsidized by government and should in principle be open to all regardless of social class, many students who qualify belong to the higher socioeconomic level of society. A case in point is the University of the Philippines, the premier state university of the Philippines, which has produced presidents, senators, justices, etc. Although tuition rates are affordable by the low-middle income families and although there are quotas for minority groups and low income levels, through the years most of its students have tended to come from private secondary schools or more affluent groups. These students, again, are at an advantage over the less affluent ones because their parents can provide them with other opportunities that can enhance their academic success, such as comfortable homes, travel and varied leisure activities.

While the NCEE scores serve as a convenient selection mechanism for students who should go to academic and professional courses, many private institutions which have very selective admission criteria do not find the NCEE percentile ranks based on national test scores as sufficiently discriminating for their purposes. Over and above reaching the NCEE cut-off scores, these institutions have their own battery of tests which they use to screen applicants. Thus an even finer school selection process occurs at this stage.

Schools as Allocators of Roles in Society

With such a school selection process in operation, those who can afford to be admitted to prestigious schools stand better chances of getting higher paying jobs. Those who can manage to take professional courses such as medicine or law or engineering earn more than those who can only afford to take vocational courses.

While it might be argued that there are scholarships and grants for students who are intellectually superior but financially handicapped, these are too few in proportion to the social class they represent.

Thus schools, far from acting as social and economic levelers of society, preserve its hierarchical structure by a selection process that assigns students to 'right levels' within a stratified school system. These levels correspond disconcertingly to their socioeconomic backgrounds and later on to corresponding strata in the world of work.

Expansion of the Education System and Income Distribution

Let us now look at the relationship between the expansion of the educational system and income distribution.

While the expansion of the educational system in our country has provided more people to go to school beyond the elementary and secondary levels, the significant increase in the years of schooling of the majority of Filipinos has not contributed significantly to a wider income distribution. This is illustrated by the fact that our socioeconomic structure over the years has remained rigid.

The attempt of many Filipinos to obtain a high school or college diploma has only succeeded to *devalue* these credentials. In the past, elementary graduates could find a job, even as teachers of lower grades or as clerks in government offices. Now it is extremely difficult for those who have finished only the sixth grade to find a decent job. They have to compete with others who have had more years of schooling. Thus we have college graduates who are employed as messengers in business offices or as fruit packers in plantations – jobs which would not even require a high school diploma. There are high school graduates who find no jobs other than assembling toys, electronic gadgets, etc. – jobs which would not require even a grade school certificate. Worst of all, Asia and Europe are now places where Filipinos with college degrees work as domestic workers. These have made tremendous adjustments in work and life styles, but they earn much more than their colleagues who have remained in the Philippines.

The problem of 'overeducation' and the educated unemployed in the Philippines and in other developing countries has been the focus of attention of the International Labour Office since the mid-seventies, prompting some social scientists to ask: 'Can manpower projections and educational plans have been so much off target? And if they have, is the reason that the economy has underexpanded, or that the educational system has overproduced?'.

The blame for the lack of correspondence between the supply of graduates and the demand of the labor market has been tossed alternately between the educational system and the economic system, thus omitting a third important dimension of the problem. Perhaps it is good for us to remind ourselves 'that economic systems do not follow manpower directions any more faithfully than educational systems follow educational plans, but, rather, that both respond to a powerful set of external factors of an essentially political nature'.

The Present Paradox

While I was writing this paper, House Bill No. 2528, which aims to fully implement the constitutional mandate of free public secondary education, was signed into law. The Chairman of the Education Committee of the Senate in endorsing this bill claimed that free public secondary education is 'premised on the principle that the advancement of a nation ultimately depends on an educated and productive citizenry'. Let me respond to this with the scholastic maxim 'never deny; rarely affirm; always distinguish'. I see a crying need to refine the premise on which free secondary education was presented for approval.

We Filipinos often boast that our literacy rate is one of the highest in Asia, yet our growth rate for the past years is lower than the Asian countries which have lower literacy rates. We can claim that we have a population that has the benefits of schooling at the same level as some developed countries; we have technocrats and leaders who have been educated in the best universities abroad. Foreign journalists who were covering the events after the February EDSA revolution were amazed at the composition of our new cabinet – it almost looked like a Who's Who of the Ivy League schools. Yet we cannot deny that our economy is in a dismal state.

These startling observations should prompt us to examine more closely the dynamics of the relationship between schooling and development, especially economic development. Perhaps we have too long regarded education as an independent variable and have habitually looked at an ineluctable causal relationship moving from education to development as if this were immutably preordained. The fact as I know it in my country, however, is that our education system continues to mirror and reinforce the structural imperfections of our society. It is therefore time to explore how education in fact can be transformed into an effective instrument for revolutionizing long-standing oppressive economic structures that have retarded our growth as a nation and demeaned our dignity as individuals.

Implications for Educators and Policy-makers

Faced with the sobering fact that the expansion of the educational system does not lead automatically to greater equality and that in fact education has not been a force for shaping the structures of society, the romantic might be tempted to close his eyes and pretend that reality is otherwise. But this is nothing but a self-deceiving way of giving legitimacy to one's work in school.

Alternatively, one could turn cynical and find no sense in sacrificing one's life for teaching if one believes that the educational system tends to act as an agent for reinforcing the status quo rather than as an agent of change. If there is not much that education can do to reverse the direction of influence between schooling and society, one might as well engage in social work with the poor and experience direct, almost instant satisfaction in the process.

Neither of these two positions, I believe, shows an adequate grasp of the dynamic relationship between schooling and society which we have talked about. Notwithstanding the fact that education is an insufficient factor for effecting change, it remains a necessary factor for change.

But education's capacity to achieve change depends upon the proper match between the priorities of the educational system and the needs of the society which the system seeks to serve. How can a proper match be achieved?

The answer to this question, in the context of a democratic nation, cannot be through regimentation. Neither can the answer be found through the efforts of educators alone. I suggest that the search for and implementation of educational priorities that can truly serve the needs of a nation, especially of economically developing and underdeveloped nations, can only be through the tripartite cooperative efforts of the education sector, the industrial and economic sectors, and government.

I am not saying that education must be reduced to a mere tool for economic development. But if leisure is the basis of culture, as I am convinced it is, education, which has for its object the development and transmission of culture, must be made to contribute to the creation of material comfort which produces that leisure where culture can thrive. Concretely, what needs to be done?

I suggest that education, industry and government must first sit down together to discover the manpower skills needed for an economic take-off that can lift the entire population out of its economic misery. The schools in turn must respond by restructuring programs and priorities so that they do not churn out hordes of graduates for whom no jobs can be found but rather graduates who are prepared to assume their share of work for national development. I am convinced, however, that the restructuring of an educational system cannot be achieved without the intervention of government. Government must play a role both in the restructuring of the system and in making the restructured system accessible to a population that cannot afford to pay for education.

First, then, there is the government's role in the restructuring of a system. And here I speak in a context of non-regimentation and where the people must be given a choice between government schools and private schools. It is easy enough for government to reorient government schools which are under government control. But government, while preserving academic freedom, must also imaginatively use the resources at its command so that the private educational system can transform itself into a more effective instrument for national development. I speak from the context of my country, where a very large proportion of education is in the hands of private schools, many of them operated for profit. I am convinced that, in such a context, government, by a combination of carrot and stick, of police power, regulation and financial incentives, can alter the program priorities of private education to make them more responsive to the needs of the nation.

Having achieved the desired reorientation of the educational system, government must next make it financially possible for the underprivileged to avail of educational opportunities. At this stage in my country's development, I do not see how this can be possible without massive subsidy from government, local and foreign, and from industry, likewise local and foreign.

Let me, however, make it clear that I am not saying that, alone, a properly oriented educational system can achieve a more equitable distribution of wealth which must accompany development as an indispensable component. Education has its role to play. But we also have to examine other factors which influence the distribution of income. Notable among these are 'the political and economic institutions of a nation, the role of multinational capital, the role of government in promoting investment and high profit and providing for repatriation of capital, the legal status and state of development of trade unionism, the degree of monopoly concentration of capital and employment, etc.' True, the values that are imported by the educational system can influence these factors. But in fact, too, in many ways, the potential or limit of educational reforms hinges very much on economic and political policy.

Finally, I hope some day when more nations have attained economic and political stability, educational systems can be appreciated and cherished not just as suppliers of skilled and knowledgeable cogs in the economic machinery but as truly human enterprises where persons learn the art of living and not just how to make a living; where ideas are born and persons become, and nations can forge their souls.

Going back to that island I spoke of, perhaps if they had had that kind of perspective, the creatures that inhabited it would not have needed to grow wings on their heels. Perhaps they might just have looked around the island and planted orchards with gold and silver fruit around them and built fountains of eternal youth right where they were, and for each other. And had they not been looking so intently down at their heels, or so seriously up at the mountain's many levels, then they might have seen a highway rising to meet them where the sky meets the sea and they might have seen the traffic – and they might have met us there. I thank you.

Sr. M. Bellarmine Bernas is President of St. Scholastica's College, 2560 Leon Guinto, Manila, The Philippines. Sr. Bernas received her Ph.D. in International Development Education from Stanford University, USA.

5

The Changing Human Dimensions of the Pacific Rim: Education for the Future

Terry McGee
The University of British Columbia, Canada

From an educational perspective, the global 'tripartite' division of the world – a concern with Canada, the USA and Europe, – is what I will call the Atlantic mindset. It might be argued that other parts of the world such as the Soviet Union, Japan and the 'Third World' form another mindset, but the Canadian educational approach to these regions is fragmented and uneven. This situation is, of course, very understandable in light of the historical development of Canada and its geographic and economic position in the world. But it is scarcely realistic, for it takes little cognizance of the emergence and growing importance of the Asia-Pacific region of the world today.

Defining the Pacific Region: A Curious Task

Attempts to define the Pacific region are legion; in fact, it is a daunting and curious task to be attempting a definition of regional components in an age of global economy. This is even more complicated if the immense geographical and cultural diversity of the Pacific region is recognized.[1] The region conjures up a kaleidoscope of images:

The word 'Pacific' involves the relaxing image of coral atolls, white beaches, waving coconut trees, and suppliant Pacific people;

the beautiful image of Javanese countryside with rice-plants reflected in the mirror lakes of rice fields that climb the terraced sides of mountains;

the progressive image of downtown Singapore or Hong Kong with office towers; temples of commerce multiply to duplicate the Wall Street of New York;

the destitute image of refugees clustered in overcrowded camps with pot-bellied children peeking from behind the sarongs of adults;

the political image of Red Guards marching under flowing red banners;

choreographed iconography well loved by the political image-makers;

the festival image of Chinese dragon dancers on Chinese New Year. The streets are full of Chinese faces. Is this Hong Kong, Vancouver or Sydney?

the philosophical image – a Japanese temple garden in Kyoto, stones raked in wave-like lines, an ocean of pebbles. Sit still and watch; eventually the pebbles begin to move like waves striking a beach.

One could go on, but let me make my first point. Most of us perceive this vast region through such images which shape our perception of the region. These diverse images are further reinforced by immense geographical diversity and heterogenity of the region.

Within the region lies the world's largest country, China, with a population of more than one billion. The region also has some of the world's smallest countries, such as Nauru which has less than 12,000 people. Within the region are some of the most historic nations, such as Korea, and some of the most recent, such as Vanuatua (formerly the colony of New Hebrides) which received independence in 1980. Within the region there is immense linguistic and cultural diversity, ranging from the Catholicism of the Latin American countries to the Islamic faith of Malaysia and Indonesia.

One could continue the list but this diversity raises the question: Can there be any unity in a region so vast? This is a region where the only unity is the geographic unity of the Pacific Ocean which stretches 12,500 miles between Singapore and Equator, and some 9,000 miles from Soviet Siberia to the South Island of New Zealand. Can there be any unity of approach to a region which includes such diverse groups of ideologies ranging from the socialist regimes of the USSR and China to the neo-conservative regime of Chile? Even by the most preliminary of counts, there are at least fifty political units divided as follows:

Asia – some nineteen units stretching from Japan in an arc bordering the Pacific through to Indonesia;

White-settler lands – Soviet Siberia, Canada, the USA, Argentina, Australia and New Zealand;

The Pacific Island States – in their multitude;

The Latin America States stretching from Argentina in the south, through Chile, Peru, Equador, Colombia, Panama, Nicaragua, El Salvador and Guatemala, to the State of Mexico.

Historical Patterns of Incorporation of the Pacific Region into the World System

Yet there are those who see great unity in the region. The America Secretary of State, John Hay, wrote in 1900 that 'the Mediterranean is the ocean of the past, the Atlantic is the ocean of the present, and the Pacific is the ocean of the future'. Today there are those who feel this prophecy has come true. They point to the fact that already the growing inter-regional trade throughout the Pacific exceeds that of the Atlantic nations and that many of the more dynamic Asian countries have been growing rapidly in economic terms, despite current slowdowns, so much so that they predict a Pacific century for 2000 AD.

Some of the more optimistic Japanese economists even envisage a Pacific Basin linked together in a manner not unlike the EEC. The combined GNP of the East Asian countries alone will exceed the EEC by the year 2000. As you will note, this is a unity perceived through growing economic growth, trade and interdependence which is seen as the basis for mutually beneficial cooperation. Whether such ambitious schemes will come about remains to be seen.

What other unifying elements characterize this vast region? Historically, the region shares the common experience of a periphery (a periphery rich in tradition, culture and art), of incorporation into a global system of economic and political relations which historically has been dominated by capitalism emanating from Europe. This process has been highly uneven both temporally and regionally, assuming different forms in different parts of the Pacific.[2] Four phases of incorporation into the global system can be delineated.

The first phase was one of *plunder*. It began with the conquistadores plundering the treasures of the Americas, the spice trade of Asia, and the sandalwood and whaling trades of the Pacific.

A second phase was *colonization* in which European powers attempted to establish political control over their regions of plunder. The Pacific was carved up between the European powers which introduced their own institutions, religions, language and culture. There were three types of society that emerged as a result of these impacts:

> the white-settler colonies which are often reproductions of the motherland – Canada, the United States, Australia, New Zealand, Siberia and Argentina;
>
> the genuine colonies directly under foreign rule, most of the Latin American countries and many in the Pacific and Asia being typical; and
>
> the countries that avoided direct colonial rule, like Japan, China and Thailand.

The third phase was one of *nationalism*, still energetic, in which political control passes to the national units, new policies of internal development are put in place, and some highly successful economic policies are applied, as in the case of Japan. This is, of course, a phase which is still of major importance. The role of the state in economic development is much more important in the so-called developing countries of the region, than was the case during the industrial revolution in western Europe.

Finally, there is a fourth phase of *economic incorporation* involving substantial economic restructuring. This phase is characterized by increasing interdependence, specialization, and the growth of the control of transnational corporations based in Japan, the USA and Europe. This has given rise to the emergence of a Pacific economic system in which there is increasing interaction in terms of trade, information, tourism and international security.

The Regional Components of the Pacific System

There are considerable problems in measuring the emergence of the Pacific economic system, apart from the obvious geographic problems of defining the spatial components of the system.[3] For instance, the economic statistics such as value of trade are subject to many qualifications. However, it may be argued that, in economic terms, the Pacific countries fall into five main groups indicated in the table below.[4] To these could be added three other groups of countries which would be the socialist economies of the Republic of Vietnam, Laos, Kampuchea and Burma; the micro-economies of the Pacific islands; and the Soviet Union, which is now attempting to establish its presence in the Pacific region in an aggressive manner.

Percentage Gross Domestic Product and Population
of Pacific Rim Countries – 1965-83

Country	1965		1979		1983	
	% GDP	% pop.	% GDP	% pop.	% GDP	% pop.
1. Supereconomies						
USA	68.7	14.3	52.6	12.3	56.8	12.2
Japan	9.1	7.2	21.8	6.3	18.4	6.2
	77.8	21.5	74.4	18.6	75.2	18.4
2. White-settler						
Canada	5.2	1.4	5.1	1.2	5.6	1.2
Australia	2.3	0.8	2.9	0.7	2.9	0.8
New Zealand	0.6	0.1	0.4	0.1	0.4	0.1
	8.1	2.3	8.4	2.0	8.9	2.1
3. NICs[a]	0.9	3.3	2.6	3.4	2.8	3.4
4. Other Asian[b]	8.2	64.8	8.5	66.0	7.9	67.7
5. Latin American[c]	5.1	7.6	6.2	8.5	5.0	7.9
Total	100.1	99.5	99.5	100.2	99.5	100.2

(a) NICs: Korea, Hong Kong, Taiwan, Singapore
(b) Other Asian countries: People's Republic of China, ASEA (except Singapore)
(c) Latin America: Mexico, Columbia, Peru, Chile, Argentina
Source: World Bank (various dates)

For the remaining five groups of countries, three facts must be emphasized. First, we see the dominance of the supereconomies of Japan and the USA in the system. In the period since 1965 they have been responsible for producing 75 percent of the gross domestic product (GDP) and value of industrial output, and over 80 percent of value of manufacturing output.

Secondly, the system has been remarkably stable over the last twenty years. Despite a much heralded rise of the NICs, the largest shifts in GDP, and in value of industrial and manufacturing output, have been in the considerable increase in Japan's share of the Pacific Rim output at the expense of the USA. Essentially, the system has seen a shift within the supereconomies, which has made very little difference to their share of the Pacific Rim's system and output. These developments have not been without growing 'friction' between the supereconomies, as the current 'trade war' attests. But the Pacific Rim economic system is still dominated by these two economies.

Thirdly, despite the very considerable focus of attention on the economic growth of the NICs, particularly Singapore, Hong Kong, Taiwan, and the Republic of Korea as major components of their own 'economic transformation', they still represent a comparatively small proportion of the total Pacific Rim output. In this respect it is interesting that the 'white-settler colonies', despite their real concerns about their industrial and economic performances, have remained stable contributors to the system.

To summarize, we are dealing with a very large region of which Canada is a small part, a region which is extraordinarily diverse. There are four incontestable facts about the region which have to be borne in mind. First of all, it has a huge and growing population. Although there are differences between countries, almost 66 percent of the world's population reside in this region. And by the year 2020, about 70 percent will be there. Secondly, this is an extraordinarily diverse region culturally, linguistically and religiously. And it is not an unimportant region within the context of world history or world significance. Great cultures have come out of this region and remain in this region. And we should not ignore this facet of it. Thirdly, if the region is looked at as an economic unit, it is dominated by the supereconomies of Japan and the USA. Eighteen percent of the Asia-Pacific population lives in these two countries, which produced about 75 percent of the region's gross domestic product in 1985. So despite being a huge region, almost 75 percent of the wealth being generated is coming from these two economies. And what is more, the situation has been remarkably stable over the last twenty years. If you look at the figures for 1965, you will see that they are not very different. The population is a little less, GDP is a little less, and this is despite all the growth that has been talked about in Korea, Singapore, Taiwan, etc. They have increased their contribution to the GDP of the Pacific region by only about 1 percent (from about 2.3 to 3.2 percent). So although they are always being paired in their 'miraculous' economic terms they are not nearly as important as the supereconomies. Canada, Australia and New Zealand, which together have about 2 percent of the population of the region, have about 8 percent of the GDP. So again they are quite wealthy components of this highly unequal world that is the Asia-Pacific region. China and the other groups, with about 67 percent of the region's population, have only about 6 percent of the GDP. So there is an extraordinarily uneven distribution of wealth in this huge region.

The major changes in the region have been concerned with the relative contribution of each of the supereconomies which have been competing vigorously for a greater share of the GDP of the region. A major shift has been Japan's increase in the proportion of GDP at the expense of the USA. Internally, major redistribution has been occurring. The rest of the region, even though growth has occurred, remains in a disadvantaged position *vis-a-vis* those supereconomies. So when we talk about the region, we must never forget the important role that those two supereconomies play in it. It affects what happens to the human dimensions of the region very considerably.[5]

Processes of Accelerated Change

Underlying all that is happening in this region is an increasing global interdependence, in economic terms and in literally every index you want to measure. This interdependence involves an increasing dominance of multinational companies often based in the USA, Japan or the EEC. Thus in manufacturing, tourism and services, multinational companies are extending their control. Now let me make it very clear that when we speak of multinational companies, we should also include national companies which are incorporated in a nation but which actually are working in a joint venture of some kind of economic relationship with a multinational.[6]

Let's take an example of one thing that I have been doing research on with some of my students. This is the issue of what is happening in the food distribution and consumption in Asian cities. If I asked you from where Hong Kong buys its wheat flour, I wonder what you would say to me. Probably you would answer that it is bought from Canada, or perhaps Australia. You might be surprised to learn that 80 percent of the wheat flour that is imported into Hong Kong comes from Japan. Now Japan is not a major producer of wheat, a fact I don't think I need to emphasize. It is, however, a major purchaser of wheat. What is Japan doing or, rather, what are the big milling companies in Japan doing? They're buying Canadian wheat, or Australian wheat, or US wheat, and they are milling it. Then by a systematic negotiation of contracts with the large users of flour in Hong Kong, by forward contracts and certain negotiating techniques, they have come to dominate the market. So this is a kind of process which is occurring throughout much of the region in which the multinationals play a major role. They of course control technology, they control marketing, and they control advertising. And all of those aspects are crucial in shaping what is happening to the people in this region.[7]

Secondly, this process of increasing global interdependence is greatly facilitated by the so-called 'telematic' revolution – the ability to move information around at great speed. Another study we did in Malaysia, just to give you an example of how this works, concerns the semiconductor industry in Malaysia, actually in Penang.[8] We were not really too concerned with the industry, for we were really looking at what was happening to the women workers who were working in the semiconductor factories, of which there are ten in Penang, and of which there are some eighteen in Malaysia, which makes it the third-largest exporter of semiconductors in the world. Of course, it is essentially an assembly operation, which imports components and assembles them using cheap labor. What we found there is that the research and development processes of that industry are located in the USA or Japan. When a problem comes about in the equipment of the production lines, what happens, for example, is that a local engineer tries to diagnose the problem, sends by fax across to his Palo Alto company a copy of the problem and what's going on, and later something comes back by fax telling him how to solve it. What that then creates is a kind of global system of production which I see the Japanese are now calling a Pan-Pacific production system. By this they mean the way different types or parts of industries are located within the Asia-Pacific region. This has important consequences for labor, because it creates a so-called international division of labor in which extraordinarily cheap labor paid at one-tenth of the wages in the USA or Japan is employed to assemble these semiconductors or textiles and clothing, etc. So these kinds of processes have to be understood as being rather crucial to what happens to people in the region.[9] Clearly, immense social and economic change is occurring in the Asia-Pacific region. These six dimensions are dealt with in the next section.

The Changing Human Dimensions of the Pacific Region

First of all, the process of growth and indeed of incorporation of this region into the global economy has historically had a disastrous effect upon the aboriginal peoples of the region. Whether you're talking about the Inuit of the North, the Indians of Peru, the Aborigines of Australia, the Samoans, the Malays, or the Maoris of New Zealand, they shared a common and disastrous experience as their regions and cultures were incorporated into the developed countries' orbit, and this process is still continuing. For instance, in contemporary West Irian, Papua New Guineans are being drawn into the orbit of another nation, Indonesia; their agricultural practices and many other things are being challenged, and they are being forced to change their ways of life.

There are also optimistic developments happening in this area. In Canada, Australia and the USA, various aboriginal communities and native coalitions are asserting their rights to land, their right to their culture, and their right to their own government. This is an exciting and important theme to take up as part of the Pacific education process.

Secondly, what about the effects of economic growth on the population food nexus; on the availability of food to the populations of this region? While I don't think anybody looking at this region today would fall back on a Malthusian view that there's going to be massive famine in the region, there is no doubt that the means to create increasing food productivity in the region has caused immense problems at the human level for all populations. This is, of course, the whole complex of agri-technology which has been delivered to the rice-growers of the region, and to the wheat-growers, and of course in Latin-America to the maize-growers. It's a process whereby increasing chemical inputs into agriculture and the development of new genetic types of rice or wheat do lead to very considerable increases in productivity. But they also greatly increase the cost of inputs. And what this has done in many of the parts of Asia which I know best – that is, in the rice-growing areas – has led to a growing inequality, a movement of people off the land, as they have been unable to afford these inputs, and a flood of people into the cities.[10]

What is more, in some cases this process has had a very serious differential gender impact. In particular, in a place like Java Indonesia, in the past women were responsible for harvesting the rice. This was done by a system which is called in Bahasa Indonesia *bagi dua*, in which they got half of what they harvested, and so had food in their hand. They could feed their families. But now women don't have that possibility. If they go to harvest rice, they get paid money. And then they may or may not have the possibility of buying food for their families. So in a place like Java women increasingly have been forced into a variety of other sorts of occupations such as trading or domestic industry, in addition to their household duties, which produces a double squeeze. This is particularly the case in the poor areas where 30-40 percent of the people are landless. The only way they are going to get their food is through this wage-labor, contracted piece-work in the home, or through self-employment such as cake-selling, etc. This is an extremely difficult situation. Their husbands are very often already in urban centres trying to earn income for the household. The household is split, leaving women looking after children and trying to survive on whatever minimal remittances they receive from their husbands and their own earnings. So some of these processes are extraordinarily devastating to the traditional family and life of this region. Of course, most of these countries are now self-sufficient in rice; that's very true. But it doesn't come without cost to the people who produce it. You have to bear that in mind as this process of increasing capital-intensive inputs into agricultural production continues.[11]

Thirdly, there are an important series of processes that relate to urbanization in the Pacific region. By about 2020, there will be at least 15 cities or metropolitan regions with populations of more that 15 million people in the Asian region alone. These already are gigantic urban complexes and the ability to build infrastructure, to provide housing for the poor, to give adequate services in such huge urban complexes which will by no means be generating the kind of wealth that Western cities do, will be a major problem.[12] What is more, the cities are spreading out. The activities that are urban are now spreading out into gigantic regions sometimes a hundred kilometres in size. Drive from Shanghai to Nanjing and you see such a region; drive through Hong Kong to Canton and you see such a region. Drive from Java to Bandung and you see the same kind of region emerging. Such regions are intensely cultivated with many crops and many small industries occur. These mega-urban regions have very large populations, often in excess of 100 million people. Also, there are immense problems with the environment in such regions. Pollutants are let into the environment and water is tapped from the ground level. It is an immensely difficult and problematic environmental impact that is occurring as these giant populations agglomerate into the cities and their extended regions.[13]

Fourthly, I have to turn to the issue of the international division of labor. I would put this more broadly, in terms of the question of the relationship between capital and labor in these regions as they develop. The history of the industrial revolution in the developed countries gave a rather special status to the role labor played as it evolved in the industrial revolution. It is not clear that this role will be repeated identically in Asian countries. First, it may not because the state in the Asia-Pacific region is desperately concerned with economic growth and is not willing to tolerate labor claims in this process. This is particularly noticeable in the free export zones. In virtually every Asian country that I am aware of, unions do not exist. I should tell you that they have legislation which enables unions to exist but they don't exist. There are now some mechanisms for ensuring working conditions are better and so on within this kind of context. Some people, of course, are very enchanted by the in-house union in Japan as a kind of coalition between management and labor which brings greater productivity. I think it's not a very significant proportion of Japanese labor which actually is organized in that way. There's a very highly significant component of unorganized labor outside such arrangements.

This process of capital-labor relations is most acute in regions such as the free export zones where cheap wage-labor is being sought and employed. I have to say from my own experience of Malaysia that the actual working conditions in the semiconductor factories which I have observed and worked in are by no means what I would call sweatshop conditions. There are serious efforts made to ensure that the working environment has some elements which are attractive. On the other hand, there are also devices which force the women (and the women are the ones who work in this industry – about 70 percent of the workforce are young women) to work under considerable conditions of stress. First, there is a reward for productivity, for a number of pieces completed in a certain time, that makes them push up their work rate. Secondly, there is a system of shift-work which puts them into eight-hour shifts, which rotate every two weeks. So they are forced to work 12.00 - 8.00 for one or two weeks, then they are on 8.00 - 4.00 each day, and so on. This is done under the understanding that everybody gets to work equally at times which are less advantageous. But on the other hand, the workers complain immensely about this kind of rotation affecting their sleep, their ability to get adequate food intake, and a number of other things. One looks at the medical data and finds that some of this comes out through the stress features that are described. I think there is also a highly significant dualistic economy in these regions where a lot of people are working outside large-scale factories or firms. Working in small-scale enterprises, they are not very well policed in terms of any kind of labor laws. People tend to see them as being important, productive and vigorous, but from a Western point of view, there are certainly problems in such situations.

Another aspect I would draw to your attention is what increased mobility in the region means to the movement of people around the region. This is very important not only in terms of refugees but also of contract labor, and we have very large numbers of people from the region going to work in the Middle East; we have the well-documented and quite well-publicized cases of

Philippine domestic servants moving around the world, and the kind of problems that this poses. Then we have a large immigration movement from parts of the region into the more developed countries. Koreans, Chinese, Filipinos and Vietnamese refugees are turning the west-coast cities of North America into very polyglot and multi-racial cities. The real task, I think, is that we must make sure that the people who live in these cities understand the implications of those developments to the social conditions of the cities, and to the relationship between people in these cities. This is not something that is going to go away; it's going to increase. And so it is important that this be on the educational agenda. It is an agenda which bridges the Pacific, not just Vancouver.

Finally, there are two other things. One is that these processes for global integration are leading to the formation of large trading blocs. The EEC will become a free-trading bloc in 1992. Canada and the USA have completed a Free Trade Agreement that will also presumably be phased in over a ten-year period. There are moves in Asia to develop similar sorts of bloc – ASEAN is one. This tendency to develop large blocs of free-trading groups within the global economy has great potential for increasing what some writers have called regional disintegration in national economics. That is, certain regions within a nation will be pulled more and more into this global system and away from the national economy. That has very important implications to people who live in those regions. We have a good example in BC in the case of Northeast coal. Here a huge investment was made in a resource which was going to be funneled into Japan, which put people into that resource, that investment, and immediately created problems in other parts of BC, *vis-a-vis* coal-selling, and so on – that is, people's employment. That is what regional disintegration does. And I think it is very important for politicians, planners and other people who get involved in these things to understand the implications for the people who are affected by that process.

The other thing which is an issue that is always on the agenda, no less important than the issue of the role of the Asia-Pacific in Canadian consciousness, is the issue of resources and environment. We find that throughout the Asia region a very rapid depletion of resources, most obvious in timber. Large areas are being virtually deforested to provide tropical timber for Japan. This is occurring in Sarawak and Sabah, in Malaysia and Borneo, where they reckon that in about twenty-five years most of the tropical hardwood should be chopped out, and we find this in other areas as well. That also rolls over into the issues of the environment, and what economic growth does to the environment. I don't need to run that list by you, because most people who are aware know what is occurring. What is important in the Asian context is that there is a noticeable growth of NGOs getting involved in concerns about these issues. You can find over a hundred NGOs in Indonesia who are concerned with environmental issues. Not all are very active, and some are small and regional, but nevertheless, within their kind of constrained political framework, that is a very encouraging tendency. The Philippines is exactly the same; one finds large and vigorous NGOs in the Philippines; Thailand is somewhat similar. These are very encouraging kinds of grassroots organizations which are trying to get at the problems underlying growth. I'm pleased to see the Canadian Federal government, in the form of CIDA, has recognized these NGOs and is funneling quite significant portions of Canadian aid to those NGOs. It's an absolutely crucial process. It's hard to convince politicians that giving money to some small group of people concerned with the loss of timber in Sarawak is better for Canada than putting money into a large tied-aid project or program somewhere or other. But there is more awareness; it's an important component and I personally think we should be quite proud of what is happening in that context.

Conclusion: Education for the Pacific Century

If there is any validity in the preceding section, then it must be obvious that one must increasingly develop an Asia-Pacific mindset in the young people of countries such as Canada. There are in fact two mindsets. One of them is a mindset that accepts the Asia-Pacific region as a vital component of the world system, and that it is just as important as Europe or the USA. I think we have a responsibility in our education system to make certain every child has the opportunity to be exposed to that fact. Not all will choose to exercise it as they proceed through the education system, but we have lived in a world which has been dominated by an Atlantic mindset. It is time for a redirection of emphasis.

The other mindset concerns the ability to recognize the fact that the growing interdependence of the Pacific region presents the opportunity for this generation to become part of the region. Shared curriculum, exchange of students, and teaching by satellite are now technically accessible to all. As is so frequently the case, the problem is to develop the institutional means to bring this about. This is the real challenge to education for the Pacific century.

Notes

[1] There have been many attempts at this exercise. In most cases the definition of the 'Pacific Rim', the Asia-Pacific region, and the Pacific region is not the same. For the purposes of this paper we have defined the Pacific Rim to comprise those countries that abut and/or are located within the Pacific Ocean. It might be argued that the countries of the Indian sub-continent should also be included but for the purposes of this paper they have been excluded. A study of the evolution of the term 'Pacific Rim' in the Canadian context is an interesting exercise. Generally, it has no precise geographic definition, having rather a conceptual meaning rather like 'the West' in nineteenth-century North America. The Pacific Rim is seen as the 'new frontier' offering Canadians the opportunity to share by entrepreneurial endeavor in the economic growth of faster-growing countries of the region (see McGee (1983)).

[2] For a beautifully written account of this process at a world scale, see Wolf (1982).

[3] For instance, it is more realistic to disaggregate national data to sub-regional components of the system. Such a procedure would place the State of California as one of the major components of the Pacific Rim system, along with BC in Canada,

and Queensland and Western Australia in Australia.

[4]The data in this table is presented for 1965, 1979 and 1983. A sample analysis of 1986 data showed that the pattern had changed very little.

[5]For example, in the transfer of aid and loans, the USA and Japan are major influences.

[6]See, for example, Taylor and Thrift (1982), and Thrift (1986). They emphasize the fact that even when national ownership may be more than 50 percent, the multinational company based outside may still effectively control the national company because of its control of global technology and distribution systems.

[7]See MacLeod and McGee (1989).

[8]See McGee (1986a), and Kamal Salih and M. L. Young (1986).

[9]See F. Frobel, Heinrichs and Kreye (1980) for an excellent distribution of this so-called 'new international division of labor'.

[10]For example, see A. Pearse (1980) and L. Trager (1988).

[11]On the effects of the 'green revolution' on women, see G. Hart (1986, and J. Momsen and J. Townsend (1987).

[12]See W. Armstrong and McGee (1985), and J. Friedman and G. Wolff (1982).

[13]See McGee (1987).

References

Armstrong, W., and McGee, T.G. (1985). *Theatres of accumulation: Studies in Asian and Latin America urbanization.* London and New York: Methuen.

Friedman, J., and Wolff, G. (1982). 'World city formation: An agenda for research and action', *International Journal of Urban and Regional Research*, Vol. 6, No. 3, 309-43.

Frobel, F., Heinrichs, J., and Kreye, O. (1980). *The new international division of labor.* London: Cambridge University Press.

Hart, G. (1986). *Power, labor and livelihood: Processes of change in rural Java.* Berkeley, Calif.: University of California Press.

Kamal Salih and M.L. Young (1986). 'The regional impact of industrialization: A case study of Penang State', in McGee *et al., Industrialization and labor force processes: A case study of peninsular Malaysia.* Canberra: Research School of Pacific Studies, ANU. 101-37.

MacLeod, S., with McGee, T. G. (1989). 'The last frontier: The emergence of the industrial palate. A Hong Kong case study', in D. Drakakis-Smith (Ed.), *The urban totem.* London: Croom Helm, in press.

McGee, T. G. (1987). 'Urbanisasi or kotadesasi? The emergence of new regions of economic interaction in Asia', *Working Paper* 87-8. Honolulu: Environment and Policy Institute, East-West Center.

_____ (1986). 'Joining the global assembly line: Malaysia's role in the international semi-conductor industry', in McGee *et al., Ibid.* 35-67.

_____ (1983). 'Canada and the changing economy of the Pacific basin. An introductory overview', in *Canada and the changing Pacific economy.* Vancouver: Institute of Asian Research, University of British Columbia, Working Paper no. 1.

Momsen, J., and Townsend, J. (Eds.) (1987). *Geography of gender in the third world.* London: Hutchinson; Albany: State University of New York Press.

Pearse, A. (1980). *Seeds of plenty, seeds of want. Some social and economic*

implications of the green revolution. Oxford: Clarendon Press.
Taylor, M., and Thrift, N. (1982). 'The geographical ramifications of multinational corporations: Introduction', in Taylor and Thrift (Eds.), *The geography of multinationals.* London: Croom Helm. 139-46.
Thrift, N. (1986). 'The internationalization of producer services and the integration of the Pacific basin property market', in Taylor and Thrift (Eds.), *Multinationals and the restructuring of the world economy.* London: Croom Helm.
Trager, L. (1988). *The city connection: Migration and family interdependence in the Philippines.* Ann Arbor, Mich.: The University of Michigan Press.
Wolf, Eric R. (1982). *Europe and the people without history.* Berkeley, Calif.: University of California Press.

Dr. Terry McGee is Director of the Institute of Asian Research and Professor of Geography at The University of British Columbia, Vancouver, Canada V6T 1W5. He has published numerous articles on urban issues in Asia, and has also spent many years in Asia.

Commentary on Section One
Kerry J. Kennedy
Curriculum Development Centre, Australia

There is a great deal of emphasis these days on the necessity for organizations to develop corporate goals and objectives so that resources can be targeted and priorities met. The assumption always is that there is a commonality of purpose within organizations that allows for a large degree of consensus about what is important and what needs to be done. It is clear from the articles in this section, however, that such a process could not be applied to Asia and the Pacific. It seems to be characterized more by diversity than by commonality, by vast differences rather than by similarities. There appears to be no single perspective. Rather, the perspective that is adopted depends on where you happen to be placed in the region and the image that you have of the future.

The article by Bom Mo Chung provides a perspective based largely on South Korea's status as a newly industrialized country. With significant increases in GNP over the past few years, the Republic of Korea now stands ready to look beyond instrumental values. The point is made that historical mass poverty was an ill that needed to be dealt with and now there is a new agenda for a new age. The Republic of Korea can now focus on the demands of an information society – the need to invest in intellectual, artistic and ethical enterprises to pave the way from an industrial to a post-industrial society.

The message from the Philippines is quite different. Increased levels of education have not delivered the promised increases in social mobility, and they have not led to a greater distribution of wealth or contributed to national development. Sister Bernas exposes the romantic view of education as being hopelessly inadequate in providing for the real needs of the Filipino people or the nation as a whole. She recommends instead an approach that links education directly to the economic needs of the nation so that graduates will always have jobs and national economic goals can be achieved. In seeking to align education more closely with economic objectives she has placed pragmatism ahead of ideology in the hope that the Philippines will be enabled to get ahead in the development stakes.

Canada's interest in the Asia-Pacific region is relatively recent. It comes after a long period when Canada's main concerns have been with Europe. Yet there is now a recognition on the part of both federal and provincial governments that the future lies not just with the Atlantic community but also in the Pacific. The statistics quoted by Pflanz demonstrate clearly the economic significance of the region to Canada and the need for Canadians to come to grips with changing trade connections. The actions taken by the British Columbian government attest to the fact that Canadians are taking the reorientation to the Pacific seriously. Nothing less than a fundamental cultural change is being put in place to enable Canada to cope with the economic realities of the twenty-first century.

In an article that moves beyond a single national perspective, McGee reminds us that there is a significant human dimension to the changes that are taking place in the Asia and the Pacific. These changes are based on the development of a global economy which incorporates all the nations of the region and which leads to increasing global interdependence. The effects may not always be positive for traditionally disadvantaged groups, the environment or for meeting the specific needs of local economies. McGee's warnings need to be heeded by policy-makers since the danger in pursuing policies designed for the national good is that the needs of individuals can easily be neglected. Economic development is not an end in itself: its impact on people and the environment must be assessed against the benefits it is able to deliver.

The articles in the section have laid out the policy scenario for the remainder of the book. They highlight both the diversity of the region and the common economic aspirations that seem to be what will tie people together in the future. It is probably true to say that at this point in history there is no shared mindset that joins Pacific peoples together – rather there are a variety of attempts to come to grips with what it means to be part of the region in the latter part of the twentieth century. Clearly, the Eurocentric views that characterized the nineteenth century have disappeared and the colonialism that dominated that period has been replaced by a nationalism that has taken different forms in different parts of the region. Yet the future, it seems, will transform this nationalism into a kind of internationalism, and while there are advantages to this there are also disadvantages for which safeguards need to be developed. As educators we need to develop international citizens who see their responsibilities not only to the nation-state but to the global village to which they will be inextricably linked. The question that faces us is how to prepare young people to make a meaningful contribution to a world that will be vastly different from the one we have known.

Kerry Kennedy is Assistant Director of the Australian Government's Curriculum Development Centre, PO Box 826, Woden, ACT 2611, Australia. He has been involved in a wide range of curriculum policy, research and development activities over the past decade.

Section Two

Curriculum Issues

6

Images and Interests in the Pacific: A Framework for Teaching and Analysing International Affairs

Steven L. Lamy
University of Southern California, United States of America

Pacific Images and Politics

Asia and the Pacific is an area of tremendous diversity in terms of economic growth, political stability, social structures and cultural orientations. It includes some of the richest trading states whose export-led economies have catapulted them into positions of international influence. To many, especially those benefiting from economic growth, it is a region of opportunity and wealth. There are, however, other images of the Asia and the Pacific. China and the Soviet Union, both major powers in military terms, are actively promoting more extensive trade linkages with Pacific trading nations in an effort to secure needed technology, investment capital and markets. Still, there are countries challenged by the problems associated with uneven and inadequate economic development. Some of the poorest states in the world, namely Laos, Vietnam, the Philippines, and Indonesia, also call the Pacific their home. For nations at the bottom of the economic ladder, the image is one of limited opportunities, inequity and exploitation.

In addition to creating a set of striking images the diversity of the Pacific helps to define the politics of the region. Increasingly the politics is shaped by trade and economic development issues, international struggles for control of policy-making processes, and the geopolitical interests of regional and international powers. Moreover, the priorities and interests of the United States and the Soviet Union collide in this area. Their geopolitical interests, promulgated through military assistance programs, development aid, economic and security alliances, and the maintenance of land, air and sea military facilities, have had a profound impact on domestic and foreign policies of most Pacific nations.

Contending Perspectives in Education

There are many 'ways of seeing' the international affairs of the Pacific. Acknowledging multiple views is particularly useful in the development of curriculum and teaching practice because it encourages students to understand how nation-states deal with international issues from a contending perspectives position. Such worldviews offer students divergent descriptions, competing explanations, a variety of predictions about the future and a range of prescriptions for policy action.

This 'contending perspectives' approach (Lamy 1988) to teaching and learning has taken on renewed importance in the United States because of the controversy surrounding educational programs that promote global understanding. Global educators in the USA have been painted as anti-American, promoting beliefs and actions that challenge some very basic American traditions and values such as the family, a laissez-faire attitude toward government, and patriotism (Caporaso and Mittelman 1988). A major criticism of global educators is that they teach issues in such a way as to promote moral and cultural equivalence. American society is presented as having the same characteristics as other countries. Thus, US leaders, like leaders elsewhere, are capable of making good and bad choices: they are not always correct. Critics believe that global education's claim that other political, economic and social systems deserve respect, and may be better than the United States in some areas of governance or international affairs, encourages disrespect and disloyalty.

Generally, critics of global education view the United States as a redeemer or protector nation-state involved in a global struggle between good and evil. This Manichean view of international relations leaves little room for alternative policy positions. The issues are seen as black or white, with a position either pro-American or on the side of its enemies. Global educators are seen by their opponents as naive and misinformed about the nature of the struggle for power in the world system. They are also sometimes considered guilty of trying to impose their political and social preferences, such as world government, pacifism, disarmament and socialism.

While criticism of global education may not be valid in all cases, educators are at times guilty of advocating a particular position. Yet, it is impossible to be value-free in discussions of complex international issues. The presentation of 'all sides of an issue' should be a primary goal of all classroom educators. Issues need to be presented comprehensively and thoroughly to students. This means making every effort to represent a variety of relevant positions along a continuum of political, economic and cultural belief systems.

Analysing worldviews when teaching international affairs is not an antidote against value-laden education. However, if worldview thinking is properly used, it is difficult to ignore any relevant policy positions. The use of worldviews in teaching encourages critical thinking without promoting one worldview over another. When applied to a specific policy problem or a complex global issue, students are encouraged to review data from sources representing relevant worldviews before deciding where they stand. What, then, is a worldview framework and how can it be used to teach contemporary issues of the Pacific?

The Worldviews Analytical Framework

A worldview is defined as a set of assumptions, core beliefs and values that an individual will use as a lens to analyse and evaluate events, the actions of other individuals, organizations or governments, and public issues in general. Thus, we react to our image of reality: the landscape of issues and events shaped by our worldview.

The international system has become more pluralistic in the last twenty years; yet, this pluralism has not resulted in a corresponding condition of international understanding and cooperation. Decision-making processes in most societies have become politicized as groups compete for resources and opportunities. Similarly, the international political arena has become a very competitive environment as states promote their interests and attempt to secure power, prestige and wealth. Nation-states are inextricably linked in their efforts to achieve these goals. In this interconnected world, the chances for controversy and disagreement increa. appreciably. An informed response to an international crisis or policy issue requires a more comprehensive understanding of the situation.

When applied to international issues of the Pacific a worldview framework encourages students to compare contrasting description, explanations and mediations from the three worldviews of maintainer, transformer, and reformer. Understanding issues requires an appreciation of contending perspectives because leaders of Pacific nations have different interests, policy goals and strategies for promoting national interests.

Some leaders will support the status quo and follow a policy strategy aimed at enhancing their power, wealth and prestige within the international system. These leaders are considered *system maintainers*. A second group of political leaders recognize the need for incremental reform of the present international system to accommodate new interests, respond to changing conditions, and resolve persistent flaws. These *system reformers* generally seek multilateral solutions to global problems and support reforms as a means of avoiding more dramatic or radical transformations in the international order. Still, there are some individuals and groups who would support nothing but a radical transformation of the present international system. Those who are *system transformers* believe that the structures and processes of decision-making that control who gets what, when, where and how need to be overhauled and not just tinkered with by those trying to protect their interests. What follows is a clarification of the foundations of each worldview.

System Maintainers

The intellectual foundations of this worldview category can be found in the writings of Thucydides, Machiavelli, Thomas Hobbes, and more contemporary writers such as E.H. Carr and Hans Morgenthau (Vasquez 1986). Simply stated, system maintainers identify political realities as power realities. From this view, states are seen as the primary actors in the international system and the more power a state has, the greater chance that it will secure its national interests. Self-interest and self-help are ruling principles in an anarchic international system. Cooperation is possible, but only if it is perceived to be a more effective means of securing a state's interests. Otherwise, states act unilaterally with like-minded states. A summary of other core assumptions follows:

Primary concern of national leaders
Maintaining power, defined usually in military terms, relative to other states to preserve a balance of power in the international system.

View of foreign relations
A zero-sum perspective (that is, what's mine is mine and what's yours is mine) is the norm in a world without rules. A country must have the capability and will to represent and then protect its national interest. Conflict is endemic in this system.

The maintenance of world order
This is best achieved through a balance of power where stability is maintained by deterrence and alliance politics.

The best strategy for economic growth and prosperity
Economic prosperity results from policies that support a liberal free-trade economic order. This involves a laissez-faire strategy with no barriers to trade and the free flow of capital, labour, etc.

The system maintainer worldview is the dominant perspective in world affairs. Most leaders support the status quo because of the uncertainty associated with any shift in power arrangements. However, those who support some reform in the system are not solely motivated by self-interest or by the desire to coopt those who advocate more radical changes. Many system reformers believe that multilateralism and international cooperation is the most appropriate strategy for securing their interests and promoting policies aimed at creating a more just, peaceful and prosperous world.

System Reformers

Most of the reform ideas are presented in response to a major international crisis. This is not a perspective based on naive idealism. Instead, it is a realization that countries of the world must work together in policy areas in an effort to avoid conflict and respond more effectively to systemic maladies such as hunger. Those who see the world through a reformer's lens believe that there are times when even rational self-interest leads actors to abandon unilateralism for multilateralism. Reformers believe that there exists a larger international moral order and states support international laws that protect the interests of the international community. States have an interest in cooperation when that cooperation prevents war and promotes the well-being of humankind. Furthermore, states will establish rules, regulations and institutions in an effort to promote the general welfare and to secure mutual gains. The writings of John Locke, Hugo Grotius, Woodrow Wilson, David Mitrany, Willy Brandt, Lester Pearson and John Holmes contribute to our understanding of this worldview.

Other core assumptions include:

Primary concern of national leaders
Developing cooperative strategies to control arms races that will lead to war. Building multilateral institutions that can effectively respond to problems associated with inequality and maldevelopment.

View of foreign relations
A minimum global social ethic exists. States now see the prospect of a mutual gain through cooperation. All states' interests are threatened by ineffective responses to common crisis situations such as global poverty. These complex problems require multilateral efforts.

The maintenance of world order
This is best achieved through the establishment of an integrated community of nation-states in which multilateralism is emphasized. This involves the integration of policy-making and collective responses to challenges.

The best strategy for economic growth and prosperity
The European Community provides a useful model of cooperation between political systems and the marketplace. States will be forced to be more cooperative and more open to public interventions to avoid neomercantilist tendencies and respond to inequities not addressed by market mechanisms.

The system reformer worldview is gaining support from leaders and citizens alike. However, leaders are reluctant to give up the control over policy-making processes that many multilateral strategies require. Additionally, leaders are less than sanguine about the possibility of replacing a system of competing national interests with a system that promotes mutual interests and burden sharing. Few leaders have the confidence to be the first to invest in these multilateral efforts. Unfortunately, it is usually a crisis situation that impels many leaders to rethink their Hobbesian orientations.

System Transformers

There are a number of individuals and groups that are not satisfied with how the present international system is ordered. These interests usually represent those who are disadvantaged in political, economic or cultural terms. Some transformers support policies that will change the system enough to give them access to power circles in the international system. These 'confrontational transformers' usually become system maintainers once they enhance their position in the international system. The challenge presented by OPEC members and their shift to status quo politics provides an example of this type of transformer.

Still, there are transformers who support a change and the establishment of an alternative system. The writings of Karl Marx, Mao and Franz Fanon provide the foundation for the 'Neo-Marxian Dependencia' perspective. These transformers see the international system as a feudal system with a core group of wealthy capitalists states in control. These states, and the economic interests they serve and protect, exploit the periphery (that is, the developing world) by supporting client governments that make it easy for them to extract resources, pay low wages for labor, and invest their surplus capital.

Another transformer worldview is that of the idealist or utopian. The World Order Models Project (WOMP) provides the most comprehensive profile of this worldview. Advocates of this position support domestic and foreign policy goals that are reflective of specific human-centric ideals such as social justice, ecological balance, peace, cultural identity, access and participation, economic well-being, and non-violence (Johansen 1980 and Falk 1975). These ideals can never be reached under the present state-centric system. Proponents argue that a more decentralized power structure is needed. One idea is a global federation of state and non-state actors where all participants act according to specific international norms guaranteed by multilateral enforcement agencies.

Additional core assumptions of both the WOMP and dependencia transformers are presented below:

	WOMP	Dependencia
Primary concern of national leaders	The need to reform institutions and policy processes that emphasize state-centric power goals over human-centric goals.	An international economic system that perpetuates inequality and an international power system that is dominated by the East-West struggle.
View of foreign relations	The goal should be a world system of state and non-state actors governed by international laws and internally recognized norms and rules of behaviour. At present, international relations are seen as state-centric and power-oriented.	The goal is to eliminate the present system in which the core states control the international policy agenda and exploit the poor states. Developing states are disadvantaged in this unequal system.
The maintenance of world order	Peace is best achieved by giving power to citizens, recognizing the role of multilateral decision-making structures.	Conflict and power struggles will continue unless a more equitable international economic system is established.
The best strategy for economic growth and prosperity	The establishment of decision-making institutions in which all states enjoy access to economic resources and opportunities. Universal rules will govern investment, labor and production processes in all states. The goal is to establish systems based on economic well-being and human dignity.	

Contending Images in Pacific Affairs

Like any geographical region, the nation-states of the Pacific face considerable policy challenges. At home citizens expect states to maintain public order, provide a stable environment for the exchange of goods and services, and discourage foreign invasions by maintaining a deterrent military force. The increasing complexity of our societies and the growth in transnational transactions have complicated and transformed the relationship between citizens and governments. It is becoming increasingly more difficult to reach a consensus on what is a country's 'national interest' in many policy issue areas. Interest groups with contending images of what is important and what should be done compete for control of the policy agenda. Two issue areas that are of increasing importance to Pacific states – international trade and regional security and defense – will be examined from the worldviews of system reformers, transformers and maintainers.

Trade Issues

In countries throughout the Pacific, private corporations and economic interest groups are looking to governmental agencies to work with them in their effort to gain access to and maintain markets, identify and acquire strategic resources, and promote and protect their investments. These states operate in a 'semi-free' market system and many Pacific states, namely Japan and the export-led economies of the Newly Industrialized Countries (NICs), have prospered in this system. These states have become major actors in the international economy. This shift in wealth and power has not been readily accepted. Those nations which have lost power and those which continue to be disadvantaged are raising concerns about the role of governments in promoting trade, the fairness of the international economic system, and the problems associated with accommodating national interest within a free-trade system. These are some of the questions that face leaders of Pacific states as they try to promote growth and prosperity within this region.

A System Maintainer Perspective

The system maintainers in the Pacific are the more affluent and influential states. The primary system maintainer is the United States. The contemporary economic system is roughly equivalent to the liberal free-trade system established by the US and its allies following World War II. The major trading states of the Pacific – Canada, Australia, New Zealand, Japan and the NICs – have benefited from this system and continue to support the principles of 'free trade' and the idea that competition and comparative advantage should be the basis of trade. Needless to say, the international trade environment is not free of public interventions. Public leaders have supported and continue to support economic interests with public resources. However, all of the maintaining states have generally agreed to control their neomercantilist tendencies, work out their differences, and maintain a relatively free trading environment.

The US position calls for a further liberalization of trade in this region. For the United States, the major problem facing trading states in this region is protectionist competitors. US officials argue that Japan must lower its trade barriers and, along with the 'Four Tigers', must take more responsibility for maintaining a free-trade system. The path to liberalization will involve a renewed commitment to trade regulations established by the General Agreement of Tariffs and Trade (GATT) and the negotiation of bilateral agreements that limit barriers to free trade.

Although generally in agreement with the goal of reducing trade tariffs and other barriers to a free flow of goods and services, the Japanese and some of the NICs are not convinced that the United States truly wants a free-trade system in the Pacific. Approximately 63 percent of the US trade deficit is accounted for in Pacific trade. American leaders are being pressured by their constituents to correct this trade imbalance and protect US industries by reducing imports and making US products more attractive to domestic and foreign markets. Thus, many leaders in Pacific states feel that reciprocity and not competition and free-trade impulses drive the US agenda. This means the more US goods they buy, the more imports the US will allow. Similar pressures and policy responses are not unfamiliar to other states like Canada, Australia and Japan. Trade imbalances and related budgetary deficits are fuelling protectionist sentiments in most of the more advanced industrial societies. The road to economic development often requires that industries be given an initial boost. This is one rationale given by political leaders in developing states for implementing barriers against imports and for seeking assistance for new industries and agricultural production.

The ideal for a system maintainer is a competitive growth-oriented free-trade system. System maintainers recognize the need for some minimal public interventions to respond to national needs; however, they are generally against any extensive restrictions that might result in 'beggar thy neighbor' competition. The actual trading environment in the Pacific is fairly competitive, in that most states either restrict or manage trade flows by offering incentives for exporters and restricting the flow of imports. National interests, cultural factors, different levels of economic development, consumer tastes, and a society's attitude toward the role of government influence a country's trade policies. In spite of the obstructions, most system maintainers are committed to bargaining and negotiating when differences threaten to disrupt the status quo. Political leaders must carefully balance the domestic interests and the goal of maintaining a stable international trade order.

There appears to be room for adjustments within the existing system. Recent examples include joint production ventures by Japanese and US firms and the building of production facilities in a number of countries. Toyota, for example, is planning to market an all-ASEAN car with parts being built and traded among ASEAN members. Still, the most common method for dealing with trade disputes is bilateral negotiation. For example, New Zealand's political leaders are constantly faced with closed markets as they try to sell their agricultural products. Since their access to European Community markets, namely Great Britain, has been restricted, they have tried to overcome quotas and tariffs that restrict free trade in dairy, beef, lamb and other primary products. New Zealand's leaders are looking to replace British and European trade by negotiating trade agreements with countries like Japan, China, the United States and Canada. Similar problems face Australia, China and many of the less developed economies trying to break into the international trade system.

Most countries want to gain access to the present system. They do not seek radical changes in the present international economic order. However, protectionist policies are continuing to challenge the 'free-trade' system in the Pacific and this neomercantilist orientation is causing some political and economic leaders to review other options.

System Reformer Options

System reformers recognize the need to shift from a self-interest trade policy orientation to a more cooperative one. This is not to suggest that national economic interests are ignored. Instead, reform advocates believe that by reaching agreements to share markets, pool resources for economic development, and jointly establish trade and production policies, their national interests can be better served. The history of cooperation that built the European Community is often used as a model for other states interested in building common markets.

According to some trade specialists, Japan is taking seriously the idea of creating an Asian trading community. Trade and investment in this community would be based on the yen and not the dollar. Such a trading bloc would be potentially as powerful as the 1989 Canada-US trade system and the forthcoming 1992 European Community. Some experts predict a world economy by the year 2000 will be dominated by these three trade blocs. In essence, Japan feels that greater economic and political integration among the Asian-Pacific nations is inevitable and it would serve its interests to coordinate or manage this process of change.

The end result may be an expansion of ASEAN, the creation of a Pacific version of the Organization of Economic Cooperation and Development (OECD), or a free-trade area loosely coordinated by existing regional organizations (e.g. ASEAN) or the Pacific Economic Cooperation Council. ASEAN, with member states Brunei, Indonesia, Malaysia, the Philippines, Singapore and Thailand, is already promoting regional cohesion in areas of trade, economic development, regional security and technological research. This group could easily be expanded by giving some sort of regular status to its 'dialogue partners': Australia, Canada, Japan, New Zealand, and perhaps the US. ASEAN, however, although founded primarily to promote regional trade, has not been as successful as the European Community in proposing joint economic ventures and encouraging more intra-organizational cooperation and trade. To ensure regional cooperation, Japan and other economic leaders will have to commit some level of political and economic support. This means sharing resources, markets and decision-making power. For example, regional projects that pool resources and expertise in energy research or telecommunication could be of immense benefit to the region. Research in these areas is expensive and there is no reason, other than national pride, to duplicate many of these industries or research and development projects.

As suggested in the Brandt Commission Reports (1982 and 1983), a reformist strategy may be the only way to close the gap between rich and poor states. Regional planning, policy coordination and collaborative ventures may be the only way to promote equitable patterns of growth and stability. Japan may be the key actor in this process.

A reformist plan would not support the establishment of an exclusive and competitive trading system made up of regional blocs promoting self-reliance and protectionist barriers. Thus, plans for creating trade zones or common markets for sections of this region may do more harm than good. Reformists would argue that any regime (that is, rules, regulations and decision-making institutions) that discourages multilateralism and promotes discriminating policies is both unwise and potentially disruptive.

Two states that should benefit from reformist efforts to encourage more economic collaboration and discourage neomercantilist tendencies are the People's Republic of China and the Soviet Union. The Chinese and the Soviets are establishing closer economic ties. In addition, membership in any 'Pacific Trade Club' would be economically beneficial and would cost less politically. It is common knowledge in international politics that bilateral agreements usually create more dependencies by giving one partner advantages over the other.

The Soviets do not see the Pacific as just another geopolitical arena for challenging US interests. The current Soviet government wants to triple its trade with countries in this region over the next twelve years. It plans to increase its trade (that is, primarily a bartering arrangement) with other socialist societies in the region – Vietnam, North Korea and China. However, in its efforts to secure technology, manufactured goods and investment capital for Soviet Asia, it is looking for trade agreements with the NICs and Japan.

System Transformer Options

Transformers favor a radical and comprehensive restructuring of the trade regime rather than the gradual reforms favored by the maintainers and the multilateral reforms supported by the reformers. There may be individuals and groups within countries advocating strategies of socialism or self-reliance; however, few national governments have taken a consistent stand for radical transformations of their economy. Burma's seemingly unsuccessful experiments with autarky and isolationism and Vietnam's little imperialism seem to be the only examples of states offering or promoting alternative systems. In both cases, the transformer's efforts were not successful. Both countries have experienced significant economic and political problems and have begun to seek connections with Western states.

It is important to note that there are political factions in many Pacific states (for example, the Philippines, Indonesia, Australia, etc.) that advocate either a path of self-reliance or a dismantling of capitalist core-periphery relations and the establishment of a more equitable international system. The latter, neo-Marxist image of the world is very prevalent in many developing states. Although these images may not be critical in the definition of any one state's official trade policies, these radical positions are heard and may have some effect on public perceptions and policy.

Images of Security in the Pacific Region

Security in the Pacific is maintained by the presence of significant naval and air forces. The Pacific is generally seen as an area where the US enjoys military hegemony. This system is now being challenged by three factors. First, the Soviet Union has established bases in the Pacific and is shifting resources to this area. Secondly, US alliances – SEATO and ANZUS – have either been dismantled or lost credibility in a post-Cold War environment. Thirdly, the US public is becoming increasingly unwilling to support military spending that they feel, correctly or incorrectly, is providing protection for states capable of providing for themselves (such as Japan). Also, many citizens within states in this region have become strong supporters of regional demilitarization and depolarization. These people do not want this region to become an arena for East-West conflict. International security concerns, as they relate to the maintenance of international order, are now discussed from each of the three worldviews.

A System Maintainer's View of Pacific Security

For the United States, order is defined by its ability to maintain a military advantage over the Soviets in this region. The United States is also concerned about potential system-destabilizing conflicts within developing states. For example, insurgencies in the Philippines, Indonesia and in the Pacific Island states concern US leaders. They are worried that these conflicts will result in shifts of power in favor of left-wing or pro-Soviet regimes. Thus, the US system maintainers support policies that will maintain a 9,000-mile arc of US military installations that indirectly involve Japan, South Korea, Micronesia, Guam, the Philippines and Australia in US geopolitical conflicts with its primary enemy – the Soviet Union (Bedford 1986).

The US strategic view of Asia and the Pacific is more than just a containment policy. It seems that the United States is interested in creating a military presence that would enable it to successfully intervene in areas of conflict (for example, the Philippines), to prepare for a potential nuclear confrontation with the Soviets, and to protect US economic interests by keeping commercial shipping lanes open and maintaining stability within the region. In the late 1980s the United States went so far as to establish a doctrine of maritime supremacy *vis-a-vis* the Soviets. The US goal was to match, weapon for weapon, every

Soviet move in the Pacific and to prepare for possible confrontations in low-intensity conflict situations (LICs). The United States aims to use economic, political and military resources to manage economic development processes and processes of political and social change in its favor.

The core assumptions of a system maintainer, such as the inevitability of a conflict in an anarchic system, the importance of national interests, and the strategies of self-help and unilateralism, to suggest a few, are very evident in US policy. What is clear about US policy is the continued emphasis on seeing most of the strategic or military issues in this area as East-West problems and not as regional or national issues. This is one reason why the United States has reacted so strongly to New Zealand's anti-nuclear position and is so concerned with Soviet 'commercial' overtures to Pacific Island states.

What may happen is an extension of ANZUS to include Japan, or the creation of a new collective defense pact manned by troops from throughout the region, supported by US hardware, and financed by the Japanese. The US is unlikely to allow Japan to extend its military role beyond home defense. Yet, there are many who are suggesting that Japan should pay a higher price for the US security umbrella.

System Reformer Views

Many of the states within Asia and the Pacific are concerned about the re-polarization of politics that occurred under the Reagan administration. Leaders in Europe, Canada, Latin America and Asia were concerned about increasing tensions throughout the world and sought to establish institutions and decision structures that emphasize shared leadership and multilateralism. Although tensions have eased under Mr Gorbachev's policies and Mr Reagan's positive reactions, other leaders of rich and poor states have not discontinued their pressures for a greater voice in decision-making.

The system reformers in the Pacific include countries like Canada, Australia, New Zealand, the ASEAN states, and many of the Pacific Island states. To some extent, Japan and the Soviet Union must also be considered system reformers in the security policy sector. China remains difficult to categorize. However, Chinese leaders did play a major role in pressuring the Soviets to push the Vietnamese to the bargaining table over Kampuchea. The Japanese seem to be seeking more linkages with both China and the USSR. The cornerstone of Japanese foreign policy is its relationship with the US; nevertheless, Japanese leaders seem to believe that by increasing trade and other exchanges, peace and order will follow. The Soviets must also be considered to be reformers. There is obviously a great deal of controversy about the meaning of the Soviet's overtures; yet, many leaders in the Pacific see the Soviets as sincere and in desperate need of trading partners, investment capital and non-communist friends. Nonetheless, the Soviets remain concerned about US military predominance in this region and minimally seek to create a credible deterrent to US forces. The Soviets seek a sense of order that results from a rough balance of forces. Thus, the Soviets expand their naval base in Vietnam, deploy more naval vessels in the region, and support regional efforts like ASEAN's Southeast Asian Zone of Peace, Freedom and Neutrality (Tow 1988). The ASEAN states, uneasy about US and Soviet involvement in their region, want to create an arena for cooperation, free of external controls and excessive influence by outside powers. If implemented, this plan would more adversely influence US strategic interests and, thus, make it easier for the Soviets to catch up and reach a balance with the US.

Reformers in the security policy sector seek more multilateral and cooperative programs for maintaining order and responding to crisis situations. Rather than unilateral military threats or actual military actions, reformers seek peace and order through international law, diplomacy and, if necessary, collective security actions. System reformers in this region tend to see conflicts in countries like the Philippines as more than East-West issues. From this worldview, the basic problems in many Pacific and Asian states are believed to be caused by a need for social and economic development and reform. These problems are simply exacerbated by US and Soviet interference. Furthermore, reformers do not believe that problems can be solved by military interventions or outside interference. For the reformer, development assistance, cooperative economic development projects, educational programs, and support for democratic reforms are the best methods for maintaining order and providing for regional and national security.

System Transformer Views

Few governments advocate a radical transformation of the international system. In the Pacific, only Vietnam posed a meaningful challenge to the status quo by its aggressive military expansion into Kampuchea and its threat to other neighbors. With China's shift in political orientations, Vietnam's decision to withdraw from Kampuchea, and the Soviet Union's new rhetoric of cooperation, only subnational groups advocate either utopian strategies for change or neo-Marxist visions of equitable societies. In security matters, Marxists and neo-Marxists tend to advocate the use of arms to overthrow repressive and exploitative capitalist systems. For example, the Marxist New People's Army has been fighting against the Filipino government since 1969. It is difficult to know whether the leaders of this insurgent group are really interested in transforming the existing order by establishing a more equitable democratic and socialist society. Many transformers simply want access to power and once this is achieved, they too become system maintainers. However, in terms of regional security, transformers would be in favour of disarmament or a collective security system controlled only by actors within the region. Most insurgent groups claim that this type of regional order is their goal. However, most rely on outside support for weapons and base their campaigns for change on military coercion and the actual use of force.

More utopian visions of international and regional security are promoted by peace and environmental groups throughout this region. Most are advocates of 'nuclear free zones' and many groups go farther by advocating more comprehensive plans for disarmament and non-military security strategies. The anti-nuclear weapons movement in the South Pacific provides an example of system transformer aims.

In 1985, the South Pacific Forum proposed the establishment of a South Pacific Nuclear Free Zone (SPNFZ). The signatories (Cook Islands, Fiji, New Zealand, Australia, Kiribati, and several others) agreed not to produce nuclear weapons. These states sought to keep the nuclear powers out of this region and to establish a regional plan for 'common security'. This system would involve regional actors focusing on regional problems. The goal would be to respond to problems and crisis situations before they become military conflicts and possibly attract the attention of outside-the-region nuclear powers (Henderson, et al. 1980). The general strategy of most utopian or idealistic system transformers is to move away from foreign policies that emphasize national interests over human interests. The diversity of interests in this region makes this goal even more difficult to achieve.

Conclusion

Leaders of states in this region face many difficult policy choices. They must decide how best to create a national and regional environment that promotes participation, provides goods and services essential to securing basic human needs, and encourage peaceful responses to crisis situations. Many would suggest that regional cooperation is an absolute requirement for growth, prosperity and peace in this region.

The anodyne may very well be an educational program that encourages students of international affairs to see an issue from a variety of value positions. This might lead citizens and their leaders to see beyond self-interest and consider the concerns of others in the formulation and implementation of public policy. In a world defined by competing national interests this call for a pluralistic policy-making process sounds rather utopian. Most leaders are rather skeptical about idealistic schemes that ask them to consider views and interests of people beyond their borders. They are also reluctant to hand over power and authority to any supranational decision-making authority without some guarantees of attention to their concerns. National interest is still the ruling concept in international affairs; however, leaders are slowly accepting more multilateral cooperative strategies as problems persist, competition increases, and tensions mount. Put simply, most leaders are now recognizing their 'micro-tools' of statecraft cannot handle the macro problems of underdevelopment, the international debt crisis, refugees, war, and pollution of the environment. The Pacific may provide us with the laboratory for working out many of these challenges. It will certainly require that we can see these issues and problems from a multitude of perspectives.

References

Bedford, Michael (1986). The strategic role of US deployments in the Pacific and Indian Ocean. In *Nuclear war and US intervention*. Ed. Joseph Gerson.

Philadelphia,. Pa.: New Society Publishers.

Brandt Commission. *North-South: A program for survival.* Cambridge, Mass.: The MIT Press.

_____ (1983). *Common crisis North – South: Cooperation for world recovery.* Cambridge, Mass.: The MIT Press.

Caporaso, James A., and Mittelman, James H. (Winter 1988). The assault on global education, *PS* 21: 36-44.

Falk, Richard (1975). *A study of future worlds.* New York: Free Press.

Henderson, John, Jackson, K., and Kennaway, R. (1980). *Beyond New Zealand: The foreign policy of a small state.* Auckland, N.Z.: Methuen.

Johansen, Robert (1980). *The national interest and human interest: An analysis of US foreign policy.* Princeton, N.J.: Princeton University Press.

Lamy, Steven (1988). *Contemporary international issues: Contending perspectives.* Boulder, Colo.: Lynne Rienner Publishers.

US Department of State (1988). Pacific development and the new internationalism. Address by Richard H. Solomon before the Pacific Future Conference, Los Angeles, Calif., 15 March.

_____ (1985). The Pacific: Region of promise and challenge. Address by Paul D. Wolfowitz before the National Defense University, Honolulu, Hawaii, 22 February.

Vasquez, Richard (Ed.) (1986). *Classics of international relations.* Englewood Cliffs, N.J.: Prentice-Hall.

Steven Lamy teaches international affairs and foreign policy of Western industrial countries in the School of International Relations, University of Southern California, University Park, Los Angeles, California 90089-0043, USA. He serves as Co-Director, Center for Public Education in International Affairs.

7

Islands in Between:
Some Social Studies Curriculum Development for Pacific Island Countries

Konai Helu Thaman
University of the South Pacific, Fiji

Introduction

> I was six when
> Mama was careless
> she sent me to school
> alone
> five days a week ...
>
> on my release
> fifteen years after
> I was handed
> (among loud applause
> from fellow victims)
> a piece of paper
> to decorate my walls
> certifying my release
>
> from 'Kidnapped' by R. Petaia (1983: 56-57)

The Samoan poet Ruperake Petaia in his poem 'Kidnapped', laments, among other things, the alienating influences of the school on many Pacific Island children. He is, of course, remembering his own school days of the 50s and 60s, yet the poem is as relevant about today's school as it was about schools in colonial times. Attempts have been made, since many of our countries became politically independent, to make the schools less alienating and curricula more culturally 'relevant'. In 1970-75, for example, a regional curriculum development project, funded by UNDP and executed by UNESCO (with headquarters at the University of the South Pacific's then School of Education), developed materials in different subject areas for use in the participating countries' junior secondary schools. Countries which took part included Cook Islands, Fiji, Kiribati (Gilbert Islands), Vanuatu (New

Hebrides), Niue, Solomon Islands, Tokelau Islands, Tonga and Western Samoa. One of the basic aims of curriculum decision-makers was the development of 'relevant' curricula, more appropriate for newly independent Pacific Island nations, but as Renner (1982: 138) warns:

> The Pacific communities, Polynesian, Melanesian and Micronesian, have long had a rich informal curriculum of their own. Unfortunately, colonialism failed to acknowledge local achievements as valid curriculum content and imposed Western courses and method on the diversity of Pacific cultures. Now, towards the end of the colonial period, the South Pacific nations are unified by their desire to free themselves from educational imperialism. But colonial dependence dies slowly. The South Pacific countries still need support and recognition of the metropolitan universities; they still depend heavily on the rimlands for financial and other forms of educational assistance.

Social Science, an integrated subject, was new to the region, but it was accepted by the participating countries, and with the exception of Western Samoa (which continued to use the term Social Studies), other countries adopted the new name, Social Science.

Some Aspects of Social Science Curriculum Development in the Pacific Islands

Curriculum development in social science/social studies in the small island countries of the South Pacific shares features and problems which are common to curriculum development in the region generally. Among such common and significant features are:

1. the central role played by national ministries of education in determining curriculum content;
2. the strong impact of external influences on decision-making; and
3. the increasing involvement of practising teachers in the planning and implementation of curriculum innovations (Thaman, 1987a: 50-60).

The central ministry of education is directly responsible for, and controls the content of, the manifest curriculum of schools throughout the small countries of the region. Central governments try to ensure that the curriculum reflects the overall objectives of the educational system. The process of curriculum development invariably begins with the ministry appointing curriculum teams/committees/panels which are normally composed of teachers, education officials and curriculum coordinators and/or administrators. Curriculum materials are produced first for trials and subsequently for wider or national implementation. The overall responsibility for this activity falls directly on senior officers of the ministry of education or on individuals specifically appointed to direct curriculum work. In some countries, there are curriculum development units. Through these agencies, the ministry of education not only produces subject-based curricula but also supplementary materials, including pupil and teacher guides. This contrasts with a system-based model used in many metropolitan countries, where curriculum developers may produce guidelines and the teachers are left to determine the details of what to teach in their own particular grades.

Most curriculum development projects in the South Pacific island countries have been or are externally funded and/or administered. In many island countries, there are a number of external aid sources involved, the major ones being the United Nations Development Program (UNDP); the governments of Australia and New Zealand, and the World Bank. Different aid sources have differing methods of administering their 'aid', but in almost all cases, foreign curriculum consultants are utilized to advise not only on how funds are to be spent, but on the actual curriculum process itself. In some cases, they do the actual writing of the curriculum units. During the past few years, concern has been expressed about the way in which external aid in education has been delivered, especially in relation to the role of some foreign tertiary institutions and consultants (see, for example, Baba, 1987: 3-11).

In almost all of these countries, the curriculum development task has fallen squarely on the shoulders of practising teachers. Their active role in designing and producing curriculum materials and implementing these has not only been encouraged, but, in some countries, demanded by educational authorities (Thaman, 1981; 1987a: 52). This trend became more obvious in the early 1970s with the beginning of the UNDP/UNESCO regional secondary curriculum development project. Regional curriculum teams, consisting mainly of teachers from around the region (with the help of a UN adviser), produced and administered the testing of new curriculum materials in their subjects. Respective national curriculum teams were also encouraged to produce units which were relevant to their cultural situations. These were to be used together with the regionally produced 'core units'.

By 1975, all the core units for a regional Form 1-4 Social Science curriculum had been written and tested. This provided the basic framework upon which each country would build its curriculum (see Appendix A). In the kinds of curriculum activities that followed, teachers continued to play an active role in writing, rewriting, revising and adapting social science materials for use by both teachers and pupils.

Renner (1982) and Baba (1979) have described and analysed the UNDP/UNESCO project and the social science curriculum respectively. In this paper I will make some observations about the work that has been done since the end of the UNDP/UNESCO regional project, as different countries have tried to continue and maintain the momentum of curriculum development in the area of social science/social studies. These comments relate to what happened in some island countries during the years 1976-86.

Aims and Objectives

The social science programs in most of the island countries have continued to emphasise the development in children of a more critical and perhaps balanced social awareness compared with what had been the case before 1970 (see, for example, Appendix B – Aims of Social Science). In the regional program for Forms 1 and 2, for example, learning was minutely prescribed in detailed lesson plans and curriculum units (rather similar to some American social studies programs) and largely reflected aspects of the work of people such as Bruner and Bloom. Objectives were defined in behavioral terms, and learning experiences were devised to reflect and achieve those objectives. This was in contrast to most pre-1970 social studies/history/geography programs where topics were identified or prescribed and the teacher had to devise his/her own methods and learning resources.

Content

The social science course devised by the regional UNDP/UNESCO project used the full range of social science subjects, and presented it as an integrated course. Since 1975, different countries have modified the basic structures to suit themselves. Fiji, for example, kept pretty much to the original structure while Solomon Islands on the other hand, changed many of the themes (see Appendix C). Pupils were introduced to different modes of inquiry with an emphasis on the use of a variety of data sources, and not just books, which, until this time, were the main sources of information for both teacher and pupils. Teachers and pupils alike were encouraged to use newspapers, films, literature, surveys, field trips, community people, statistics, etc. to obtain information about the different societies they were studying, including their own, of course.

Method

There was a general move away from teacher-centred to pupil-centred methods of teaching. Discovery learning, fashionable at the time especially in metropolitan countries, demanded that the teacher became a 'facilitator' rather than a 'director' of learning and curriculum units contained many 'pupil activities' designed to stimulate students to discover things for themselves and hence develop their own capacities for learning. Resources were wide-ranging, and such things as photographs, audio tapes and films, together with teachers' guides and pupil booklets, provided what many curriculum officers referred to as the 'teacher-proof' curriculum, in the sense that it was hoped that children would learn something even if the teacher should be ill-prepared to implement the curriculum.

Evaluation

Evaluation in the new social science programs include teacher-made tests and school examinations as well as standardised national examinations, usually sat at the grade 9 or 10 level, as part of national school-leaving examinations. In some countries, such as Tonga and Fiji, students could choose from social science, history and geography. It was generally found that students who opted for social science as an examination subject tended to score better grades compared with those who did history and geography (Puloka, 1983:

pers. comm.). Many teachers felt that this was partly due to the fact that social science was more interesting and meaningful for students, and they therefore liked it. Baba (1979), for example, concluded that students in Form 1 (grade 6 or 7) in Fiji schools found the activities in the social science curriculum easy to understand and they also found them interesting.

Issues and Problems

By 1985, Fiji, Tonga, Western Samoa, Vanuatu and the Solomon Islands had integrated social science programs at least up to Form 4 (or grade 10). However, in two of these countries major teaching changes, relating to changes in the pattern of examinations, have been brought in and have affected the content of Form 3 and 4 social science. In Fiji, parts of the Forms 3 and 4 program now includes topics originally found in the history and geography curricula, with the social science units relegated to 'optional'; and in Tonga, history and geography became once more compulsory subjects for the secondary leaving certificate, which meant dropping social science from the list of subjects offered at Form 3 and above.

It is not known why social science has become a target for criticism in Tonga, especially among senior educational officials and some principals. According to social science teachers I interviewed, students preferred social science because it was based on content they could relate to and, moreover, it was 'fun'; history and geography means 'going back to memorising facts and figures again, and is boring', they said. Furthermore, many students performed better in the school leaving exam in social science compared with history and geography. Whatever the reasons, it is certain that many students are going to find that the change is not to their advantage, judging from the poor student performances in history and geography examinations generally.

Since 1975, a number of problems have become apparent in relation to work in social science/social studies. These may be grouped into three main areas: pupil-related problems, teacher-related problems, and curriculum-related problems.

Pupil-related Problems

Much remains to be learned and understood about the readiness of children to understand various aspects of social relationships. For example, the prevalent use of the spiral model of curriculum development, much influenced by the work of Piaget, sometimes lead to studies which may underestimate the ability of children to understand different kinds of social relationships. For example, one critic of the regional social science, a New Zealand teacher, claimed that the study of the complexities of family relationships in grade 7 was unrealistic. She was later amazed at the ability of Tongan children to fully understand the content of their unit on 'The Family', complete with definitions and explanations of different kinds of kinship relationships. She had complained to me earlier that she did not come across such content until her anthropology class at university! Tongan children and adults alike, however, have lived within this intricate kinship network and associated descriptive terminology for centuries.

On the other hand, much remains to be done in finding out how different students respond to the social science curriculum. Baba (1983: 480), for example, found that, in Fiji, Indian students generally expressed more favorable attitudes than Fijian and 'other' students. Moreover, he found that there were differences between rural and urban schools in that rural schools perceived the activities in one social science unit as significantly easier than students in urban schools did. More research is clearly needed in this area.

Teacher-related Problems

Many teachers are not well prepared to teach an integrated curriculum. There is a need to include other subjects besides history and geography in teacher education programs. There are many cases in our schools where the head of the Department of Social Studies does not understand the social science curriculum. This may because she/he does not teach it or went through an undergraduate program which concentrated only on history and geography. Many of these kinds of people are either indifferent or even hostile towards the teaching of an integrated curriculum. In many cases, teacher training has not kept up with curriculum development, a point that cannot be overemphasized, especially in our region.

In terms of teacher participation in curriculum development, many teachers have favorable attitudes towards their active role in curriculum development, but many do not have the necessary skills to fully and effectively take part. Again, teacher education programs generally show a lack of consideration of this new aspect of the teacher's role in the region. A survey of teacher training programs in Fiji, Tonga and Western Samoa highlighted the lack of courses relating to curriculum theory and practice (Masih, 1978). Teacher education programs at the University of the South Pacific include such courses, but the majority of teachers currently teaching in junior high schools in the region do not have the opportunity to go to university.

The amount and degree of teacher influence in curriculum decision-making depend, of course, on the country under consideration, as well as the educational level reached by the majority of the teachers. In many situations, the major decisions and much of the actual production work seem to rest with a few, enthusiastic members of the curriculum committee. Limited data available from Tonga, Western Samoa and Vanuatu would suggest that there would probably have been a more positive attitude from teachers in respect to implementation if they had participated in curriculum-writing workshops. Perhaps the important thing is for teachers to feel that they have contributed to the preparation of curriculum materials, rather than major curriculum decisions *per se*. Tongan teacher trainees at the USP in 1978-83, as part of their curriculum studies course, were required to write curriculum units using themes from the Tonga Social Science program. The best of these were sent to the curriculum development unit in Tonga, and were later incorporated in the curriculum. Many of these students later became social science teachers, and provided much needed support to other, less fortunate teachers through in-service training activities organized by the social science teachers' association.

However, there are still very few incentives offered to teachers throughout the region to involve themselves in curriculum development either as writers or trial teachers, despite ministerial proclamations about the need for their involvement. The nature of incentives varies from country to country but, generally, teachers are expected to give up their school holidays to attend curriculum workshops, and to use their own time to complete writing curriculum units. Many practising teachers throughout the region lack the necessary professional and material support to be actively involved in curriculum development.

Curriculum-related Factors

Some people feel that the social science curriculum materials developed since 1970 are too parochial, in the sense that so much emphasis is placed on the societies from which students come. This is an unfair criticism, in my view, and one which is the result of a superficial examination of many social science programs. Comparative studies are a part of many programs, and perhaps the criticism has come about because some teachers either fail to include these in their teaching or because of lack of time and/or resources.

We are still unsure as to which strategies are more effective in inquiry-based learning, especially given differing cultural contexts. Moreover, much of our curriculum work tends to ignore the research dealing with the development of attitudes and values, and although attitudinal objectives are included in many units, learning experiences tend to focus only on the development of knowledge and understanding of concepts and thinking skills.

Perhaps from a Western perspective, it is possible to view the content of many social science programs in the islands as being too deterministic, in that they overemphasize people's adaption to their physical and social environments and do not adequately deal with people's role in bringing about change to their environments. Furthermore, some countries tend to censor out conflicts of one kind or another, suggesting that these would be detrimental to harmonious living. Examples of this are trade unionism in social science units in Tonga and land issues in units in Fiji.

There is also the problem of incorporating new content in existing social studies/social science programs. There continues to be an increasing number of new ideas related to currently championed areas of development which various experts (usually United Nations ones) have deemed important for inclusion in the school curriculum. Most people tend to single out social science or social studies as the appropriate subject in which to 'inject' such 'new' and important areas. A number of projects, for example, under the main headings of population education, environmental education, ocean resource management and, most recently, tourism education (mostly funded by one or other of the UN agencies) have developed resources which need to be incorporated into existing social science programs. The problem arises as to how these resource materials are to be incorporated, without completely obliterating the original curriculum.

Finally there is the question of whether the social science curriculum ought to address social and moral issues which are relevant to Pacific island societies. Because the underlying values and assumptions of our school curriculum are still basically foreign, liberal and middle class, many curriculum consultants do not address social and moral issues, believing that these are not really their concern. As a result, the school curriculum continues to 'reproduce' neo-colonial situations, such as the overemphasis on academic/intellectual skills, and the stress on individuality and competition.

Such a relative neglect of the social and moral aspects of curriculum development is contrary to the expectations of both parents and teachers in that they regard the school as a proper place for social and moral training (Thaman, 1980 and 1987b). The problem is further complicated by the indifference of many teacher training programs to this particular issue, not to mention many teacher educators. Character training is not fashionable in educational literature because of its 'subjectivity' and its connotations of indoctrination and social engineering. Yet many social science programs claim to aim at 'citizenship' education, and one often wonders what kind of society citizens are being prepared for.

A recent study I conducted in Tonga, for example, showed that primary and secondary teachers emphasized their social and moral roles more than their role as teachers of subjects. This is in line with traditional Tongan notions of *ako* (learning), for the purpose of becoming *poto*, knowing what to do and doing it well (in the context of Tongan life). Teaching and learning of subjects is therefore seen in the context of Tongan society as important for the purposes of passing examinations, which would enable one to proceed to higher levels of schooling, or to gain employment. This is regarded as necessary for meeting family, church and other social obligations or *faifatongia*. The purpose of learning therefore is basically social and the role of the teacher is seen as facilitating the learning of the child so that he/she is prepared for his/her future role as a responsible, contributing member of a group or several different groups.

Within such a context, intellectual skills such as those laid down by curriculum planners form only a part of the overall requirement of *poto*. Independent thinking, although necessary, needs to be exercised within the contexts of life in a particular society. A 'democratic' society such as in the USA or Australia or New Zealand is not quite the same as a 'democratic' society in Western Samoa, Vanuatu or Tonga. Yet the assumptions made by (curriculum) models utilized, planners and designers are the same in all. The results may not always be beneficial for Pacific island pupils and societies.

Towards a Culture-sensitive Model of Curriculum Development

In a model of the decision-making process in SSCD, Lawton (1981: 37) refers to three important 'influencing factors', namely, society's needs and priorities, students' needs and priorities, and the organized bodies of knowledge. He also stresses the importance of what he calls 'cultural analysis' (defined by him as the systematic process of examining a particular society in its social and historical context) in the process of curriculum planning. Such a cultural analysis would involve the examination of a society's culture, language, technology, knowledge, beliefs and values, in order to make better judgments about what ought to be transmitted to the next generation – in other words, what is worthwhile to teach and learn.

In my view, SSCD in the Pacific islands has often neglected the most important aspect of cultural analysis. Quite often, people are in a hurry to get on with the work of producing materials, because of the constraints associated with the funding, and therefore the administration, of many projects. Furthermore, because most curriculum projects are externally funded and most consultants are foreign, it is often assumed that because curriculum teams consist of local people, they would provide the necessary local input and cultural analysis. However, in my experience, most curriculum team members do not have the time, skills or inclination to be openly and constructively critical, from their own cultural perspectives, of what most foreign consultants may suggest. Consequently, many of the social science/social studies programs closely resemble curriculum structures in metropolitan countries, complete with underlying values and assumptions.

A more culturally sensitive model of SSCD would include basic questions such as:

1. What are the underlying values of the curriculum that is proposed, and do they agree with the prevailing values of the society?
2. What role does the language of the curriculum play in the social education of children, where English predominates as the language of instruction, at least in theory, while the language of the home and of socialization, in most cases, is different? and,
3. What important knowledge, skills and values are contained in a curriculum of social education?

The answers to these three questions relating to the proposed curriculum's underlying values and assumptions, the language used, and important cultural knowledge, skills and values, would assist persons involved in SSCD to be more sensitive to the importance of cultural analysis. It would also assist them to develop more appropriate strategies both for teaching and for learning.

One reason why cultural analysis is so important in our small countries is because of the contrasting nature of our traditional models of education with more Western models. Furthermore, the kinds of things which our peoples value and therefore influence the scope of their thinking (what I call 'valued contexts' of thinking), seem to me to be different from those which are emphasized in Western cultures, although, through modernization – including formal education – what may be held to be valuable is changing. Unfortunately, as mentioned earlier, most Pacific islanders involved in curriculum development work in their countries, have not had the time to seriously consider the differences between what their curriculum may be advocating and what their traditional cultures (which still largely affect the way both teachers and pupils behave) expect.

In the Pacific islands we need to pay more serious attention to what our cultures value in order to carry out more effectively the work of cultural analysis, from our *own* perspectives. This is not to suggest that ours would necessarily be 'right' or 'correct', but it will be different, because we have the best of both worlds. In my view, curriculum decisions resulting from more rigorous cultural analysis and synthesis would be more soundly based and, perhaps, would transmit to the next generation the best and most appropriate knowledge and cultural values for a given non-Western culture.

Most of our curriculum planners have not consciously tried to identify those things which their cultures emphasize and regard as valuable and worthwhile to be passed on to the next generation. This is unfortunately true of most formal education systems. What follows therefore, is an attempt to address this question, using Tonga as an example. My reason for choosing Tonga is twofold; first, I have been a teacher in Tonga and have, more recently, been involved in curriculum development and teacher education there; and secondly, I am a Tongan.

Valued Contexts of Thinking: The Case of Tonga

The following contexts have been identified as some of the most important which Tongan people value and therefore *emphasize* and which form their ideal model for behavior. They include the emphasis on: (1) the supernatural/spiritual; (2) concrete context; (3) formal conformity; (4) rank and authority; (5) social relationships; (6) kinship relationships; (7) Tongan traditions and customs; (8) the concept of '*ofa* (compassion or love); and (9) restrained behavior.

The emphasis on the supernatural in Tonga is still very strong. *Lotu* (religion/church/prayer) permeates every facet of Tongan life and together with 'traditions' forms a powerful force in the life of almost all Tongans, whether they admit it or not. Religious and traditional values provide the rationale for almost every family, village, school, church and indeed national *kavenga* (function/organized activity) in which individuals as well as groups are expected to participate.

Most people emphasize concrete and specific contexts in their thinking. This is not to say that they are not capable of abstract thinking but rather that many abstract ideas are expressed in concrete ways which symbolize them. For example, the concept of reciprocity is expressed as *maka fetoli'aki* (a rock being chipped on both sides) or the idea of doing one's duty is *fua kavenga* (bearing a burden or heavy load). Modern abstract ideas such as democracy, development, investment, human rights, individualism, etc. have to be translated into concrete contexts before they can be made more meaningful to people, especially children.

Formal conformity to written as well as unwritten social norms is still highly regarded in Tonga and helps to sustain and maintain the uniqueness which many Tongans believe characterize their culture. And so is the emphasis on *'ofa*. Although they obviously do not have a monopoly on compassion and sharing, they nevertheless believe that their brand of *'ofa* (or *aloha/aroha/alofa*) is different and more potent (see Kavaliku, 1977, for a detailed discussion of *'ofa*).

Social relationships are very important and are determined through a complicated network of kinship relationships. Such relationships influence both social and political behavior and, together with an introduced system of law and order, provide the necessary sanctions for people's behavior. The metaphor of kinship is pervasive, even among Tongans who do not live in Tonga. As most Tongans know, outside of Tonga everyone belongs to the metaphorical *kainga Tonga* (Tongan extended family), and is expected to behave accordingly. Individuals who are not close kin are generally considered less important than even distant kin relationships, and close friendships are usually with persons who are related to one another.

Finally, restrained behavior is often emphasized, particularly in relation to overt praise as well as criticism. Such an emphasis may give rise to what many non-Tongans have observed to be a weakness in the spirit of criticism among many people, including both teachers and students. This is manifested, for example, in a general unwillingness to speak out or question the ideas of elders or those in authority. Such a questioning attitude is highly valued in Western societies, and is reflected in the aim of social science to develop independent and critical thinking among children.

In my view, knowledge and understanding of the above emphasized contexts of thinking would assist persons who are involved in curriculum decision-making, especially if they are non-Tongans. Tongans themselves would benefit from comparing such valued contexts that are generally held to be important in their culture with the underlying values of new curricula.

In multicultural situations, such as the one existing in Fiji, for example, the same kind of cultural analysis would seem beneficial. Curriculum planners would at least have an opportunity to decide which common values ought to feature in the curriculum, and if it is decided that mutual respect and understanding is valued, then the content and strategies of the curriculum ought to reflect this.

Cultural analysis, therefore, is a way in which SSCD may be made more appropriate and meaningful for Pacific students. Furthermore, it may help curriculum planners to find solutions to problems often associated with implementation, especially those relating to teachers' attitudes and reactions. Many may not publicly reveal inadequacies in the curriculum, especially to curriculum officials or any type of official for that matter. They would prefer to seek assistance from their peers, or none at all. I believe that subject teachers' associations seem to work better in providing help for teachers in Tonga, for example, than the normal educational inspectorate.

Conclusion

In this paper, I have tried to identify various features of, and problems associated with, SSCD development in South Pacific island countries since 1970. I have also tried to point out that many of the problems may be related to the conflicts inherent in the kinds of curriculum development models which we have adopted, usually those which have been imported from outside. Finally, it is argued, following Lawton's suggestion, that cultural analysis is a vital input in curriculum decision-making. We in the Pacific islands would benefit from a serious questioning of those values and assumptions inherent in curriculum models and structures which have been and are being introduced to our countries. As part of this cultural analysis, it is suggested that we need to systematically identify what we consider to be those values and beliefs which our various cultures emphasize, in a process of a continuing search not only for worthwhile knowledge and skills to be passed on to the next generation, but more importantly, perhaps, for a common set of values. In this way, social studies would not only emphasize intellectual skills but also important cultural values and beliefs, which would help our young people create a cultural identity of which they would be proud. This, in my view, is a prerequisite for effective and responsible citizenship.

References

Baba, T.L. (1979). An evaluation of the UNDP social science curriculum in Fiji secondary schools. Unpublished PhD thesis, Macquarie University, Sydney.

Baba, T.L. (1987). Academic buccaneering Australian style: the role of Australian academics in the South Seas, *Directions* 9(1): 3-11.

Baba, T.L., and Fraser, B.J. (1983). Student attitudes to UNDP social science curriculum in Fiji – personal and environmental influences, *International Review of Education* 29: 465-483.

Kavaliku, S.L. (1977). *'Ofa, Pacific Perspective*, 6(2): 47-67.

Lawton, D. (1981). Foundations for the social studies. In *Handbook for the teaching of social studies*. Paris: UNESCO. 36-58.

Masih, V. (1978). A comparative study of the education programmes at three teachers' colleges and the Diploma in Education Programme at the University of the South Pacific, *Directions* 1: 3.

McCrae, C.J. (1986). Problems in educational development in the Kingdom of Tonga. Unpublished PhD thesis, University of London Institute of Education, London.

Petaia, R. (1983). Kidnapped. In *Seaweeds and Constructions* 7: 56-7.

Puloka, M. (1984). Principal, Queen Salote College, Tonga. Personal Communication.

Renner, J.M. (1982). Curriculum development in a cross-cultural setting: social science in the South Pacific, *New Zealand Journal of Educational Studies* 17(2):

128-141.

Thaman, K.H. (1980). Community expectations of secondary education in Tonga, *Directions* 4: 27-36.

_____ (1981). Teachers as curriculum developers. Unpublished paper presented at the First Teacher Educators' Seminar, Apia, Western Samoa.

_____ (1987a). Curriculum development in Pacific island countries with specific reference to Tonga. In K. Bacchus and C. Brock (eds), *The challenge of scale: Educational development in the small states of the Commonwealth*, London: Commonwealth Secretariat. 50-60.

_____ (1987b). 'A teacher's story', *International Review of Education* 33(3): 276-82.

Appendix A:
Structure of the UNDP/UNESCO Social Science Curriculum

The Social Science Curriculum Framework		
Year	Annual Themes	Theme for Each Term
1	Living Together	Family and Kinship Community and Nation Race and Migration
2	Making a Living	Human Needs Using Resources Competing and Cooperating
3	Freedom and Control	Rules, Regulations and Customs Sanctions Rights and Responsibilities
4	Planning and Changing	Urbanization Making decisions Community and National Planning

Source: Social science in the South Pacific: An introduction for teachers, August 1974: 10.

Appendix B:
Appropriate Aims of Social Science

That pupils should:

1. Be knowledgeable about their cultural inheritance.
2. Appreciate and understand the changes now occurring in their country's social and economic life.
3. Adapt to the changes without losing their cultural identity.
4. Be committed to play, with reasonable efficiency, imagination and integrity, a role appropriate to a member of a contemporary community in a rapidly changing world.
5. Appreciate the diversity *yet* interdependency of peoples in the national and international communities.

In short:

– pupils should be well-informed about their society

– able to think intelligently about it
– put it in world perspective
– and be interested and concerned about it.

Source: Social science in the South Pacific: An introduction for teachers, August 1974: 6.

Appendix C:
Social Science Themes and Sub-themes for Form 1-4: Fiji and Solomon Islands

	Fiji	Solomon Islands
Form 1	*Living Together* – Family and Customs – Community and Nation – Race and Migration	*Social Change* – Our School – Families – Communities
Form 2	*Making a Living* – Human Needs – Using Resources – Competing and Cooperating	*Economic Change* – Physical Environment – Use of Resources in Solomon Islands – Use of Resources Overseas
Form 3	*Freedom and Control* – Rules, Regulations and Customs Sanctions – Rights and Responsibility	*Political Change* – Aspects of Solomon Islands History – Leadership and Government in Solomon Islands – USSR and USA – Development and Change
Form 4	*Planning and Changing* – Urbanization – Making Decisions – Community and National Planning	*Environment* – Conflict – Cooperation – Man and His Environment

---

Konai Helu Thaman is Senior Lecturer in Education at the University of the South Pacific, Suva, Fiji. She was Director of the University's Institute of Education from 1985 to 1987. Her main academic interests are curriculum development, teacher education and indigenous educational ideas. She also writes poetry as a hobby.

8

Schooling and Citizenship in Malaysia

Thunguvala Marimuthu
University of Malaya, Malaysia

This article focuses on the strategic role played by education to bring about national integration in the plural Malaysian society. It discusses the processes of schooling and socialization in developing values and norms which are relevant for a multicultural nation. The paper also attempts to assess the effectiveness of these educational processes in the development of the civic culture and citizenship in Malaysia.

Malaysia is one of the plural societies that constitute the Pacific Rim countries. It has a diversity of ethnic groups, religions, languages and cultures. Of the total population of 15.8 million in 1985, the ethnic distribution was 60.1 percent Malays and other indigenous groups termed as Bumiputeras, 30.9 percent Chinese, 8.4 percent Indian and 0.65 percent Others. The Malaysian ethnic pluralism is notable amongst the emergent Pacific countries in that the minorities in the country are relatively numerous when compared with the indigenous groups, a situation which prevails elsewhere in the Pacific Rim only in Fiji. The development of the Malaysian ethnic plural society was the result of large-scale immigration of Chinese and Indians during the British colonial period (1786-1957), particularly in the late nineteenth and early twentieth centuries to assist in the development of the rubber and tin industries.

This ethnic and cultural pluralism was sustained and reinforced by residential segregation, geographical isolation and occupational segmentation based on ethnicity. The indigenous population – that is, the Bumiputeras – were confined to the low-income, subsistence and agricultural occupations, while the non-Bumiputera groups such as the Chinese and to a lesser extent the Indians were located in the urban areas and involved in commerce and manufacturing. This occupational segmentation by ethnicity was supported by a colonial education system which performed a divisive rather than an integrative function. Although this pattern of identification of race with economic activities is fast changing, it is still a significant feature in the occupational distribution of community groups in Malaysia.

Education and National Integration

With the achievement of independence for Peninsular Malaysia in 1957 and the formation of Malaysia in 1963, the tasks of social reconstruction and national integration in the plural society became urgent social policy priorities. It was in this context that education was perceived to be an important instrument of national development and social cohesion. It was called upon to perform several functions. Education was seen as a catalyst to bring about the necessary social change in the Malaysian plural society as well as to meet the manpower requirements of the developing economy. It was also expected to equalize opportunities and provide better life-chances for the population as a whole. Education was also seen in terms of a basic human right and not as a privilege. This belief that education can solve many of the social and economic problems confronting developing societies boosted educational expansion and expenditure. Malaysia spends about 5-6 percent of its gross national product on education, which compares favorably with the educational expenditure of developed countries.

The objective of nation-building and forging national unity amongst the various ethnic groups in Malaysia ranks as one of the highest priorities in both the political and educational agendas of the country. Education is expected to create a nation out of disparate ethnic groups whose differences in language, religion, history and culture provide few common bases for national integration. Educational goals are expected to submerge conflicting interests and at the same time meet the aspirations and needs of all sectors of society (Arahad, 1986). The idea that the educational system could be used effectively to meet some of the challenges of nation-building in a plural society is a phenomenon of the post-colonial independent Malaysian society. Prior to this, the colonial policy towards education was one based on welfare and social consideration rather than as an instrument for national development. Thus, education, which was not considered important for development during the colonial period, assumed greater importance, that is, it took on a greater degree of 'coterminality', which is the simultaneous convergence of interest by the government and all other ethnic community in the country.

With independence there was a need to restructure the education system incorporating the national aspirations and the recommendations contained in the Razak Report (1956) which formed the basis of the new education policy. The disparate education sub-system that evolved during the colonial period, with multilingual schools (that is, English, Malay, Chinese and Tamil) have been unified in stages, to form one national education system. The present educational structure has two types of schools – the national schools and the national-type schools. The national schools use Bahasa Malaysia (the national language) as the medium of instruction while the national-type schools use Tamil and Chinese as the media at the primary level. Secondary and tertiary education is only available in the medium of Bahasa Malaysia. All schools use a common-content curriculum and the pupils appear for common national examinations. The present educational system of Malaysia is the result of a series of compromises and negotiations between the various ethnic groups and reflects the intercommunal understanding and accommodation.

The overriding objective of national unity is to be achieved through the implementation of the educational policy as well as the two-pronged strategy of the New Economic Policy (NEP). The two areas of the NEP is the eradication of poverty by raising income levels and increasing employment opportunities for all Malaysians, irrespective of race, and accelerating the process of restructuring Malaysian society to correct economic imbalances, so as to reduce and eventually eliminate the identification of race with economic function. Education is expected to play a vital role in achieving these aims. The educational philosophy and objectives are guided by the *Rukunegara* (the National Ideology), the tenets of which are: belief in God, loyalty to king and country, upholding the constitution, the rule of law, and good behavior and morality. The educational strategy to achieve national unity is to emphasize, encourage and develop common values and loyalty among all the ethnic and social groups in the country from all regions. Let us now consider how the process of schooling creates conditions for good citizenship in Malaysia.

Schooling and Citizenship

For T. H. Marshall (1950), citizenship constituted three basic elements and they are the civil, political and social rights of an individual. These rights included the freedom of speech, thought and faith; the right to participate in the exercise of political power; the right to economic welfare and security and share in the social heritage and live the life of a civilized being according to the standards prevailing in the society. He also stated that citizenship is an important factor in the process of social integration.

Morris Janowitz (1983), focusing on education for civic consciousness, points out that Marshall has emphasized the rights of citizens to the neglect of one's responsibilities. Citizenship means both rights and obligations. He feels that the school is the central agency for the development of civic consciousness and advocates national military service as a form of civic education. The process of schooling contributing to social integration and national unity draws support from Dreeben (1968). He states that the school is the dominant mechanism for social change, where differences can be subordinated and new equalities and similarities can be learnt. He suggests that the learning norms in schools occur not only through what is taught but also the way in which it is taught. Dreeben considers equality as the most important basis for national unity.

How does the process of schooling contribute to the attainment of a common citizenship in a plural society like Malaysia? It has been pointed out earlier that the restructuration of the colonial education system, the introduction of a common curriculum, a common language, and a common examination for all schools are strategies that have been employed to achieve values relevant to common citizenship.

At the school level the inculcation of common values is to be achieved through the common curriculum, the extensive use of the national language and participation in extracurricular activities which is made mandatory. Children in Malaysian schools also wear common uniforms, possess common textbooks and are schooled in similar school buildings. The teaching of common citizenship values are to be achieved through the school curriculum in subjects such as Islamic education, moral education, civics education and social science education. In moral education sixteen moral values have been identified and they are good-naturedness, courtesy, gratitude, mutual respect, love, justice, freedom, valor, honesty, diligence, cooperation, moderation, rationality, community-spiritedness and purity of mind and body. These moral values are not only clarified in moral education classes but are also dealt with in other subjects. In Islamic education, which is taught only to Muslim pupils, the emphasis is on the teachings of the Koran. Through the study of Malaysian history, responsible and loyal citizens are expected to be nurtured. History also emphasizes the affective values which would develop good citizenship qualities. In geography, too, the values and norms relevant to good citizenship are inculcated.

The study of civics is being replaced by citizenship education which lays emphasis on history, culture and the development of the nation. It also attempts to inculcate values and practices of good citizenship that are necessary for social cohesion in a plural society. Through the study of citizenship education, it is expected that the pupils will develop awareness, sensitivity and understanding of social issues which would contribute to nation-building. The elements of citizenship education are incorporated into the total school environment. They are integrated into all school subjects and co-curricular activities. The approach taken in the inculcation of moral values and good citizenship qualities is that these are not only taught in the classroom but also taught in the prevailing moral culture and environment of the school.

The inculcation of common citizenship values entails the development of the affective domain of the individual, which includes the development of feelings, emotion, sentiment, attitudes and values towards nationally desired norms. The participation in co-curricular activities such as sports, games, clubs and societies provide opportunities for greater social interaction and for the development of some of the moral values in the curriculum agenda.

A common national language is also used as a strategy to develop social cohesion and national identity in plural societies of the emergent Pacific. In Malaysia, the successful implementation of Bahasa Malaysia as the main medium of instruction from primary to university levels has contributed towards greater inter-ethnic communication and understanding. The national language also provides the basis for the development of and participation in a common culture.

There is some evidence to support that the process of schooling, in terms of non-cognitive outcomes, does in some measure succeed in passing on some of the universalistic values which can contribute to social integration and the development of a sense of national unity in plural societies (Bacchus, 1987). Another study has shown that the exposure of students to civics curricula was associated with lower levels of political chauvinism and greater support for democratic principles (Litt, 1963). But whatever evidence that is available in the Malaysian context shows that the curriculum as a whole has not contributed effectively towards the development of common citizenship values.

Since curriculum is seen essentially as a selection from the culture of a society, it is not only expected to transmit knowledge but also modify attitudes, behavior and values. In Malaysian schools the transmission of knowledge and skills has been more successful than the development of common values. A study on the relationship between the lower secondary school curriculum and national unity found that the relationship was weak; the textbook examined contained ethnic biases and stereotypes and teachers interviewed were least concerned with issues of national unity but were very concerned in helping the pupils to pass examinations (Mukherjee, et al., 1984). It has also been acknowledged that the educational system has produced unintended outcomes such as racial polarization and a sense of parochialism in educational institutions (Arahad, 1986).

The Curriculum Development Center (CDC) of the Malaysian Ministry of Education has admitted certain weaknesses in the Malaysian secondary school curriculum. It states that the present secondary school curriculum does not provide sufficient emphasis on values and skills that would enable the pupils to become good and patriotic citizens; there is also not enough focus on the development of character and personality. The present curriculum is too concerned with the transmission of knowledge and the preparation of the pupils for higher education. Hence a review of the present secondary school curriculum has been undertaken so as to remedy the weaknesses in the new secondary school curriculum. The new curriculum is being introduced in stages from 1988 (Ministry of Education, 1987).

Notwithstanding the weaknesses and problems encountered in the achievement of the educational objectives, particularly with regards to the development of common values and social integration, both the new primary school curriculum introduced in 1983 and the new secondary school curriculum introduced in 1988 reiterate the objectives of promoting national unity and social integration through education. The new secondary school curriculum emphasizes the need to develop the full potential of the individual so that he or she would play an effective and productive role in national development and contribute towards national harmony and peace. This underlines the continuing faith and confidence that policy-makers have in the power of education for national development in a plural society.

The very issues that are considered to be critical factors in the process of nation-building also become issues of conflict and tensions in a plural society. In Malaysia, areas such as education, language, religion and culture continue to be problematic. Since plural societies are inherently conflict-laden, such issues exacerbate the tensions and conflicts in society. It needs political skills to manage these tensions. One strategy that has been used successfully in the management of tensions is by the committee system where important issues are resolved through discussions, negotiations and compromises.

For example, in the area of education, the policy of positive discrimination in favor of the Bumiputera students, especially in higher education, has created a sense of relative deprivation and anxiety amongst some of the non-Bumiputera groups. This has led to the creation of dominant and assertive groups. The concepts of domination and assertion are used by Vaughan and Archer (1971) to analyse educational change in England and France between 1789 and 1848. In the process of restructuring the Malaysian society, the Bumiputeras have become the dominant group at the tertiary educational level while the non-Bumiputera have become the assertive group. The assertive group has engaged itself in instrumental activities, such as the provision of alternative educational facilities, thus possessing a measure of bargaining power and subscribing to a meritocratic ideology. These three factors – the instrumental activities, bargaining power and ideology – are necessary conditions for obtaining educational concessions from the dominant group. In the context of the Malaysian plural society the dialectics of domination and assertion usually result in a 'truce situation' – a situation of compromise.

Another recent example in this tradition of tension-management is the setting up of the National Economic Consultative Council (NECC) in January 1989 to review the New Economic Policy (NEP) and to suggest a national economy policy after 1990. The 150-member Council includes representatives from various political, social, economic, educational and professional organizations. A significant feature of this Council is that it is made up of 50 percent Bumiputeras and 50 percent non-Bumiputeras. About one-third of the Council is made up of practising politicians who are from both the ruling and the opposition parties. The rest of the members represent the interests of business, education, medical and legal professions, trade unions, banking, consumer associations, farmers, fishermen, lorry drivers, petty traders, employers' associations, youth council, rubber planters association, insurance, housing developers association and other minority groups.

The area of education is well represented. The educators in the Council include university vice-chancellors, professors, lecturers and practising school teachers. Educators make up about 14 percent of the membership of the Council.

It is expected that the Council will review the progress made in the last two decades, identify strengths and weaknesses of NEP, and suggest educational policies and strategies for national development and social integration for the Malaysian plural society, based on equality and social justice.

Discussion

There is some supporting evidence that education in Malaysia as a whole has contributed to the achievement of some of the national development goals. The incidence of poverty has declined and income levels have been raised; ethnic imbalances in employment and corporate ownership has been reduced to some extent (Aziz, 1987). Impressive progress has been made in the democratization of educational provision in the last three decades. Available data show that Malaysia has attained universal primary education. The imbalances in access to the different levels of education among the various ethnic and socioeconomic groups have been redressed significantly. Greater equality of educational opportunity has resulted in increased upward social mobility for all social groups, but the middle socioeconomic group has benefited the most (Rabieyah bte Mat, 1988).

It has been pointed out earlier that education has been less than completely successful in developing common values as the basis for nation-building. The pursuit of national unity through education is a complex process. As Reid (1988) points out in her analysis of politics of education in Malaysia, education as an agent of integration has somewhat been negated by other wider institutional environments. The common educational socialization may be a necessary condition but not a sufficient one for national integration. The transmission of values and skills for good citizenship relies heavily on a direct socialization model in school and neglects the social, economic and political forces that determine the 'life chances' of individuals within each community.

Some of the educational issues discussed above are areas which cause genuine concern to policy-makers and educationalists. Educational policies and practices are reviewed periodically to keep in line with the aspirations and expectations of the population. The national philosophy of education which was announced in 1987 reflects the values and beliefs of contemporary Malaysian society. The philosophy of education focuses on the total development of the individual who is expected to contribute to nation-building. Other themes to be found in the statement of the philosophy of education include the development of persons who are knowledgeable, who possess high moral standards and who are responsible and productive citizens. This shows a shift from the macro-concerns of the relationship between school and society to the micro-level of the individual, whose development is to be based on the belief in and devotion to God. The moral and religious elements in the philosophy of education show how education is responding to societal changes in Malaysia. The faith in education to alter the social condition continues.

References

Arshad, Abdul Rahman, in ISIS (1986). *The bonding of a nation: Federalism and territorial integration in Malaysia.* Kuala Lumpur: Institute of Strategic and International Studies.

Aziz, U.A., Chow, S.B., Leo, K.H., and Banyai, T. (1987). *University education and employment in Malaysia.* Paris: IIEP.

Bacchus, Kazim (1987). *Education, equity, cultural diversity and national unity in multi-ethnic societies,* Kuala Lumpur: Institute of Advanced Studies, University of Malaya (mimeo.).

Dreeben, R. (1968). *On what is learned at school.* Reading, Mass. Addison-Wesley.

Janowitz, Morris (1983). *The reconstruction of patriotism: Education for civic consciousness.* Chicago: The University of Chicago Press.

Litt, Edgar (1963). Civic education, community norms and political indoctrination, *American Sociological Review,* 28: 69-75.

Malaysia. Ministry of Education (1987). *Rancangan kurikulum borsepadu sckolah monengah.* Kuala Lumpur: Pusat Perkembangan Kurikulum.

Marshall, T.H. (1950). *Citizenship and social class.* Cambridge: Cambridge University Press.

Mukherjee, G.H., *et al.* (1984). *The Malaysian lower secondary school curriculum and national unity.* Kuala Lumpur: Department of Social Foundations, Faculty of Education, University of Malaya.

Rabieyah bte Mat (1988). Educational opportunity, social mobility and poverty reduction in Peninsular Malaysia (1972-1982), *Negara,* Vol. XII, No.1: 29-37.

Razak bin Hussain (1956). *Education Committee report.* Kuala Lumpur: Government Printers.

Reid, Linda J. (1988). *The politics of education in Malaysia.* Hobart: Political Science Department, University of Tasmania (Monograph Series).

Vaughan, Michalina, and Archer, Margaret Scotford (1971). *Social conflict and educational change in England and France (1789-1848).* Cambridge: Cambridge University Press.

Professor Marimuthu is Head, Department of Social Foundations, Faculty of Education, University of Malaya, 59100 Kuala Lumpur, Malaysia. He has written extensively on citizenship and national unity in Malaysia.

9

Making Asian Women Visible in Curriculum

Machiko Matsui, Yuanxi Ma and Catherine Cornbleth
State University of New York at Buffalo, United States of America

Our focus is on the intersection of two, usually separate concerns: Asian cultures, particularly those of China and Japan, and women's experiences, perspectives and issues. International or global understanding and comprehension of world issues require attention to women's experiences and points of view, as well as men's, within and across cultures. Ignorance fosters misconceptions and stereotypes, for example, of the submissive Asian woman. There has been important change in the situation of women in China and Japan as well as continuing exploitation. Even patriarchal Asian cultures are not simply male cultures, and even traditional Asian cultures are not static. In teaching and learning about Asian cultures, we should recognize male and female, tradition and change – in interaction and sometimes tension or conflict with one another.

Towards these goals we offer brief sketches of the historical contemporary situations of women in China and Japan and conclude with several recommendations for making Asian women visible in elementary and secondary global studies curricula and in secondary and college women's studies programs. Our emphasis is on incorporation or integration into regularly offered or required programs, rather than separate courses or units of study, for two reasons. One is practicality. Given the constraints of knowledge, time and other resources, it is not feasible to add courses or units to most school programs. (The situation may be different at the university level and warrant separate courses.) And, at least in the USA at the present time, non-mainstream topics such as this are not viewed very favorably by many people.

A second reason for recommending integration is interpretive or political but not without practical aspects. It is that we should be revising our stories of our own and other cultures to include women – not just to add them on in photographs, special features, or isolated units – and to include recent and continuing changes and issues. The practical aspect is that integration of women's experiences and perspectives makes them available to most if not all students, not just those who choose to take elective courses or do extra credit work. Also, what is added on is rather easily dropped, as is evident in the declining number of separate women's studies (and black and ethnic studies) courses in US secondary schools during the past decade. In contrast, what is integrated is less easily disposed of when personal or political winds change.

As you consider the following sketches of Chinese and Japanese women's experience, note that generalization across Asian women's experience is risky because of major political and socioeconomic as well as historical and cultural differences. Beyond the common Confucian heritage in East Asia and the presence of contemporary women's movements that often are in conflict with other progressive movements, differences across Asian nations are at least as salient as similarities.

China

When we talk about Chinese women, we have to consider Confucianism, the doctrine of Confucius, a Chinese philosopher living between 551 and 478 BC. Confucianism became the dominant ethical doctrine, almost synonymous with traditional Chinese civilization. It is a comprehensive ideology and social system, in which everyone is supposed to know and assume a proper place, that was designed and propagated to stabilize a hierarchical social order in peace and harmony. Confucianism has established a set of ideas about women, including the following:

Women are as different from men as earth is from heaven ... Women are, indeed, human beings, but they are of a lower state than men.

Woman depends on the light of her husband to shine.

Woman's virginity and chastity are more important than her life.

Woman's greatest duty is to produce a son.

The most important principle of traditional ethics for women was 'the three obediences' – to father before marriage, to husband after marriage, and to son after the death of husband – and 'the four virtues' – chastity, proper speech, modest manner and diligent work. There is a whole literature educating women on self-discipline; etiquette; relationships with in-laws, husbands, children, friends; household management; humility; and chastity. All this set the tone and determined the position of women in society – economically, politically and morally. We can sum up the essence of Confucianism for women in three points: woman should be dependent upon and subordinate to man; woman should observe loyalty and fidelity to man; and woman should serve man to the end of her life.

Early Women's Movements

Over the centuries, things have changed tremendously. Chinese women, along with their male supporters, have been fighting their way out of the shackles of Confucianism. It has been a hard and protracted battle; the struggle is still going on. Although Confucius died long ago, his doctrine on women is far from being extinguished. It takes on different forms and more subtle ways. What is most important is not just the changes on the surface, but changing what is deep-rooted in people's minds.

If there has ever been a women's liberation movement in China, it would be the one emerging from the May Fourth Movement in 1919. The May Fourth Movement also is called the New Cultural Movement. It directly demanded the abolition of Confucianism and the traditional values that accompanied it. It fiercely attacked the patriarchal clan system and feudal codes of ethics and sought changes in family structure. The slogan of the Movement was 'Down with Confucius and his disciples!'.

A group of women, who were active members in the Movement, came out and stood up for women's rights. Supported by a number of male revolutionaries, these women raised almost all the important issues concerning women's rights: equal pay for equal work; equal right to election; equal access to college education; equal opportunity for employment in government offices; reexamination of all legal codes to ensure equal rights for both sexes; elimination of footbinding, child brides, female infanticide, sale of girls, concubinage and prostitution. They advocated open contact between men and women, freedom of love and marriage, and freedom of divorce and remarrying. This was a movement that emerged from the people, mostly initiated by intellectual women and then involving a number of women workers.

Contemporary Conditions

After 1949, Marxism was established as the guiding ideology in China. The basic view on the question of women is mostly clearly expressed by Engels in his *Origin of the Family, Private Property and the State*: 'Emancipation of woman will only be possible when women can take part in production on a large, social scale, and domestic work no longer claims anything but an insignificant part of her time' (p. 148). It also is maintained that the liberation of women is just part of the liberation of mankind. Therefore, it is not necessary to have a separate movement for women's liberation. Definitely, it is not encouraged. Chinese women have been told that, in socialist countries such as the Soviet Union and China, women enjoy every right equally as men. Mao Zedong told the Chinese people, 'Women hold up half the sky; whatever men can do, women can do too'.

Unfortunately, however, women in China are not totally freed from subjugation, servitude and dependence once domestic labor is socialized and industrialized, and they enter the workforce. In China, over 80 percent of women work outside their homes. It is greatly to their advantage because they can at least gain some economic independence. And it also is true that, in the cities, if men and women are doing exactly the same work, they get the same pay. Nurseries and kindergartens are widespread, and most are well run and inexpensive. However, if we probe deeper into the situation of women, we will see that women still hold a lower social status than men. Due to historical factors and traditional views, women are doing mostly unskilled and menial jobs.

Professional women only constitute 5.5 percent of working women. They still have less access to higher education, thus less opportunity to obtain better jobs and promotions. In most cases, women shoulder a triple burden of a job outside the home, housework, and child care. Naturally, they will have less time than men to study and improve themselves.

For many women, there exists the acute conflict between family and career. A job does not necessarily mean a career. Women's participation in some economic and political activities does not automatically eliminate traditional values and the force of habit established thousands of years ago and handed down from generation to generation. Conventions die hard.

In recent years, female infanticide has reappeared due to the one-child policy as most people still want a son to carry on the family line. In principle, people have freedom to choose their own spouses, but parents still have a large say in their children's marriages. In the cities, more than 60 percent (more in the countryside) of marriages are arranged through go-betweens. Many women in their late twenties and early thirties are pushed into marriages by their parents or friends. People's standards of a good wife are not much different from the past. A survey in 1987 among male students in a university in Beijing asked the question, 'What kind of wife do you want?'. More than 70 percent of the students wanted their wives to be beautiful in appearance, gentle in temperament, good in housework, and unchallenging in intelligence and in academia. Double standards still exist for men and women with respect to virginity, extramarital affairs, divorce and widowhood. Prostitution is prohibited, yet the number of underground prostitutes has been growing in the last few years.

Recently, debate has ensued as to whether women should go back to doing housework and taking care of children full-time. Many people agree to this because, with women going back home, their jobs can be given to men, thus solving some of the unemployment problem. Another argument is that men will be able to work better as they can take their minds entirely off household affairs and children and concentrate on their work. They say that division of labor is necessary, and that this will be a good arrangement. Quite a number of women like and support this idea as it will reduce their burden. People who oppose the idea consider it a major setback for women.

Progressive forces are emerging in China. Since 1980, a group of women, mostly intellectuals, have become more and more conscious of women's problems. A number of women writers are writing about women's issues in short stories, novellas and novels. They raise questions about the position of women, write about women's plight, agonies, bitterness and sufferings in coping with love, marriage, family and career. Never in Chinese history, at least since 1949, have women characters been so distinctly depicted and dealt with in such abundance and variety in Chinese literature. In fact, in recent years, a new women's literature has appeared in which we find a whole spectrum of women characters and their experiences. This women's literature has attracted considerable attention and discussion in literary circles. In the last two or three years, a group of women teachers, journalists and writers have been getting together to read and discuss books on women or feminist books from the West and to talk about women's problems. One of the goals they are pursuing is to establish women's studies programs in the universities.

In China today, the official view on feminism is one of criticism and occasionally condemnation. It is considered that feminism is an invention of the West and it is a manifestation of bourgeois liberalism. Feminists are characterized as loose women who advocate free sex and have little sense of morality.

Ever since Confucius, Chinese culture has reinforced and justified the supremacy of man over woman, holding women as the inferior sex. It is most essential to have people, especially women, better educated so that they will be aware of the damaging force of this ideology and do their best to shatter it so that women can be freed from all shackles – physical and mental, visible and invisible, external and internal.[1]

Japan

The Meiji Restoration of 1868, an epoch-making incident in Japan's modernization, brought many changes to women's lives. Under the restored Emperor system, patriarchal family values were reinforced in order to transfer family loyalty toward the Emperor by identifying Emperor-loyalty with filial piety. Nationalist ideologues identified the nation as a large 'extended family' sanctified by the Emperor as a patriarchy 'sacred and inviolable'.

Within this family state, women's status severely deteriorated. The Meiji government imposed Confucianism as a state ideology through the modern compulsory education system. As a result, peasants and lower-class women, who enjoyed more egalitarian relationships between sexes, lost their autonomy as the patriarchal ideas became more widespread.

Under the Meiji Civil Code of 1898, although women had the right to divorce, custody belonged entirely to their husbands; parental consent was required for the registration of marriages; adultery by women was made a criminal offense; women had a property right but once they married it was transferred to their husbands. Moreover, the Police Security Regulations of 1890, especially Article 5 that prohibited women from participating in any political organization, severely curtailed their mobility.

Early Women's Movements

The Japanese feminist movement was born out of the resistance to repressive political and family systems. In 1911, Hiratsuka Raicho published a literary magazine, the *Seito* (Bluestocking) with other prominent intellectual women of the upper-middle class.[2] In her Proclamation of Emancipation, Raicho stated:

> In the beginning, woman was really the sun.
> She was a true person.
> Now woman is the moon.
> She depends on others for her life.
> And reflects the light of others.
> She is sickly as a wan, blue-white moon.
> We, the completely hidden sun, must restore ourselves.
> We must reveal the hidden sun, our concealed genius.
> This is our constant cry and inspiration of our unified purpose.
> The climax of our cry, this thirst, this desire will impel the genius in ourselves to shine forth.

Raicho tried to revive women's power and creativity which once existed in the ancient maternal society and was supressed for a long feudal period. Although the *Seito* started as a literary magazine, in which women could express their inner selves freely, later it evolved to consider broader social issues such as freedom of love and marriage, prostitution, abortion and women's oppressive status under the patriarchal family system. Because of its increasing social concerns and radical criticisms, the magazine often was censored and banned by the government.

Despite the difficulties, the *Seito* became a forum for prominent feminist activists, thinkers, writers, poets and artists. In its emphasis on women's creative talent, sexuality and individual freedom, the *Seito* was an awakening of Japanese feminist consciousness. The *Seito* members established the New Women's Association in 1920 and worked for the registration of maternal protection laws, suffrage, the abolition of Article 5 and the Meiji Code, and improvement of women's education.

Apart from the *Seito*, women were active in the socialist movement. Fukuda Hideko published her own journal, the *Sekai Fujin* (Women of the World) in 1907 (Sievers, 1983). Until it was banned in 1909, it covered women's issues not only in Japan but also internationally and became a forum for socialist men and women to debate the question of relationship between socialism and feminism. While prominent male socialists posited that women's liberation could only come through socialist revolution, Fukuda and other socialist women maintained that economic liberation did not necessarily lead women to real emancipation.

The new Peace Preservation Law of 1925 banned all leftist ideas as dangerous thoughts. During the so-called 'Dark Valley period' in the 1930s, all the progressive movements died out. Unfortunately, most Japanese feminists supported the totalitarian government and its policies. Contemporary feminist scholars have begun to explore the relationship between feminism and fascism in order to avoid its recurrence.

Contemporary Conditions and Movements

Since World War II, women's status in Japan has been dramatically improved in accordance with democratization policies under the US occupation. The New Constitution of 1946 entitled women to equal access to education, the right to vote, and complete equality in legal status. The New Civil Code abolished the traditional family system based on the patrilineal inheritance. Yet, gaining legal equality did not necessarily lead women to real emancipation.

The contemporary feminist movement started from the criticism of the gap between the post-war democratic ideals and the actual status of Japanese women. Under the influence of American feminism, in the early 1970s women who had been active in the various New Left movements (for example, minority civil rights, anti-Vietnam War, environmental protection) became critical of their degraded status as housekeepers and sex objects. They started to organize themselves into grassroots, consciousness-raising groups, conducting workshops and demonstrations to protest against rampant sexism in male-dominated Japanese society.[3] In 1972, a group of radical feminists opened the 'Lib Center' in Tokyo, which functioned as a core of the women's liberation movement by disseminating information on contraceptive technology, abortion and other women's issues, and by providing counseling services for women seeking divorce and shelters for battered women.

Since 1975, activist coalition groups such as the Kokusai Fujin-nen o Kikkake ni Kodo o Okos Kai (International Women's Year Activist Group) and the Asia no Onna-tachi no Kai (Asia Women's Association) were established (Mackie et al., 1980). In the 1980s, women in these activist groups have been engaged in the issues around sexuality such as anti-pornography campaigns, protest against sex tourism and international traffic of women (import of Southeast Asian women as prostitutes or mail-order brides) and reproductive freedom.

Middle-class housewives in suburban nuclear families shared the same type of problems as their American counterparts in the 1960s. In the 1980s, they became increasingly active in organizing study groups, running women's small businesses such as bookstores, craftshops, and restaurants to create women's networks throughout Japanese cities. They have been active participants in the various grassroots social movements around the issues of anti-nuclear power, consumer products, peace and ecology (Chizuko, 1984).

Education and Work

Before World War II, women's access to education was very limited. Athough Japan had achieved universal primary education during the early twentieth century, gender-related differences in secondary and tertiary education were considerable. At the secondary level, females had to attend separate girls' schools where the content of teaching, quality of teachers and facilities were inferior to those for boys' schools. Higher education was largely closed to women. While more than 30,000 men attended prestigious imperial universities before the war, only 40 women attended (Paulson, 1976). A very few private women's universities were open to women of privileged backgrounds.

Nowadays, nearly 40 percent of high school graduates, both men and women, go to college in Japan (Nihon Fujin Kyoiku Kenkyu kai, 1987). This figure is similar to that in the United States. Yet, 60 percent of women go to two-year junior colleges, whilst almost all men go to four-year universities (Nihon Fujin Kyoiku Kenkya kai, 1987). Junior colleges are exclusively for women and offer limited subjects such as home economics, nursing, education, art and literature, which are considered good to prepare them to be better mothers. The ideology of *ryosai kembo*, a good wife and wise mother, has dominated Japanese women's education since the Meiji era. Despite the postwar democratization of the educational system, this ideology is still kept alive in most of the female junior colleges. Consequently, women's occupational opportunities are severely restricted.

Most Japanese corporations usually prefer female junior college graduates to university graduates because the latter are considered overqualified for proper women's jobs such as making copies, operating phones, serving tea – in short, acting womanly and making the workplace pleasant for their male colleagues. Ironically, the more women are educated, the fewer opportunities they have in the Japanese occupational structure.

In the 1980s, however, there have been some changes in Japanese women's status. Since the late 1970s, more and more women have entered the workforce. Since a single income hardly sustains the average family living standard, especially since the oil crisis inflation of the mid-1970s, working wives have become the norm. Today, nearly 40 percent of Japan's workforce is made up of women (Robin-Mowry, 1983; Rodosho Fujin Shonen Kyoku, 1986). Yet the growth in the number of working women does not indicate an advance in women's emancipation. According to Sohyo, Japan's major labor union, 20 percent of female workers are part-timers, working under poor conditions, with minimal wages and no fringe benefits, social insurance or job security. The average women's wage is only 51.8 percent of that of men (Nihon Fujin Kyoiku Kenkyu kai, 1987). The so-called Equal Opportunity Bill of 1985, which was opposed by feminists and progressive parties, prohibited some discriminatory practices, but cut back protective regulations and only called on companies to 'make efforts' to treat female workers equally.

In the field of education, the most hopeful sign in the 1980s is the opening of women's studies courses in many colleges. In 1983, 94 courses concerning women's studies were offered in 75 colleges. In 1986, 204 courses were offered in 113 colleges throughout Japan (Nihon Fujin Kyoiku Kenkyu kai, 1987). These courses are related to women's history, literature, sociology and anthropology, and to Western and Japanese feminism. Women's Studies Associations were established in Tokyo and Kyoto by concerned feminist scholars who were actively promoting feminist scholarship and organizing study groups including housewives and workers to make women's studies a lifelong education.

Although the situation of Japanese women has improved in recent decades, it remains to alter underlying assumptions and values that are the root causes of inequality. Reforms to date have been top-down changes undertaken by men. At the national level, gender equality tends to be a non-issue in Japan because legal equal opportunity is assumed to be synonymous with everyday equality.

Curriculum Recommendations

The integration of Asian women into global and women's studies curricula that we recommend is conceptual and issue-oriented. A conceptual base or framework provides a powerful means of organizing, interpreting and comprehending a large array of data – events and experiences, perceptions and actions – across time and place. An issue orientation points not only towards problems and conflicts but also towards their resolution. By issues, we refer to persistent human problems that are the subject of public policy decisions such as discrimination on the basis of race or gender. An issue orientation provides structure for comparative, cross-cultural study, for value exploration and analysis, and for multidisciplinary studies. It also stimulates systematic inquiry, rather than description alone or unthinking acceptance of others' conclusions.

Examples of concepts and issues that are (a) important to understanding the experiences and perspectives of Asian women, and (b) important to global studies and well illustrated by the experiences and perspectives of Asian women include the following: tradition and change, interconnectedness or interdependence, similarities and differences, equity versus protection or exploitation, opportunity versus pseudo-opportunity, and attaining social justice. In any consideration of Asian women, it is important to probe beneath the surface appearances, for example, of modernity in Japan and of socialist equality in China. The present situation is neither as it has been nor as it might seem to be.

These are just a sampling of possibilities for making global studies global in the sense that they not only encompass cultures and nations worldwide but also include both male and female experiences and perspectives.

Notes

[1] This section drew on the following sources: Croll (1983); Johnson (1983); Stacey (1983); Lee Yao (1983); *Women of China* (1987).

[2] Raicho's Proclamation of Emancipation appeared in the first issue of the *Seito* in 1911. It was translated by Robin-Mowry (1983).

[3] In the early 1970s, feminists edited *Japanese Women Speak Out* to protest sexism in a male-dominated Japanese society and presented it at the United Nations Women's Decade Conference in Mexico City in 1975.

References

Croll, E. (1983). *Chinese women since Mao*. London: Zed Books.

Johnson, K.A. (1983). *Women, the family and peasant revolution in China.* Chicago: University of Chicago Press.

Mackie et al. (1980). Women's groups in Japan, *Feminist International*, 2.

Nihon Fujin Kyoiku Kenkyu kai (1987). *Tokei ni kmiru josei no genjo* (The present status of women in statistics). Tokyo: Kakiuchi.

Paulson. (1976). Evolution of feminine ideal. In J. Lebra et al. (Eds.), *Women in changing Japan.* Boulder, Colo.: Westview.

Robin-Mowry, D. (1983). *The hidden sun: Women of modern Japan.* Boulder, Colo.: Westview.

Rodosho Fujin kyoku (1986). *Fujin rodo no jitsujo* (The situation of women in work). Tokyo: Okurasho Insatsu Kyoku.

Sievers, L.S. (1983). *Flowers in salt: The beginning of feminist consciousness in modern Japan.* Stanford, Calif.: Stanford University Press.

Stacey, J. (1983). *Patriarchy and socialist revolution in China.* Berkeley, Calif.: University of California Press.

Task Force (1975) *Japanese women speak out: White paper on sexism in Japan.* Tokyo: International.

Ueno Chizuko (1984). Genesis of the urban housewife, *Japan Quarterly*, 34(2), 130-42.

Yao, E.S.L. (1983). *Chinese women: Past and present.* Mesquite, Tex.: Ide House.

Women of China (1987) (journal published in the People's Republic of China, Nos. 1-12).

Matsui is a Ph.D. candidate in Comparative Education in the Buffalo Research Institute for Education and Training (BRIET) at the State University of New York (SUNY) – Buffalo. Her address is BRIET, 208 Baldy Hall, SUNY – Buffalo, NY 14260, USA. Yuanxi Ma is a Ph.D. candidate in American Literature in the English Department at SUNY – Buffalo. Previously she was an Associate Professor of English in Beijing, China. Her address is English Department, Clemens Hall, SUNY – Buffalo, NY 14260, USA. Catherine Cornbleth is Professor of Education and Director of BRIET at SUNY – Buffalo. Her address is BRIET, 208 Baldy Hall, SUNY – Buffalo, NY 14260, USA.

10

Education for the Twenty-first Century: A Japanese Perspective

Akio Nakajima
Kumon Institute of Education, Japan

Japan is often characterized as a land of tradition and change. For centuries cultural values and religious practices have dominated Japanese thinking and ways of life. These periods of tradition are followed by times of drastic transition, in which educational reform tends to be an outgrowth of social and economic changes. The lessons learned from tradition and transition are forming the basis of new directions for Japanese education.

Educational Reform in Japan

An historical overview reveals two major reform movements in Japanese education. The first took place immediately after the creation of a modern national state under the Meiji restoration, when the Government Order of Education was promulgated in 1872. The Order and its accompanying statutes laid the foundations of Japan's modern national system of education by establishing the principle of equal educational opportunity. Six years of elementary education became compulsory for all children and a range of educational institutions at the levels of secondary and advanced education developed. By the beginning of the twentieth century, 90 percent of all Japanese children were attending elementary school.

The second major reform took place immediately after World War II with the enactment of the Fundamental Law of Education, which defined the aims of education and set forth basic principles for education in the new democracy. Under this law and related School Education Law, compulsory schooling was extended from six to nine years, co-education was introduced, concepts of the social studies were included in classrooms, and a new '6-3-3-4 system' was introduced. This system was derived from the principle of equal educational opportunity for all, which was more extensive than in the period before the war. Under this new system, education opportunities were extended and improved with support from the Japanese people whose national character placed high value on education, and with the help of increased revenues brought about by the improved economic growth of Japan.

Both the introduction of a modern system of formal education in the Meiji period and the educational reform after World War II accompanied a major political reform within the government and social structure of the nation.

The present educational reform represents a change in 'times of peace' following no major political upheaval. However, after a hundred years of 'catch-up' efforts in modernization since the Meiji era, Japan is at the threshold of a major transitional period in the history of civilization.

Today, the third reform movement is underway in which the Ministry of Education, Science and Culture is making efforts to guide Japan into the twenty-first century. This represents a transition to an age of internationalization characterized by the spread of information and to a time of social maturity, never before experienced by Japanese people. Educational reform, while representing a political ideal, is strongly supported by the majority of Japanese people who have expressed considerable dissatisfaction with the present education system for some time. Government initiatives are reflected in two master plans for reform – the report of the National Council on Educational Reform, a body established by Prime Minister Nakasone in 1984, and the report of the Curriculum Council, commissioned by the Minister of Education, Science and Culture in 1985.

The National Council on Educational Reform

During three years of activity, the Council submitted a series of interim reports for public discussion and debate. Eight basic principles for educational reform were identified during the early stages:
1. Greater respect for individuality
2. Emphasis on fundamentals
3. Cultivation of creativity, thinking ability and power of expression
4. Expansion of opportunities for choices
5. Humanization of the educational environment
6. Transition to a lifelong learning system
7. Coping with internationalization
8. Coping with the information age.

For its final report the Council identified three principles it considered significant for educational reform. They were:
1. Emphasis on individuality
2. Transition to a lifelong learning system
3. Coping with internationalization and the information age.

Both reports for educational reform were submitted in 1987. The report prepared by the National Council is more idealistic and future-oriented, while that of the Curriculum Council is directed toward actual school changes.

Currently the Japanese government is in the midst of educational reform, implementing new national curriculum standards, introducing new teacher training programs, making the secondary education more flexible, and establishing a University Council.

Japanese Education Today

The rapid changes in Japanese social environment and the immense expansion of education have had a great impact upon education in our country. A number of problems have arisen, such as insufficient effort to identify and develop the personality, abilities and aptitudes of individual students; the uniformity of the content and methods of teaching in schools; excessive competition in entrance examinations resulting in overemphasis of student scores in standardized achievement tests; and the uniformity, rigidity and closed nature of formal education.

In the present situation all students of differing abilities, aptitudes and interests are given homogenous instruction with a similar curriculum, similar teaching materials and similar teaching methods. As a result, children whose pace of learning is relatively slow are unable to keep up with classroom learning and are labeled as 'failures' while those who learn more quickly feel that classroom teaching is not challenging enough.

Let me draw your attention to the expansion of our senior schools after World War II. Our pre-war secondary school system accepted selected students who wanted to continue to university. After the war, Japan introduced a new type of secondary school called the 'comprehensive high school', a North American concept. 'Secondary education for all' was the slogan for this new type of school, and the number of students attending such a school rose dramatically. For example, ten years after the end of the War, 50 percent of students continued on to comprehensive high schools. Ten years later, 70 percent attended. By 1973 attendance exceeded 90 percent. Today, 94 percent of students within the same age group attend senior high schools, while 47 percent enrol in higher institutions of learning.

However, the intense competition to get into prestigious universities pressured the high school curriculum to become more academically oriented and stereotyped. Thus, it has moved away from one of the basic ideas of the comprehensive school: a broad-based curriculum for a variety of students. To correct this situation, the National Council on Educational Reform has stressed in its report the principle of individuality for Japanese education.

Characteristics and Issues of Japanese Education

Japanese education has a reputation for its high standards and its attainment of substantial equality. I think it is true. Japanese people are proud of the system in which all children, wherever they are born and no matter what their family situation, have equal opportunity to acquire the basic skills of reading, writing and arithmetic. In our modern democratic society, free competition is important, providing that all youngsters have equal opportunities to learn basic skills. My vision is to see a very equal and high standard of elementary education, followed by a secondary education system which acknowledges individual differences in its programs.

In order to facilitate the accomplishment of the new education priorities, the Japanese government is providing subsidies to local governments to help maintain national curriculum standards. Government money is used to supply free textbooks for students. It also covers half the money paid for local schoolteachers' salaries and the cost of school buildings, facilities and equipment. Such national support ensures a high standard of education conditions throughout Japan. Slightly less than 50 percent of the cost of operating elementary and secondary education is financed by the Japanese government.

The School Education Law regulates the subjects taught and the hours of instruction. Objectives and major content topics in each subject are listed in the course of study set as the national curriculum standards for each school level. Although textbooks are published privately, all must be authorized by the Ministry of Education as supporting the the established course of study. Because Japanese teachers base their teaching on textbooks, courses throughout the country are relatively uniform in content.

While rigidity and uniformity may be a prerequisite to learning basic skills identified in elementary school curriculum, they are not appropriate for secondary schools. Japanese schools have tended to be characterized as 'cramming schools' which emphasize student memorization. In the next decade, the ability to apply acquired knowledge in creative ways, as well as the ability to think independently, must be stressed. Creativity can be fostered only when individuality is encouraged.

Looking into the Twenty-first Century

There is no doubt that Japan will continue to stress a high degree of interdependence with other nations. If our country is to survive as a member of the international community, then we need to develop a global outlook among Japanese people that will be respected in the international community.

To this end it is essential for us to acquire both the proficiency to express the individuality of Japanese society and culture, and the ability to appreciate the diversities of other world cultures. While respecting the values and identity of our own country, we should avoid making judgments of others based on national self-interest. Fostering global understanding will facilitate international communication and our ability to understand peoples of other cultures.

In December 1987, the Curriculum Council submitted its final report for revising national curriculum standards at all levels of schooling for the twenty-first century. One of the main issues cited by the Council was the difficulty of coping with rapid social changes, especially the issue related to internationalization and the information age. The greatest emphasis was placed on internationalization of the school curricula. The Ministry of

Education has been revising the courses of study following the Council's direction.

One of the expected changes related to the internationalization will be in the upper secondary school social studies courses. Under the current curriculum standards the objective of social studies is 'to make students deepen their understanding and awareness of society and human beings from a broad perspective, and to develop their qualities necessary as citizens which are essential to a democratic and peaceful nation'. In its report the Curriculum Council emphasized greater international understanding that would be of help to Japanese people as they enter the the twenty-first century.

To strengthen the objective of international understanding, the Curriculum Council divided social studies into two new required subjects of geography and history/civics at the senior high level. The new required world history course, for example, will stress the diversity of history, lifestyles, customs and values of other countries in the world.

Another subject area that the Ministry of Education is strengthening is that of foreign language. To improve English proficiency, numerous programs have been started. They are:

1. In 1976 a five-week English immersion program for leading secondary school teachers began. The program emphasized listening and speaking comprehension.
2. In 1977 the Monbusho English Fellow Program was initiated to bring young American university graduates to local school boards to assist consultants in English language instruction.
3. In 1978 the British Teacher Program started, in which young British fellows with a bachelor's degree were assigned to secondary and tertiary schools to help in English language instruction.
4. In 1979 the English Teacher Abroad Program was established, in which leading Japanese teachers of English who finished the five-week training started in 1976 were sent to the United States and Great Britain for eight weeks of study.
5. In 1987, the Monbusho English Fellow Program and the British Teacher Program were amalgamated to form a new Japan Exchange of Teachers (JET) Program that brought to Japan young English teachers from the United States, Great Britain, Australia, New Zealand, Ireland and Canada. By 1988, 1,400 overseas teachers were brought to Japan for one year to teach English to Japanese students and teachers. The program hopes to attract 3,000 teachers each year in the near future.

As Japanese people, we are fully aware of the responsibilities of an internationalized society of the twenty-first century. Centrally located in the Pacific Ocean at the eastern end of the Asiatic Continent, Japan is the meeting place of East, West, North and South connections. Continued personal contacts and cultural understandings will help the Japanese to fully participate in the international community of the twenty-first century. Thus, the Pacific Rim is a kind of micro-laboratory for the world where the elements essential to peace and prosperity can be examined. It is our national wish to educate our young people so that they may serve as bridges between Japan and other Pacific nations. Let us all try to make the large Pacific a small basin in the twenty-first century.

Akio Nakajima is Director of the Kumon Institute of Education, 5-bancho Grand Building, 3-1, 5-bancho, Chiyoda-ku, Tokyo 102, Japan. He is also President of the Education Future Institute. Mr Nakajima acted as Deputy Director General in charge of elementary and secondary education from 1986 to 1988, after twenty-five years of service with the Ministry of Education, Science and Culture.

11

The Evolution and Direction of South Korean Social Studies Curriculum since 1945

Se Ho Shin
Korean Educational Development Institute, Republic of South Korea

Introduction

Education in the Republic of Korea has experienced drastic changes during the period of forty years since independence from Japan in August 1945. The most conspicuous of these is the series of changes in the school curriculum. Behind these changes are changing national and social demands, and the effects of pedagogical research and educational development activities.

In contrast to other subject areas, it is in social studies that the needs of a nation and a society are most often directly reflected. National and social needs are often mirrored in the goals and objectives of social studies, and in the selection and organization of its contents and in the teaching of its methods.

This close relationship between society and curriculum is most evident in the South Korean social studies curriculum, which has undoubtedly reflected the distinct and dramatic political, social, economic and cultural changes experienced in South Korea during the past four decades. The social studies curriculum has, in fact, shown some distinct characteristics of South Korean society in different periods of its development.

With this perspective in mind, the present paper will examine the changes in, and distinct characteristics of, the South Korean social studies curriculum in six successive periods of recent curriculum development. The paper will discuss the distinguishing characteristics of the social studies curriculum at each stage, and furthermore will discuss such characteristics in relation to their formative factors.

1. Teaching Guideline Period (1945-55)

One of the common aspirations of South Koreans after the liberation from Japanese colonial rule in August 1945 was to achieve massive reforms in education. The 'Educational Council', founded immediately after the liberation, established the basic goal of South Korean education: 'to cultivate citizens of a democratic state, with whole character and thorough patriotism based on the educational ideal of Universal Benefit to Mankind'. With the cooperation of the US military government, the Council established a new set of educational goals and selected and organized the contents of the curriculum of the new education system. But the effort ended merely in providing a set of Teaching Guidelines, rather than a formal curriculum, largely because of insufficient time and lack of professional manpower needed to design and develop the curriculum.

One of the distinct features of the Teaching Guidelines used during the period was the appearance of a 'Social Life' subject in the primary and middle schools curricula. 'Social Life' was a comprehensive subject which included contents of geography, history, civics, natural sciences and vocational education. This subject was expected to play the role of cultivating citizens of the newly independent nation. Previously, schools were used as instruments of colonial educational policy.

The conceptual basis of 'Social Life' was adopted from the American 'Social Studies'. Its subject area had significant implications for all Korean social studies education which was to follow. The establishment of 'Social Life' can also be understood in the context of the 'New Education Movement', initiated by teachers as part of research activities on teaching methods aimed at the cultivation of citizens through child-centered or experience-centered education.

The spirit of establishing 'Social Life' subject was strongly reflected in supplementary teaching materials used at the time in elementary schools, especially in the supplementary materials used by fifth-grade and sixth-grade children. The teacher would act as a guide to students and would lead his or her pupils to the farm with a book in one hand and a hoe in the other. He or she would help children to learn the meaning of creation and production through experience, and at the same time would strengthen their desire for work, cultivate their spirit of endurance and thereby help them feel the satisfaction of creation and production. The materials provided the following teaching-learning contents:

> *Fifth grade:* Soil, plowing, farm tools, good seed, barley, processing of rice straw, the fowls, mulberry tree, spring, summer and fall, silkworms, disease of silkworms and prevention manual, seedbed, flower garden, vegetable, chemical fertilizer, home-made fertilizer, German (Italian) millet, beans, and so on.
>
> *Sixth grade*: Seed picking, cotton, vegetables, storing and processing of vegetables, vegetable damage by blight and harmful insects, fruit trees,

rice harvest, agricultural handiwork, chemical fertilizer, pig breeding, egg and chicken, cattle, afforestation and forest protection law, rice seedbed and planting young rice plants, mowing the rice plant, damage by blight and harmful insects, barley harvest.

2. The First Curriculum Period (1955-63)

The Teaching Guidelines, which were transitionally promulgated immediately after South Korea's liberation, and which were subjected to partial revision, finally became the first documented curriculum in September 1955. The first curriculum was promulgated with the nation's foremost task of reconstruction from the devastation of the Korean War (1950-53) well in mind. Such concern was well reflected in the social studies curriculum.

The subject of 'Social Life' as offered in the primary school mainly dealt with basic issues related to the social requirements and basic needs of children. It particularly emphasized the promotion of understanding of interpersonal relationships in various groups, the significance of group life, intergroup relationships, the recognition of one's proper position in group life, and the importance of forming desirable attitudes according to one's own position. As a curriculum, 'Social Life' in primary schools placed emphasis on the importance of group life in achieving the restoration of social order, which had been greatly disturbed during and immediately after the Korean War.

'Social Life' in the middle school emphasized moral education as an extension of its counterpart in the primary school level. Moral education, which was mainly included in 'Civics', was centred around anti-communism education. Considering the social need for reconstruction from the Korean War, a chapter entitled 'Rehabilitation and Reconstruction' was newly included in 'Civics' for third-graders in middle schools. In geography areas of the curriculum, contents dealing with economic livelihood, productivity by adapting to natural environments, and the utilization of natural resources were added. Also added was content on preserving natural resources.

In the high school, the educational aims of social studies included education for mental and skill training through experience, diligence and frugality, willingness for hard work, wise and rational management of economic life, and rational selection of one's career, as bases for independent livelihood. Under these aims, educational contents in social studies included those suitable for development of skills, attitude and habits required for recognizing and solving problems faced by the society. In geography, a more positive interpretation of various worldwide phenomena was encouraged in an effort to eradicate the inferiority complex of many who had been victims of colonial education under Japanese rule. In addition, a new unit entitled 'Comprehensive Plan for National Land Development' was included in line with the reconstruction effort after the Korean War.

3. The Second Curriculum Period (1963-73)

The second curriculum attempted to reflect the experience-centred educational philosophy that had been widely advocated ever since the Teaching Guidelines had been provided in a more practical and refined manner. In other words, the second curriculum defined the school curriculum as a totality of all kinds of learning activities that pupils experience under schools' guidance. In effect, the second curriculum accommodated, in practical terms, an experience-centered progressivism, an educational philosophy which put emphasis on building up one's character and experiences through daily living. Accordingly, emphases on autonomy, productivity and usefulness were the core of the revised curriculum.

The most conspicuous characteristic of the second curriculum was that 'Anti-communism and Moral Education' became an independent subject in middle school. Previously taught within 'Civics', the contents of this new stand-alone subject were aimed at the acquisition by students of a firm basis of anti-communistic and moral thoughts by enabling them to understand how the principle of free democracy operates in all areas of human life and having them learn by experience how this principle contributes to improvement in human dignity, freedom and welfare. The separation of 'Anti-communism and Moral Education' as an independent subject was a reflection of the commitment of the Third Republic, which came into being in 1962, to the establishment of a new social order. The change in name of the high school subject 'Moral Education' to 'National Ethics' was in the same vein.

4. The Third Curriculum Period (1973-81)

The basic principle of the third curriculum was the acceptance of discipline-centred curriculum, in place of an experience-centred one. The second curriculum was primarily geared to educational contents oriented to the present, with a functional utility suitable in the confused period which had resulted from the aftermath of both the Japanese colonial rule and the Korean War.

Yet the explosion of innovations in science and technology and the dramatic expansion of knowledge made it impossible to teach all types of knowledge to students. Furthermore, it had to be acknowledged that the new knowledge of yesterday quickly becomes the obsolete knowledge of today.

Therefore, the argument for emphasizing discipline-centred or academically-oriented curriculum was to improve the effects of school education by teaching learners the general structure of knowledge embodied in the mother discipline of a given subject area, rather than delivering a massive volume of facts and knowledge, and thereby develop learners' attitudes to explore and inquire into relevant contents of education.

Parallel with this trend, the social studies curriculum adopted a structured system of knowledge as a content of learning and placed heavy emphasis on a problem-solving approach based on inquiry and discovery.

This was also the period when Korea was launched into the international community and the conflict between North and South Korea became more acute. 'Korean History' was established as an independent subject in middle school with an aim of promoting the self-pride and identity of Koreans. The basic philosophy of establishing 'Korean History' was to preserve and inherit cultural integrity, to accommodate the inflow of foreign culture on top of a firm awareness of the native culture and the legitimacy of national history.

5. The Fourth Curriculum Period (1981-87)

The fourth curriculum best realized the spirit of integrated curriculum for social studies. In the first and second grades of primary school, Korean language, social studies and moral education were integrated into a 'Daily Life' subject. In third grade through sixth grade, existing contents were reorganized into a more integrated subject. But in the case of middle school, subject integration was rather incomplete in form and degree. 'Civics' and 'Geography of Korea' were integrated in the first grade, 'World History' and 'World Geography' were integrated in the second grade, and 'World History' and 'Civics' were integrated in the third grade. However, the contents were merely bound together in a textbook, and units respective to different subject areas were clearly distinguished.

Though the integration was incomplete, integrated social studies started to be taught on the premise that school education should contribute in solving various problems occurring in daily social life. Because the most problematic situations in real social life are in integrated form, relevant to many subject areas of school education, teaching of such subjects should naturally be done in an integrated manner.

Another factor behind the advent of an integrated curriculum for social studies was an effort to overcome a widespread criticism of the third curriculum. As the third curriculum was heavily discipline-centred, overly emphasizing the structure of knowledge in related subject areas, the educational evaluation (entrance examination) based upon such a curriculum tended to become rote-memory-oriented and inhuman. The fourth curriculum adopted so-called human- or child-centred educational philosophy as its basis as one way to overcome the educational crises that were reaching climax level at the time.

6. The Fifth Curriculum Period (1987-   )

The two distinct features in the revision toward the fifth curriculum have been the systemization of teacher-learning contents and the improvement of economic education. The fifth curriculum was the product of a new attempt at improving and developing the scope and sequence of teaching-learning contents.

For the first and second grades of primary school, where Korean language, social studies and moral education had been integrated into 'Daily Life', Korean language once again became an independent subject. This change was a response to the call that the Korean language should be an independent subject to bring about substantiality in Korean language education.

In middle school, a 'Human Life and Social Phenomena' unit was included as an introductory unit in the first grade. Its aims were to improve the level of understanding of the contents and methods to be taught in the integrated social studies subject. The unit is followed by contents such as the regional geography of Korea and the world and the history of the East and the West, from prehistorical times to the middle ages. In the second grade of middle school, students now learn about the history of the East and the West in modern times up to the present, as well as about the fundamentals of politics, economics, law, society and culture. Teaching-learning contents in the third grade are much more systematized. First, students learn about politics, economics, society, culture, natural environment and inhabitants, and utilization of national territory and protection of the environment within the limited geographical scope of Korea. After these, they learn about natural environment and human activities in the rest of the world. Finally, students are introduced to a unit entitled 'Developing Korea and the Future'. Such an organization of teaching-learning contents reflects the effort to integrate more practical contents, but, at the same time, to avoid meaningless repetition of interdisciplinary contents of civics, geography and history.

In high school, attempts are being made to further distinguish the characteristics of different subject areas. In this effort, the titles of the former Social Studies I and II were changed to 'Politics and Economy' and 'Society and Culture' respectively, and those of Geography I and II to 'Korean Geography' and 'World Geography' respectively.

A major characteristic of changes in the fifth curriculum is the major emphasis given to the qualitative improvement of economic education in schools. Previously offered economic education in schools was mainly through civics courses and partially in subject areas such as geography, history and national ethics (moral education). Most of the teaching-learning contents in economic education were geared to public information or propaganda statements on the government's economic policies and to indoctrinate the superiority of a free-market economic system. And, because such contents were dispersed into too many subject areas, systematic learning of economic concepts and phenomena was very difficult.

In the meantime, as the scope of Korean economic activities were greatly expanded, and as their structure became more complicated, the importance of economic education received much more public recognition. It has been increasingly contended that democratic society requires more than blind loyalty and patriotism from its members. And that the teaching-learning contents of economic education based on such a viewpoint should be related to cultivating the learner's ability to make rational decisions in daily economic life.

Of course, the basis of economic education in schools is in laying its foundation on preserving and developing democracy and a free-market economy.

In short, basically four themes were developed as the guiding objectives of the new economic education system. The economic education system will help the students of elementary, middle and high schools in:

1. understanding the basic principles and workings of the free-market system;
2. cultivating rational decision-making abilities in their daily economic life;
3. enhancing their interests in economic subject-matter and phenomena; and
4. cultivating sound economic behaviors in a modernizing industrial society.

On these bases, teaching-learning contents of economics within social studies, as reflected in the fifth curriculum, include: basic characteristics of the economy, basic principles of the free-market system, as well as contents aimed at understanding various types of economic phenomena, and developing rational attitudes and habits in economic life.

Important activities in the major revision of economic education in schools began with the total revision of the entire chapters on economics in social studies textbooks and related teachers' guides at both the primary and secondary school levels. It was accompanied by new design, development and diffusion of slide packages, reference books, children's stories and other teaching-learning materials on economics for school children. Also conducted at the national level was an extensive teacher-training program on newly revised curriculum for economic education. In the coming years, these activities will continue to be expanded and upgraded on the basis of continuing feedbacks from the field.

Conclusion

As reviewed in this paper, changes in the social studies curriculum in South Korea have directly reflected the drastic changes in larger political, social and economic changes occurring in the country during the past forty years. This characteristic can be readily observed when one examines the stated purposes and contents of social studies curriculum in successive periods of curriculum revision. Looking ahead, some distinct trends can be expected with respect to the characteristics of future social studies curriculum.

One of the major changes in educational climate which the South Korean social studies has to consider is the trend towards the internationalization of Korean society. The status of Koreans in the international, economic, cultural and political spheres has been greatly elevated in recent years. With this comes the increasing importance of 'education for international understanding' as an important objective for social studies to pursue. Furthermore, the emergence of the Pacific region in international political and economic arenas has given added regional weight to education for international understanding. Of course, attention was given, even in the past, individually to the North and South Americas, Japan and China. But the attention placed on the Pacific region as an entity was lacking.

Along with the emergence of the Pacific region, the increased importance of Korea as the new focal point of possible ideological reconciliation between the East and West is another factor in the educational climate which South Korean social studies education must pay attention to. In the past, social studies education in South Korea in this respect has been based mostly on anti-socialism and anti-communist education. Now, with the increased thaw in conflicting ideological postures, there is an ever-increasing need to direct education toward promoting an increased understanding between nations with different ideologies. This development has serious implications for the ways in which children are being taught about nations with opposing ideological postures. This general climate certainly is not one that social studies educators will find easy to adjust to, and much research and development activities need to be carried out.

Another conspicuous change in South Korean social studies curriculum is the new emphasis given to improving and extending economic education. This trend is not unrelated to two previously mentioned trends occurring in recent years. The recent reconciliatory mood between the East and the West has greatly pushed the expansion of the Korean economic policy toward the Eastern bloc economies. Together with this, the so-called Newly Industrializing Countries (NICs), including the Republic of Korea, of the Pacific region are receiving world-wide attention. In this context, South Korean social studies education, as pointed out earlier in this paper, is giving more weight to economic education in schools. At the individual level, emphasis is being given to cultivating a more rational economic livelihood based on an enhancement of economic literacy. Also emphasized are contents related to social and national needs which are basic to the understanding of domestic and international economic issues and problems.

As briefly summarized above, education for international understanding, ideology education and economic education are three major areas which have evolved as major areas which have gained new attention and weight in the social studies curriculum of South Korea. And such emphases are expected to continue for some time to come.

References

Cho, Do-Keun (1987). *School-based economic education and in-service and pre-service teacher training*. SaeGyoyug, April, Seoul: Korean Federation of Education Associations.

Gang, Hwan-Kook (1985). *Introduction to the social studies*. Seoul: Hackyeonsa.

Ihm, Chon-Sun et al. (1988). *A study on basic directions and improvement strategies of economic education in Korea*. Seoul: Korean Educational Development Institute (KEDI).

Jung, Young Soo, et al. (1985). *Ideologies in Korean educational policies (I): Beginning of national education and establishment of democracy education from 1945 to 1960*. Seoul: KEDI, 1985.

_____ (1987). *Ideologies in Korean educational policies (III): 1980-86*. Seoul: KEDI, 1987.

Ministry of Education, Korea (1986). *Curriculum revision in primary and secondary schools (1946-81): the social studies and history*. Seoul: Ministry of Education (MOE).

_____ (1986). *Curriculum revision in primary and secondary schools (1946-81): Master guidelines*. Seoul: MOE.

_____ (1987). *The 5th curriculum revision of elementary school*. Seoul: MOE.

_____ (1987). *The 5th curriculum revision of middle school*. Seoul: MOE.

_____ (1988). *The 5th curriculum revision of high School*. Seoul: MOE.

Moon, Yong Rin, et al. (1987). *A comprehensive report on the revision of school economic education in Korea*. Seoul: KEDI.

Shin, Se Ho (1981). *Research and development of curriculum revision*. Seoul: KEDI.

Se Ho Shin is President of the Korean Educational Development Institute (KEDI), 92-6 Umyeon-dong Seocho-gu, Seoul, 137-791 Korea. He has served in a number of positions with KEDI during the past eighteen years, as well as had postings with the national government and with South Korean and US universities. As an educator, Dr Shin has been closely involved in the development of social studies curriculum in South Korean schools.

12

Curriculum Reform and Teaching Materials Development in China

Wu Yongxing and *Wan Dalin*
Curriculum and Teaching Materials Research Institute
People's Republic of China

Education in the People's Republic of China is directed by the State Education Commission (SEdC), formerly the Chinese Ministry of Education. Two institutions, the People's Education Press (PEP), established in 1950, and the Curriculum and Teaching Materials Research Institute (CTMRI), founded in 1983, develop and publish teaching materials for primary and secondary schools according to the national teaching plan. Both institutions share the same staff of about 220 editors and researchers.

These institutions are directly responsible to the State Education Commission. In addition to their responsibility for providing curricular materials they supply paper matrices to printing houses in various provinces, municipalities and autonomous regions for mass printing of textbooks. They also serve as centres of research compilation, data collection and publication. Textbooks prepared by PEP for primary and secondary schools are comprehensive and cover all subject areas in the individual disciplines, languages and the arts. Teaching materials such as workbooks, teachers' manuals, extra-curriculum readers, dictionaries and audio-visual materials are also developed as supplements to textbooks. Our institutions are now engaged in the preparation of the eighth round of teaching materials for primary and secondary schools since 1950. Other publications are developed and distributed to teacher training institutions, universities and colleges and vocational schools.

Since 1950, 14,000 different book titles have been published. Approximately twenty billion copies of these titles have been printed. CTMRI carries out extensive work in both theoretical and practical educational issues. Examples of recent research programs at national level include:

> During the Sixth Five Year Plan (1981-85): Experiments and Research on the Reform of Primary and Secondary Schools in Relation to System,

Curriculum, Teaching Materials, and Teaching Methods. Articles on the program are collected and published as a book entitled *Reform on Primary and Secondary Education.*

During the Seventh Five Year Plan (1986-90): Experiments and Research on the Integrated Reform on Primary and Secondary Schools. This program is aimed at studying and drawing up the curriculum structure, teaching syllabi, a teaching material system and teaching contents for the Nine Year Compulsory Education and senior secondary schools. A monthly magazine entitled *Curriculum, Teaching Materials and Methods* is published for distribution at home and abroad as the official publication for the two institutions.

Guidelines for Curriculum Reform

In China, curriculum reform is based on a set of national positions and principles. Seven basic guidelines are:

Education should be directed to modernization, to the world and to the future.

Laws of physical and intellectual development of children and youth should be respected.

Students should be developed morally, intellectually, physically and aesthetically. Students should form a correct attitude towards labor.

Theory and practice should be combined.

The difficulty of textbooks should be adjusted.

The burden placed on students should be lightened.

Teaching requirements should be clear and concrete.

Basic principles for developing teaching materials are:

1. *Correctly handle the relation between education and student development.* Primary and secondary education should not only be compatible with physiological and psychological development of students but should also encourage further development.

2. *Correctly handle the relationship between knowledge and skills teaching and capabilities cultivation.* All courses should cultivate the capability of students' thinking through the concrete teaching contents of individual courses. Teachers should deliberately develop students' creative thinking in order to cultivate creativity.

3. *Correctly handle the relationship between traditional knowledge and modern scientific knowledge.*

4. *Correctly handle the relationship between the depth and breadth of teaching contents.* Teaching materials for each course should respect the physiological and psychological development of the children for whom it is designed, but at the same time challenge them.

5. *Correctly handle the relationship between theory and practice.* The combination of theory with practice not only enables students to learn gradually how to apply the knowledge, but also facilitates understanding. Such a combination also helps students develop thinking skills and cultivates their capabilities. Therefore, the teaching materials should allow for introduction of locally referenced materials that relate to the local geography, with respect to nationality and history.
6. *Correctly handle the relationship between knowledge education and moral education.* Moral education should be part of various school activities and underlie the teaching of various courses. It should relate to content without distorting the knowledge itself.

Textbook Development

The People's Education Press and the Curriculum and Teaching Materials Research Institute develop teaching materials according to the school curriculum, syllabus and guidelines of the primary and secondary textbooks after they have been approved by the National Evaluation Committee for Primary and Secondary School Textbooks (NECPSST), a branch of the State Education Commission.

In China, primary and secondary textbooks have been developed only by the People's Education Press for more than thirty years. In 1985, the SEdC declared that institutions and individuals were encouraged to develop teaching materials in all subjects according to the school curriculum, syllabus and guidelines of the primary and secondary textbooks.

Our PEP and CTMRI have fifteen editorial departments, including politics, mathematics, foreign languages, chemistry, history, geography, painting and pre-school education. Each department develops a manuscript for a textbook using the following process:

1. The authors are composed of PEP and CTMRI editors and experienced teachers (from primary and secondary schools as well as colleges) with writing ability.
2. The development of textbooks must be strictly based on the educational policies and requirements of the State, and also on the curriculum, syllabus and guidelines for textbooks. The content outlines and manuscripts for each subject, drafted and revised by the responsible editor, must be discussed and researched again and again under the leadership of the chief of the department. After the department chief reads the guidelines of contents and manuscripts for each subject, the materials are submitted to the editor-in-chief or the vice-editor-in-chief for approval.
3. Well-known experts are invited to act as advisers in the process of textbook development. They are consulted throughout the development process.
4. Opinions are extensively gathered from relevant department members through interviews and discussion. Problems are resolved by

consultation with relevant departments in the State Council, the Academy of Sciences of China, the Academy of Social Sciences of China, as well as colleges.

5. Experienced teachers are invited to read through the textbook manuscripts and attend discussions throughout the process of textbook development. If necessary, the revised textbook manuscripts are piloted in certain schools, and may be further revised according to these findings.
6. Attention is directed to the accuracy, development and sequencing of content within each text. Each text must also follow on from the texts used in lower grades and be consistent with those used in higher grades.

It should be pointed out that according to the 'Working Regulations of the National Evaluation Committee for Primary and Secondary School Textbooks (NECPSST)' issued by the SEdC in 1987, all textbooks to be used on a national scale, developed either by institutions or individuals, cannot be published and distributed without the prior approval of the NECPSST. Locally developed, adapted, or supplementary textbooks must be approved by the educational authorities in their province, municipalities or autonomous region and their use reported to the SEdC.

People's Education Press publishes and prints textbooks and guidebooks approved by the SEdC. The People's Education Press printing house makes paper matrices and sends them to the local printing houses in respective provinces, municipalities and autonomous regions for mass production of the textbooks. Textbooks are distributed by the local Xin Hua Bookstores to schools so that every student is able to get the textbooks before each new school term. The textbooks are also translated and printed into minority languages and then distributed to the minority nationality regions.

Textbooks Relating to the Pacific Region

The teaching of geography and history is offered in alternate years in primary schools, beginning in Grade 5, and throughout junior and senior secondary schools. Moral education, laws, social construction and development are offered to students in certain periods in each grade at the primary and secondary schools. In addition to the teaching of geography and history, social studies occupies 7 percent and 16 percent of school time in primary and junior secondary schools respectively.

The Pacific Region is mainly covered by the geography and history textbooks produced by CTMRI.

Geography Textbooks

In the geography textbooks for primary schools, pupils are taught the position and scope of the Pacific Ocean; geographical features such as volcano and earthquake belts; climate, vegetation and natural landscapes in the torrid, temperate and frigid zones; and populations, races and countries. Pupils are expected to have some general knowledge about environments, local production and life in the Pacific.

For junior secondary schools, knowledge about the Pacific Ocean occupies a small part of the *World Geography* text. Students are taught in detail the Pacific part of Asia, Oceania, North America, South America and Antarctica; and natural geographical outlines, economic development features and local lives in some countries. Students learn how the local people use the geographical environment to improve production and daily life. At the same time, they learn about transportation, trade, economic and cultural links between China and other countries in the Pacific.

Geography textbooks for junior secondary schools also deal with the structures and features of the geographical environment; the exploration and application of resources and energies; the agricultural production; the development and distribution of population and cities; and environmental problems. Students learn how the people of the Pacific address problems that arise from economic development and their effects on the environment and the world economy. In particular, the students will understand the linkages between the development in China and that in the Pacific. This knowledge provides a basis for participation in international cooperation and world environment protection.

History Textbooks

The history textbooks for primary schools introduce the famous navigators such as Zheng He (1371-1435), Christopher Columbus (1451-1506) and Ferdinand Magellan (1480-1521) who explored new routes in the Pacific Ocean.

In the history textbooks for secondary schools, there is a detailed account on the frequent exchanges between China and Korea, Japan, India, etc. in the fields of economy, politics and culture when China ruled by the Tang Dynasty (618-907). China had more links with the Pacific Ocean area during the Ming Dynasty (1368-1644). From 1405 to 1433, Zheng He navigated the Pacific Ocean and Indian Ocean seven times. He travelled to what we now call Indo-China, Indonesia, the Philippines, Malaysia, Bangladesh, India and Iran, as well as to the Arab and African countries. He took with him Chinese silk and porcelain and brought back gems and perfume. The secondary textbooks also stress the fact that since Zheng He's navigation, many Chinese have gone overseas to other countries in Southeast Asia, and that they have brought with them Chinese productive skills and traditional culture and have taken an active part in the creation and development of various countries.

The *World History* textbook includes not only the ancient histories of Korea, Japan and America, but also the modern histories of Asia, Africa and Latin America. The textbook stresses the awakening of the Asian countries and the struggles for national independence of the Latin American countries.

Peace and development are two main problems in the world today. The countries around the Pacific Rim share a common natural environment and have many political and economic connections with each other. China is centrally situated in the Pacific Region. Its long Pacific coastline has been classified as the most important economic zone in the country's drive to modernize. It is hoped that increasing awareness of the Pacific area will have a positive effect on the reform of social studies education in China as well as on the educational reform of other countries.

Wu Yongxing is director of the Curriculum and Teaching Materials Research Institute (CTMRI) and Wan Dalin works as an editor at the same institution. CTMRI is located at 55 Sha Tan Hou Street, Beijing, People's Republic of China.

13

Exploring Pacific Issues through Small-group Cooperative Learning

Don Northey
The University of British Columbia, Canada

Education with a Global Perspective

In our world the television camera brings us face to face with the joys of the 1988 Olympic Games in Korea, the reality of floods in the Philippines and the growing demand for consumer goods in China. Governments link visions of our brighter economic future to creating and maintaining beneficial trade links with Pacific nations. Concurrently within our education system, greater emphasis is being placed on learning 'about' other Pacific countries.

This growing interest in the Pacific encourages and necessitates a renewed questioning of the approaches of social studies. For example, as educators how do we create a learning environment which models in its practice a deeper understanding of our interdependent roles in the Pacific? This article contends that small-group cooperative learning has much to offer students in their investigation of Pacific issues from a global perspective.

Education with a global perspective encourages participants to become more aware and appreciative of the perspective of others and of how others perceive them. Thus learning about the Japanese concept of family helps Canadians to understand their own family relations more deeply. Further, this understanding enables more conscious and effective interaction with others. This process necessitates focusing on the cooperative learning while at the same time recognizing the need to develop and apply skills in dealing with conflict situations, as required in examining such issues as trade tariffs and immigration policies among Pacific nations.

The following diagram illustrates the interrelationships among value orientation, conceptual content and skills which are necessary to be meaningfully involved in education with a global perspective.

By actively dealing with issues arising out of the interdependent action among various political, economic, technological and social systems in the

Pacific, participants are encouraged to analyse alternatives, make decisions and by doing so enhance their sense of empowerment. These decisions are directed towards making mutually beneficial decisions dealing with current life situations and to creating a worthwhile future for all countries of the Pacific. Thus, there is concern for the well-being of the *campesino* in Nicaragua and the hospital worker in the Philippines as well as individuals in one's own country.

Education with a Global Perspective

Cooperative Group Learning Approach

Introduction

A distant voice can be heard asking: 'Sounds like a nice idea in theory, but how can education with a global perspective work in my social studies class of thirty students? I'm in the real world and have to be practical!'. To investigate this question let us enter a classroom where this challenge is being encountered during a lesson on international trade in the Pacific Rim. Students are sitting in neatly arranged rows patiently listening to their teacher who asks: 'Why do you think Pacific nations tax items coming into their countries?'.

The proverbial Johnny responds with a lengthy response: 'I think that taxes are important because...' A few students listen while others dream about the upcoming break or the next episode of their favorite TV program.

The teacher and Johnny continue in their interaction as the teacher inquires: 'What role do you think our government should play with regards to import quotas on cars coming into Canada from Korea and Japan?'. After the 'discussion', the teacher gives directions for the assigned seatwork: 'Answer the questions in your notebooks. The assignment mark will be used as part of your report card grade. Work quietly on your own. Any questions?'. Johnny tackles the task instantly. Other students search for erasers, or whisper secretly to their neighbor about the upcoming school dance. A few students frantically raise their hands and ask the teacher to explain the assignment again. The lesson ends with the ringing of the bell, a flash of closing textbooks and a rush for the door.

In this scenario we see a teacher with honorable intentions whose teaching/learning structure actually impedes the pursuit of a global perspective while dealing with Pacific issues. The statement 'Work quietly on your own' implies that it is neither productive nor right to help or work with other individuals. In this learning structure and the resulting interaction, the emphasis is not on cooperation but on individualistic and competitive learning. The concept of interdependence involved in the topic of international trade in the Pacific is not reflected in the interaction within the learning environment itself. Rather, in practice interdependence is discouraged while individual competition for limited resources and rewards is fostered. In this setting the teacher regulates these rewards and the access to knowledge. John Goodlad (1983) characterizes such teachers as 'emphasizing their own talk and monitoring of seatwork – the prevailing instructional group is the total class; small-group activity is rare – classroom contingencies encourage and support minimal movement, minimal student-to-student or student-to-teacher interaction' (p. 558). Although educators may talk about cooperation, students quickly see what is valued and witness the contradictions evidenced in classroom practice.

What creates and sustains this situation? It grows in part from the individualistic learning approaches that teachers have experienced in their own education. An alternative to this approach is offered by cooperative learning which is a pedagogic approach consistent with the goals of education with a global perspective. As such it speaks clearly to an exploration of issues in the Pacific. Some educators will say: 'I tried group learning once but all havoc broke loose! I'm not going to try that again!'. It is hoped that the following discussion will provide support for further implementation.

Definition

Cooperative learning is defined as a teaching/learning approach in which heterogeneous groups ranging from pairs to groups of five or six interact with each other as they work on a task to reach a common goal. This common goal can only be reached by each person in the group contributing in joint mutual action. In this process intercommunication is required to understand the designated tasks and to decide on a plan of interdependent action. Peer instruction is used to convey the lesson content which creates the feeling that participants can help themselves by helping others. This contrasts with an individualistic approach whereby one individual's win means another person's loss. At the same time, merely putting individuals together or assigning independent tasks within the group does not reflect the cooperative approach. Instead, this approach is characterized by a cooperative task structure, a group incentive structure and an individual accountability system.

Cooperative Learning: An Example

By looking at a specific example of a cooperative activity, the characteristics noted will be illustrated. The example chosen illustrates an adaptation of the jigsaw cooperative approach originally developed by Aronson (1984). Each member in a group (five or less) would be given different materials and resources. In order to provide opportunities to clarify the assignment, to discuss procedures and to exchange ideas on possible ways to teach the material, one person from each group meets with members from other groups who have the same topic. After this preparation time, members return to their respective home groups to lead their part of the group task and to participate in tasks organized by other group members. The material shown below is a sample of what one group member would teach and organize.

Japan and Trade

Japan is a country that has small amounts of natural resources such as coal and oil. To get these raw materials Japan must buy them from other countries. When these materials are brought into a country, they are called imports. Companies in Japan use the coal and oil to help make many different manufactured goods such as ships, cars and steel. These products are then exported (sold and sent to other countries).

Japan is only able to use about 15 percent of its land for growing food. Some of the crops that are raised are rice, vegetables such as cabbage and broccoli, and oranges. Japanese farmers produce a lot of food from a small area. As well, fish from the sea play an important role in the Japanese diet. However, Japan is not able to produce all the food that its people need. To pay for imported food Japan sells its manufactured goods to other Pacific countries such as Australia, Canada and the United States.

Activities
1. In your group have students make a list of Japan's exports and imports that you gave in your presentation. Have the group recorder write these items on a chart.
2. As a group make a list of the products that you have in your homes that are imported from Japan.
3. Discuss the impact that trade with Japan has had on your lives.

In this learning situation we see that the cooperative task structure is implemented by assigning each group participant an organizing/teaching task. In the above example this individual has information on Japan's trade which the other group members do not have. In order to complete the common assignment and meet the group goals, that is, completion of the chart and lists, other group members need to listen attentively to their peer's instruction on

Japanese trade. Students' own ideas are discussed and incorporated into this assignment. In the ensuing interaction participants take on the assigned rotating role of organizer/teacher and ongoing interactive roles such as encourager, summarizer and praiser. It is critical that these roles be taught early in the cooperative learning program.

Within the group learning environment, participants can see the ongoing operation of a particular system. They observe and experience the interdependence of roles. Conflict is also a part of this interaction process. However, a cooperative learning approach encourages participants to work towards solutions to common problems. Hence, a mutual interdependency is required by the task structure and by the peer instruction which is the vehicle for meeting the task goals. Consequently, a framework is provided for gaining an understanding of Pacific issues.

A Comparison

The chart on page 136 shows relationships between cooperative learning strategies and the concepts and values of education with a global perspective.

The focus on interdependence is a focal point of cooperative learning and education with a global perspective. Both are grounded in similar beliefs: each person has the right, ability and desire to contribute to the progress of oneself and others, personal and collective growth is linked to and dependent upon interaction with others, and empathetic understanding is necessary for cooperative interaction. Cooperative learning recognizes and builds upon the belief that students can learn from and with each other. Through this interaction, participants come to understand others' perspectives. As a result, differences are more respected and understood and new commonalities demonstrated. Based on an education with a global perspective this coming to know and appreciate other individuals and groups is critical to dealing with issues encountered among the nations in the Pacific.

Teacher's Role

The implementation of a cooperative learning approach changes the teacher's role 'from being the imparter of knowledge, maintainer of classroom control, and validater of thinking to helping students gain confidence in their own ability and the group's ability to work out problems, thus relying less upon the teacher as the only source of knowledge' (Parker, 1985, p. 54). Consequently, investigating Pacific issues with this approach does not mean providing more direct instruction about such areas as trade balances, geographic features or group cultural values. Rather a facilitator role is required which entrusts students to make decisions, to focus on tasks, and to instruct others. A cooperative learning study by Sharan (1980) supports this role as students reported a greater sense of freedom to express themselves and increased feelings of responsibility because the teachers trusted them. In this way the teachers are called upon to put democratic principles of participation into practice in their classroom.

Relationship Between Cooperative Learning and Education with a Global Perspective

Values and Concepts of a Global Perspective	Cooperative Learning Strategies
Interdependence	Common group end-product; shared materials; jigsawed materials and tasks; group rewards
Perspective	Communication skills taught and implemented in group interaction; meeting common goals necessitates consideration of others' perspectives; engaging in different group roles; tasks require increased participant interaction
Community	Sense of ownership in meeting common goal; consensus form of decision-making; awareness of others' perspectives; development of 'we' relationship
Responsibility	Individual and group self-evaluation; individual accountability (tests, presentation to group, signing group form to show knowledge of task); jigsawing of material; group marks (one mark for common project, averaging of individual test results, bonus group marks)
Diversity	Heterogeneous small groups (academic abilities, gender, ethnic group membership)
Action/empowerment	Active contributing role required in the learning process; degree of group autonomy; individual and group evaluation process – action required to deal with improving group process
System	Group membership roles and responsibilities; each group as an operating system with inter-dependent tasks and roles
Leadership/power	Leadership distributed and rotated; consensus form of decision-making; social interaction skills taught and developed; degree of group autonomy
Cooperation	materials jigsawed; materials limited; materials shared; tasks divided; common product produced; direct student-student interaction promoted; social interaction skills taught

Research Findings

Much of the current movement in cooperative learning has grown out of investigations in social psychology and issues dealing with ethnic conflicts. Although the early work of researchers such as Allport did not speak of cooperative learning *per se*, their findings offered direction and support for the small-group cooperative learning approach. In his focus on the contract theory of intergroup relations Allport (1954, p. 281) stated that prejudice 'may be reduced by equal status contact between majority and minority groups in the pursuit of common goals. The effect is greatly enhanced if this contact is sanctioned by institutional supports . . . and if it is of a sort that leads to the perception of common interests and common humanity between members of the two groups'.

These major characteristics outlined by Allport are aspects of cooperative learning. For example, members are of equal status; that is, each individual's contribution is required to complete the task, common goals are fostered by task and incentive structures, and institutional support for cooperation is evidenced by the formation of heterogeneous groups in which teachers give students responsibilities in the learning process. In the ensuing social action students find a basis for sharing as they work towards common goals. In this way participants come to know each other in a deeper way. If students are able to interact with their immediate world on this basis, then there are possibilities for similar student action in addressing Pacific issues.

A growing body of research has reported on the impact of small-group learning. In a meta-analysis of cooperative learning research, Johnson and Johnson (1982) found that 'students with cooperative experiences are more able to take the perspective of others, are more positive about taking part in controversy, have better developed interaction skills and have more positive expectation about working with others than students from competitive or individualistic settings' (p. 23). Aronson's (1984) research indicates that cooperative learning increases positive self-esteem, positive attitudes about one's own group and other ethnic groups. Research by Slavin (1983) has shown that cooperative learning approaches increase participants' understanding of the perspectives of others, empathy skills, and feelings of being in control. Although not specifically developed to test the impact of education with a global perspective *per se*, this research offers support for employing cooperative learning as a pedagogy for addressing a global perspective.

Conclusion

If social studies programs are to do more than simply increase students' knowledge 'about' the Pacific area, then there is a need to explore alternative learning approaches. The present public and educational interest in the Pacific provides opportunities for educators to ask meaningful questions about the direction and approaches of social studies.

Education with a global perspective provides a way to approach, to focus on and to organize learning experiences which foster an understanding of, and responsibility for, world issues. For example, the growing population of Pacific nations is making increasing demands upon scarce resources. At the same time, economic disparity exists among these nations as evidenced in the lives of the rice farmer in the Philippines, the *campesino* raising corn in Mexico and the Japanese auto worker. This raises questions dealing with social justice and equality: On what basis should resources be shared? Who should make decisions on the use of resources?

In order for a global perspective to develop, individuals need to identify the feelings, needs and values of others and by doing so come to see things from the other's point of view. Through this examination of what makes us human, we come to recognize that we share some common bonds with others. In this way we recognize our similarities and the universal values which bind us. At the same time cultural diversity is honored.

A cooperative learning approach fosters this development through mutual striving to meet common goals. In this way the pedagogy of cooperative learning is consistent with and supportive of education with a global perspective. A cooperative learning approach encourages participants to think globally and act globally. This cooperative learning approach is necessary both within our classrooms and among the Pacific community of nations if we are to mutually create a more just and peaceful society.

References

Allport, G. (1954). *The nature of prejudice*. Reading, Mass.: Addison-Wesley.

Aronson, E., and Bridgeman, D. (1984). Jigsaw groups and the desegregated classroom: In pursuit of common goals, in *Reading about the social animal*, Ed. E.Aronson, New York: Freeman, 312-22.

Chapman, J., Becker, J., Gilliom, M., and Tucker, J. (1982). National Council for the Social Studies – Position statement on global education. Vol. 46, No. 1, 36-8.

Goodlad, J. (1983). A Study for schooling: some implications for school improvement, *Kappan*, 3, 556-62.

Hanvey, R. (1982). An attainable global perspective, *Theory Into Practice,* Vol. XXI, No. 3, 162-7.

Johnson, D., and Johnson, R. (1982). Cooperation in learning: Ignored but powerful, *Lyceum*, 9, 22-6.

Johnson, D., and Johnson, R. (1984). *Circles of learning*. Alexandria, Va.: Association for Supervision and Curriculum Development.

Parker, R. (1985). Small group cooperative learning – improving academic, social gains in the classroom, *NASSP Bulletin*, Vol. 69, No. 479, 48-57.

Sharan, S. (1980). Cooperative learning in small groups: Recent methods and effects on achievement, attitudes and ethnic relations, *Review of Educational Research*, Summer, Vol. 5, No. 2, 241-71.

Slavin, R. (1983). *Cooperative learning*. New York: Longman.

Don Northey teaches elementary social studies methods courses, conducts cooperative learning workshops for teachers, and is coordinator of the Multicultural Teacher Education Program, Faculty of Education, The University of British Columbia, Vancouver, BC, Canada V6T 1Z5.

14

Mapping Asia and the Pacific

Angus M. Gunn
The University of British Columbia, Canada

School days are a powerful influence in shaping perceptions of and attitudes towards places and peoples. The mental images retained from maps are foremost among these influences because, like television, they are visual. When the words of textbooks have faded from the memory, these mental images persist, delineating for years to come a student's spatially-fixed world.

In the classroom, the staple place diet has long been an atlas with maps centered on Europe, oriented to that continent in both design and content. World maps show North America at the far left of the page, and India, China and the rest of Asia at the extreme right.

From a North-American point of view, these 'far-eastern' countries are just about as remote as anything on planet earth could be. The corollary is that they have little significance for us.

In addition to the problem of orientation, atlas designers have frequently chosen rectangular or cylindrical projections; that is to say, maps with straight latitude and longitude lines. Each parallel of latitude is equal in length to the equator, while the longitude lines have the same length as the one that passes through Greenwich, near London, England.

Rectangular and cylindrical maps are reasonably accurate for places near the equator because the lines of latitude and longitude represent real distances. At places nearer the poles, however, severe distortion takes place, so that Greenland appears much bigger than either the United States or Canada, even though in reality it is less than a quarter of the size of either country. During World War II, Winston Churchill liked to use a cylindrical-type map in meetings with Franklin Roosevelt, because it presented Canada, a member of the British Commonwealth, as being much bigger than it really is.

Fortunately the distortions of traditional maps need not be a problem any longer. Over the past two or three decades, profound changes have taken place in the science of cartography, enabling us to represent earth features with degrees of accuracy that far surpass those of earlier maps.

Additionally, the advent of color television and the computer have, together, forced a complete rethinking in the design of maps. Viewers have become so used to television that cartographers, if they wish to attract readers, must use color to create attractive, uncluttered images of places, instead of employing color solely to augment the quantity of information stored. Similarly, computers have transformed the process of recording information since they are far more effective than maps for storing and retrieving areal data. These developments have given rise to a new type of map characterized by pleasing appearance and greatly reduced content.

Dr Thomas Poiker of Simon Fraser University, near Vancouver, Canada, has been pioneering this new type of map for many years. In 1980, using computer-cartography techniques, he created a special space-age map for the National Film Board of Canada (NFB). It measured sixteen feet by two and a half feet, fitting the space above an average chalkboard, and presenting an image of Canada as it might appear from a satellite over Central America.

In 1987, Canada's Asia Pacific Foundation asked Tom Poiker to design a wall map for schools, one that would combine the new cartography with more traditional maps. His response was the composite map of different projections and scales (see Figure 1), all designed to bring new perspectives to the Asia-Pacific Region. In the corners of the map are four global views, centered at different locations, providing the kind of view an astronaut would get from time to time as his or her spaceship circled the earth.

Peripheral to the new-style central map, and placed alongside their counterparts in the center, are several bonne projections, representing the kinds of maps commonly found in school atlases. These maps provide a familiar frame of reference to assist in the transition to the newer displays. They deal with relatively smaller areas when compared with the vast reaches of the region portrayed on the central map.

These traditional bonne projections must, of necessity, be limited to, say, the scale of North America or Europe, in order to maintain reasonable accuracy across the map for any one element – scale, direction, area, or shape. The computer-generated central map, on the other hand, is not constrained in these ways. All that is needed is a decision on which elements are critical; the map is then designed to maintain accuracy across the entire area for one or two critical elements, even when the territory in question is as vast as Asia and the Pacific.

The new central map (see Figure 2) is an azimuthal-equidistant projection, and the critical elements are true orientation from both eastern and western North America with respect to the rest of the region, true scale from the center to all of the countries within the region. At the outer edges, beyond the rim nations, there is considerable distortion.

The azimuthal-equidistant projection used in Fig. 2 is particularly popular, because it faithfully represents air distances in any direction from the center. Since this center is close to Hawaii, the map has special value for Hawaiian teachers and students. A similar map, centered near London,

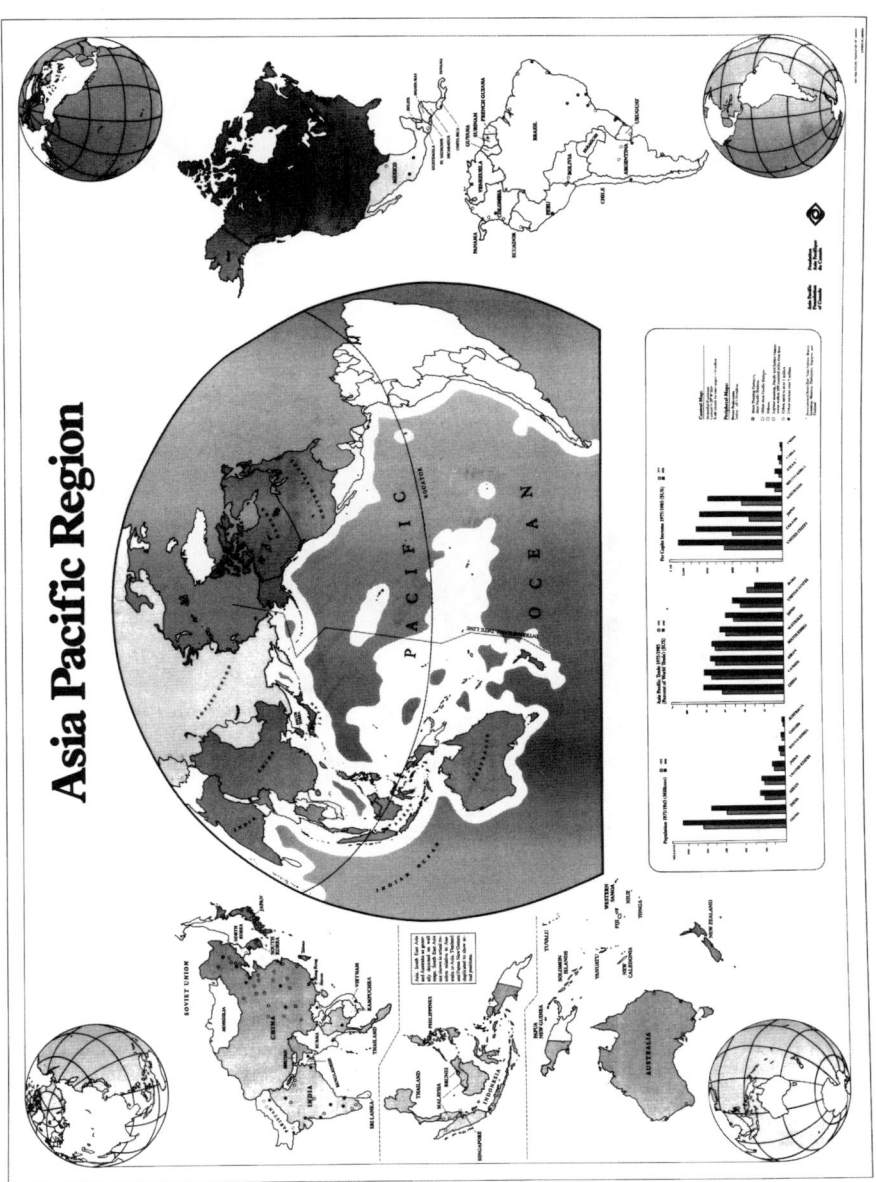

Figure 1: Global, bonne and azimuthal-equidistant maps of Asia and the Pacific.

England, might provide a useful frame of reference for the study of Asia and the Pacific. It could highlight distortions of the past and help us make the intellectual switch from 'a far east' view of Asia to the more realistic 'near west'.

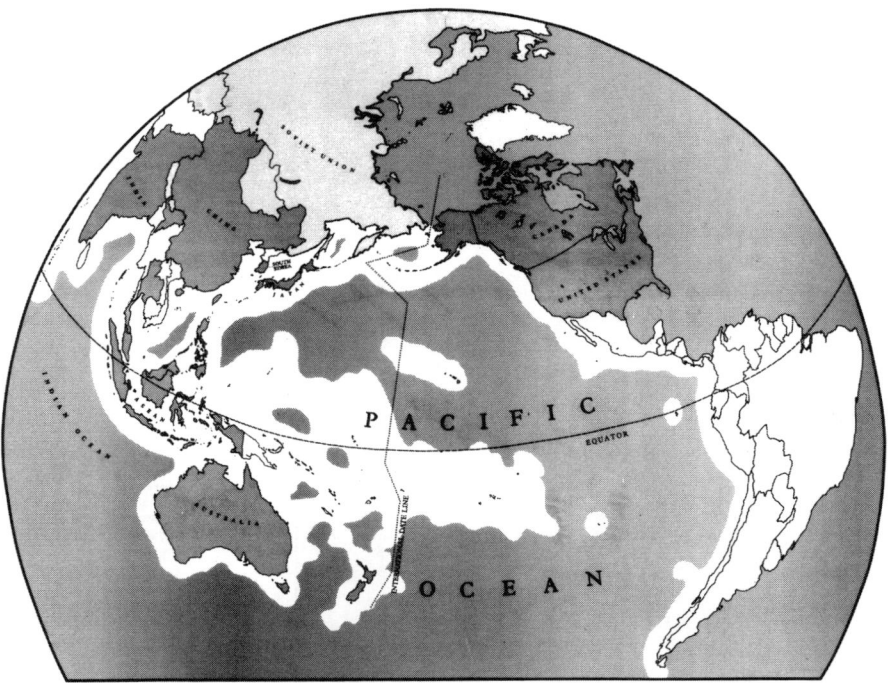

Figure 2: Azimuthal-equidistant map of Asia and the Pacific.

Typical questions that can be asked about the new map include the following:

Measure the distance from Panama to Singapore and compare it with that given in other maps in your atlas.

2. Why is the equator not a straight line?
3. When it is noon in Chicago what is the time in Tokyo?
4. Make a list of the nations that border the Pacific Ocean, the ones often described as Pacific Rim countries.
5. Five of the world's most populous nations border the Pacific. Name them.
6. For a ship, what is the approximate distance from:
   Vancouver to Shanghai
   Tokyo to Auckland
   Panama City to Sydney
   Singapore to Honolulu
   Manila to Los Angeles
7. Identify the advantages and disadvantages of the various maritime entry points (ports) into the Pacific Ocean, historically and present-day.

8. Where have there been recent earthquakes and volcanic actions? How does the study of plate tectonics help predict similar future actions?
9. Historically, there has been little interchange of goods across the breadth of the Pacific. Why? What changes do you see today and what caused them?
10. Name four of the biggest trading nations that border the Pacific Ocean.

Angus M. Gunn is Professor Emeritus, The University of British Columbia, author of several geographical texts and a former Assistant Director, High School Geography Project of the Association of American Geographers. He resides at 771 Westcot Road, West Vancouver, BC, Canada V7S 1N8.

Commentary on Section Two

David L. Grossman
East-West Center, United States of America

In the second section of this book, we turned from the more lofty discussion of various rationales for teaching Asia and the Pacific of the first section to more practical issues of curriculum and instruction. In the first paper, Lamy offered a conceptual framework of 'contending perspectives', which involves the analysis of competing worldviews, for teaching contemporary issues in the Asia-Pacific region. Five of the subsequent papers (Thaman, Marimuthu, Wu and Wan, Shin, and Nakajima) looked at curriculum development and reform efforts in Pacific Island nations and four countries (Malaysia, China, South Korea and Japan), and the implication of these efforts for teaching about Asia and the Pacific. Another paper examined the issue of the representation of Asian women in the curriculum in a case study of China and Japan (Matsui, Ma and Cornbleth). Northey's paper explored the relationship between small-group cooperative learning techniques and teaching Asia and Pacific issues. Finally, Gunn examined the underlying mental images of Asia and Pacific conveyed through maps.

With such a wide range of topics covered, is there anything we can conclude from this section? One fundamental point that emerges from this section is the fact that Asia and Pacific curricula needs have to be related to larger issues of curriculum development and reform in each country. Teaching about Asia and the Pacific must be seen as contributing to the national agenda of producing a competent citizenry for the twenty-first century. In this regard, the papers in this section reflect a substantial difference in emphasis among the nations discussed. This diversity of emphasis seems to be related to a country's stage of development. In less industrialized countries (such as Malaysia and China), the emphasis seems clearly on citizenship goals related to the issue of nation-building. In highly developed countries (such as Japan) or newly industrialized economies (such as South Korea), there seems to be a broader agenda which allows for the inclusion of the international dimensions of citizenship education. Given the pressures on scarce resources and the need for nation-building in developing nations, this should come as no surprise. However, it is perhaps fair to conclude that if the study of Asia and the Pacific is not seen as an integral part of the national, state or provincial agenda, we are not likely to find curricula which refect the new international realities of the

Pacific era.

This raises a related issue, that of the political context within which educational reform takes place. In many countries of the Asia and Pacific region, educational policy is formed within an authoritarian political context. While such a context may facilitate the development of an agenda supporting educational or curriculum reform, one has to evaluate the price that must be paid for the lack of public debate in determining such important societal agendas. To what extent do the sources of the pressure for educational reform determine the effectiveness of resulting policies?

In this regard, as the Lamy paper suggests, it is important to consider carefully what conceptual framework is used in analysing a region as vast and diverse as Asia and the Pacific, and what biases, political or otherwise, we bring to our analysis. Where do Asia and the Pacific fit? How can we relate the study of Asia and the Pacific to important educational skills, such as critical thinking? Whether we adopt Lamy's model of contending perspectives or not, it is incumbent upon us to identify the significant themes, concepts or issues that will help students build a framework for analysis that includes an understanding of their own national perspective or perspectives. Further, when pursuing our analyses, we must be wary that a potential of political bias always exists, and that multiple points of view must be taken into account.

One form of bias that is easy to miss is that of omission. If, when we teach about Asia and the Pacific, we omit women from the curriculum, if we fail to include the smaller or less powerful nations of the region, or if we focus only on the highly industrialized countries, in effect we are teaching students to have a very limited 'mental map' of Asia and the Pacific. Given existing textbooks and curriculum units, it is very easy to err by omission rather than commission, and we must help students understand the full complexity of Asia and the Pacific by making the perspectives of commonly omitted groups and nations more visible.

Finally, we must not forget the relationship between the content of Asia and Pacific studies and instructional strategies. Interactive educational strategies such as small-group cooperative learning, simulations and role plays have a great potential for enhancing student understanding of Asia and the Pacific. Passive strategies are not as likely to produce the kind of learning outcomes that will contribute to the development of a participatory and competent citizenry who will have to deal with the changing world of the twenty-first century. In this section the Northey and Gunn papers provide illustrative examples of approaches which emphasize direct involvement of students in the learning process. In the next section we present some sample lessons which encourage interactive learning about Asia and the Pacific.

David L. Grossman is the Project Leader of the Consortium for Teaching Asia and the Pacific in the Schools (CTAPS) located in the East-West Center, 1777 East-West Road, Honolulu, Hawaii 96848. Before taking up that position he was the Director of the Stanford Program on International and Cross-Cultural Education (SPICE) at Stanford University.

Section Three

Classroom Activities

15

Living in Japan

Mary Hammond Bernson
University of Washington, United States of America

Level: Grades 5-8
Time: 1 to 2 class periods

Introduction

An introduction to Japanese homes and furnishings allows students to experience one aspect of population density and to compare the different choices consumers make in Japan and the United States, two modern, wealthy nations.

Objectives

- Students will become acquainted with the basic spatial unit of Japanese homes.
- Students will compare Japanese preferences in the purchase of household appliances and furniture with their own.
- Students will explore some of the implications of limited residential space.

Procedures

1. Explain to the class that the average Japanese house or apartment is much smaller than its American counterpart. There are many reasons for this.

    (a) Japan's overall population density is 12 times as high as that of the United States. Since much of Japan is not suitable for building cities, urban population density is extremely high.

    (b) Most of Japan's people live in cities, where land is very expensive. The percentage of people who live in urban areas is 77 percent in Japan, compared with 76 percent in the United States.

    (c) Energy costs for building or maintaining homes are very high. Japan must import 80 percent of its energy, compared with 14 percent for the United States.

    (d) Cultural and historical factors affect people's housing choices. People may have limited options or may prefer to spend their money in other ways.

2. Ask students to read the '*Tatami* and Japanese Homes' reading or read it aloud to them.
3. Ask them to identify which characteristics of Japanese homes, either apartments or houses, are the same as in the United States and which characteristics are different. Point out that both countries have a wide variety of housing.
4. Create a 6-mat room in the classroom. This is the most common-size room, although many homes may have larger rooms. Create the room by marking the space on the floor with masking tape or by arranging six 6-foot lengths of 3-foot wide butcher paper. Two common arrangements are:

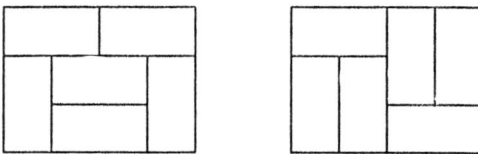

Using tape or markers on the paper, outline a table in the middle of the 'room'. A traditional arrangement would be a low table with no chairs.
5. Ask small groups of students to sit in the 'room'. Discuss questions such as:
   (a) How big can the table be?
   (b) Where should they put their legs? If they were guests, it would not be polite to stick them straight forward. The most polite option is to sit on their feet until the host invites them to relax. Then boys may cross their legs and girls may either sit on their feet or sit with both feet out to one side.
   (c) How many people can fit in the room Japanese style?
   (d) How many people can fit in the room American style?
   (e) Where would they put appliances or furniture?
   (f) How would two families' activities differ if one spent its evenings in a room of this size and the other spent its evenings in a larger room or several separate rooms?
6. Brainstorm as a group what qualities they would look for in furniture to use in small rooms. Possible characteristics include small size, pleasing appearance, and multi-purpose use. The group can identify solutions to space shortages in their own homes, such as the use of bunk beds or shelving which reaches to the ceiling.
7. Using an overhead projector or handouts, ask students to read the chart.
8. Ask the groups whether their choices of appliance and furniture would be the same as those reflected in the chart they read. Why or why not?
9. Because energy is very expensive and central heating is rare, many Japanese homes have *kotatsu* (low tables with heaters underneath them). If the students and their families spent their evenings gathered around a

kotatsu, how would their activities differ from what they do now?
10. Conclude this lesson by asking students to write three facts about Japanese homes and three opinions or feelings about what they learned.

Extension Activities

1. Ask students to find examples of Japanese design in magazines or books.
2. Show the students films or videotapes which include scenes inside modern Japanese homes. A good example is the series entitled *Video Letters from Japan* (Asia Society, 725 Park Avenue, New York, New York 10021, USA). Identify solutions to space shortages, such as multi-purpose furniture or simply piling possessions higher and higher.
3. Research traditional Japanese furniture designs. Possibilities include a *futon*, which serves as a bed; a *tansu*, a storage chest; a *kotatsu*, a low table with a heater underneath it; and a *hibachi*, a piece of furniture used for heat or for heating water for tea. A *tokonoma* is an alcove with shelves which is used to display flowers or art objects.
4. Research comparative statistics for households in the United States and one other country and make charts or graphs of the information about all three countries.

Student Reading
Tatami and Japanese Homes

Tatami are mats used to cover the floors in a traditional Japanese home. They are made of two inches of thick straw padding which is covered with a mat woven from reeds. The padding and mat are sewn together at the edges with cloth strips. The *tatami* are about six feet by three feet in size and form a smooth, greenish-gold surface for the floors.

The custom of using *tatami* is over a thousand years old. Originally they were just used as a place to sleep. Eventually they were arranged to completely cover the floors, in the same way that some Americans use wall-to-wall carpeting. Each room in a traditional Japanese house was designed to contain a certain number of *tatami*. Common sizes were 4 1/2-mat rooms and 6-mat rooms.

People were expected to take their shoes off before stepping on the *tatami*. It is still the custom to leave shoes at the front door when entering a Japanese home.

Old Japanese houses did not have much furniture. People sat directly on the *tatami*-covered floor. A low table was used for eating and other purposes, and then put away at bedtime. The same room was then used as a bedroom. Soft mattresses and quilts were stored in cupboards or chests during the daytime and spread out at night.

Traditional Japanese houses were simple and often very beautiful. The colors were the natural colors of wood, reeds and plaster. A corner of a room was often set aside as a place to display a piece of artwork or a flower arrangement. People around the world have copied some features of Japanese house design, such as the alcoves for displaying art.

Nowadays in Japan, houses that have *tatami* and just a few pieces of furniture are becoming rare. More and more people live in city apartments or in houses that are very international in style. Still, traditional house design can be found in country inns, rural houses, designer homes like those shown in magazines, or in special places such as teahouses used during tea ceremonies.

Many people choose to have a combination of *tatami* rooms and other rooms in their houses or apartments. More than 90 percent of modern apartments have one *tatami* room.

The size of the *tatami* continues to be used as a unit of measurement even when a room does not actually have any *tatami* on the floor. Newspapers often carry ads for 'one 4 1/2-mat room, one 6-mat room, and a combination dining area and kitchen'. That ad tells the room sizes in an apartment, but not whether the apartment actually contains any *tatami*.

Think about the furniture and appliances a Japanese family might buy to furnish that apartment.

Chart: Appliance and Furniture Ownership

This chart shows the kinds of appliances and furniture now found in Japanese homes. A family's possessions must fit into house and apartment sizes which average about 900 square feet per family. Homes are larger in rural areas than in the cities, but the overall Japanese average is much smaller than the average in the United States.

The following percentage of Japanese households owned at least one of each item in 1988:

color television	99%	refrigerator	98%
washing mahine	99	stereo	59
microwave oven	57	videocasette recorder	53
piano	20	sewing machine	82
table and chairs for dining	65	bed	61

Japanese homes generally do not have:

conventional ovens	dishwashers
central heating	clothes dryers

Sources: *Japan 1989: An international comparison*, published by the Keizai Koho Center, Tokyo, and *The Japanese consumer*, published in 1983 by the Japan External Trade Organization, Tokyo.

This lesson is © 1989 by Mary Hammond Bernson. Excerpted from *Japan through art activities*, © 1988 by Mary Hammond Bernson, Janet Graves, Elaine Magnusson and Sonnet Takahisa and available from the East Asia Resource Center, Thomson Hall, DR-05, University of Washington, Seattle, Washington 98195, USA. Mary Hammond Bernson is the East Asia Outreach Director at the University of Washington.

16

Mental Maps of the Pacific

David Dufty
University of Sydney, Australia
Theodore Rodgers
University of Hawaii, United States of America

Level: Upper elementary to senior high
Time: At least 2 class periods

Introduction

Despite the skills of modern cartographers, maps are not exact representations of reality but social constructs which reflect the assumptions and often biases of the makers. They influence the images which we have of our own countries and that of others. This exercise can be used to explore both our mental maps and the printed maps which have helped to produce these maps. It raises critical questions as to what our more ideal maps might look like in the future. Examples will need to be chosen according to the location of the school in the Pacific region.

Objectives

- To examine the spatial pictures of the Pacific which we hold in our minds.
- To understand that maps are human made and reflect the viewpoints of the makers.
- To try to view the Pacific from other viewpoints than our own.

Materials

At least one map of the Pacific and ideally a collection of different maps taken from publications of different types – for example, advertising brochures as well as atlases, and from different countries. A wall map should *not* be displayed during the initial exercise. A foolscap sheet of paper for each student would assist.

Procedures

1. To set a context, ask the students to name the world's oceans (Arctic, Atlantic, Indian and Pacific). Ask them which is the largest. The answer, of course, is the Pacific, which covers a third of the earth's total area (more than 64 million square miles or 166 million square kilometres), which is 46 percent of the earth's water area and more than the earth's total land area.
2. After making sure that there are no maps or globes visible, distribute a blank sheet of paper to students and ask them to do a sketch map of the Pacific region as best they can. Tell the students that this is not a test, and not to worry about being right or wrong. Ask them just to sketch in broad outlines their mental picture of the landforms of the Pacific region. Tell them that the objective is to show their own image of the relationship of major landmasses and not exact squiggles of coastline or definitive political boundaries. They should label the names of as many landmasses, countries and cities as they can. Suggest that they may like to add some distinctive features, such as Mount Fuji in Japan, the Great Wall in China, or the Great Barrier Reef off Australia, to their sketches.

   Suggestion: In order to assist them in this task, suggest that they fold the blank piece of paper into four sections or quadrants. The horizontal dividing line then becomes the equator. If they are stuck, suggest that they might start by simply numbering the quadrants and listing which countries/continents/landforms fall primarily into each quadrant.
3. Divide the students into small groups of four or five, and ask them to choose a recorder and a spokesperson. (You may also wish to provide them with marking pens and poster paper to record their discussion.) Tell them the small-group task is to share their maps with each other and to include in their discussion the questions below. Tell them to be prepared to report the outcome of their discussion to the rest of the class.

   Questions
   (a) Which parts of the Pacific region were clearest, or most commonly included?
   (b) Which parts were most unclear, or most commonly omitted?
   (c) How do the individual maps of each group member compare and how do they differ?
   (d) What did the maps suggest about the images your group has of the Pacific region?
4. Ask each of the groups to report on their discussion to the class. Record the answers to the last question on the board or on poster paper. Ask the class to summarize or draw generalizations about their images of the Pacific based on the map exercise.

Period 2

1. Using at least two maps of the Pacific, such as wall maps or other maps which you have gathered and perhaps prepared as student handouts,

overhead transparencies or slides, provide opportunities for the students to observe how maps of the Pacific may vary greatly according to such features as:

(a) What country they were prepared in.

(b) What purpose they have e.g. physical maps, population maps, political maps, etc.

(c) Artistic and print features, e.g. the use of color or various kinds of shading or lettering. How does this affect our image of the country?

(d) Use of any sketches or illustrations that attempt to make the image more graphic.

(e) Different kinds of projections, e.g. Mercator which tends to exaggerate the size of countries distant from the equator.

(f) Other features, e.g. . . . .

2. 'Sit in your seat in a relaxed position, close your eyes and breathe deeply for a moment or two. Now let's go on a voyage of the imagination.

'First, let's imagine you live in a village in the Kingdom of Tonga which consists of a number of small tropical islands right in the middle of the South Pacific Ocean. (More detailed description might follow of a Pacific country you are familiar with.)

'Try to imagine how you might view the Pacific from your location in Tonga. How do you view your immediate surroundings, how do you view your neighboring countries, how do you view the big countries that are on the Pacific Rim, and the people who live there?'

3. A second location is then chosen and a similar exercise is undertaken. For example: 'Imagine you live in a big city like Vancouver, San Francisco or Shanghai in the northern part of the Pacific. Or imagine you live in a city on the west coast of South America such as Valparaiso. How would your view of the Pacific and of other Pacific countries differ from the view you have from your present location?'.

4. A third viewpoint would be for students to imagine they were astronauts flying high above the earth and looking down on the Pacific Ocean. 'What would you notice about the Pacific? What would be your feelings about this part of the earth as you gazed down on it.' A variant might be to imagine that they are visitors from another planet flying over the Pacific. The aim here is to ensure that the Pacific is seen as a large system and also as an integral part of the whole planet and not as something separate.

Debriefing

Give the students the opportunity to discuss in small groups how they felt about being a person living in the Pacific in a location very different from their own and what they learned from the exercise.

Conclusion

Share with the whole class the conclusions of the exercise. For example, refer to the aims and see if class members became aware of the way in which maps are constructed by people and reflect the views of those people and the way in which maps can be very influential in helping to create the images which are in our minds. How could we ensure in the future that maps provide a more diversified image of the Pacific. What sort of maps could be designed for tomorrow's world?

Follow-up Activities

With the help of penfriends or computer pals students might try to make direct contact with people in other Pacific countries. They could ask them to send maps of their country and to give their own descriptions of life in their own countries from their viewpoint.

This lesson is an amalgamation of submissions by Dr David Dufty, Faculty of Education, University of Sydney, New South Wales, Australia, and Dr Theodore Rodgers, Curriculum Research and Development Group, College of Education, University of Hawaii. Dr Dufty resides at 243a The Scenic Road, Killcane, NSW 2256, Australia, while Dr Rodgers may be contacted at CRDG, Castle 114, College of Education, University of Hawaii, Honolulu, Hawaii 96822, USA.

17

The Yin *and* Yang *of the Asia-Pacific Region*

Charles Hou
Burnaby North Secondary School, Canada

Level: Grades 7-12
Time: 2 class periods

Introduction

In the broadest sense, the Asia-Pacific region can be defined to include all the nations in or bordering on the Pacific Ocean or Indian Ocean. With this view the region would include all the countries of South, Southeast and East Asia, North and South America, Australasia, the island nations of the Pacific, and the USSR. The basic unit of study in geography is the region, and geographers generally define region in terms of an area that displays unity in terms of selected criteria. These selected criteria or characteristics can distinguish a region from other areas. However, the Asia-Pacific region encompasses a vast area, which includes, to cite just one example, peninsulas as diverse in climate, culture and language as those of Kamchatka, Malaysia and Baja California. How are we to help students conceptualize a region with such variety and difference? What set of criteria can we use to define this vast region with all its complexities?

One way of dealing with this problem would be to employ the Chinese concepts of *yin, yang* and *tao* as tools to understand the Asia-Pacific region. These concepts, derived from traditional Chinese philosophy, propose that the core of the universe (or nature, or reality) is *tao* (pronounced like 'dow' in Dow-Jones), or unity. But the universe is also composed of two opposite but at the same time complementary principles: *yin* (pronounced like 'een' in keen) and *yang* (pronounced like 'yahng').

... *yang* is ... light, hot, positive, *yin* is ... dark, cold, negative. Unlike the dualism of the Mediterranean world, in which good and bad are in perpetual conflict, *yin* and *yang* are mutually complementary and balancing. The greater *yang* grows, the sooner it will yield to *yin*; the sun at noon is starting to give way to night. The interdependence of the two principles was well symbolized by an interlocking figure, which today, for example, is used as the central element in the flag of the Republic of Korea.

> Edwin O. Reischauer and John K. Fairbank, *East Asia: The Great Tradition*, Boston: Houghton Mifflin (1960), pp. 76-7.

Tao is the principle which unites these opposing and balancing forces of *yin* and *yang*.

If we apply these traditional concepts to analyse the Asia-Pacific region, *yang* represents those forces (e.g. similarities) which tend to promote the unity of the region, while *yin* represents those forces (or differences) which tend to promote the disunity of the region. *Tao* then encompasses the totality of the region, or the interplay of the forces of *yang* and *yin*.

Objectives

- To examine the geographical concept of a region.
- To introduce students to the similarities and differences found within the Asia-Pacific region.
- To involve students in using the traditional Chinese concepts of *yang*, *yin* and *tao* as a means of helping students understand the complexities of the Asia-Pacific region.

Materials

One copy per student of a blank *yin-yang* diagram.

Procedures

1. Discuss the concept of region with the class. Start with a small region, say the classroom, and progress to successively larger regions. Discuss why we divide the world into regions, and the problems we run into when we do so. Why do the problems of defining a region increase as the size of the region increases?
2. Ask the students to define the largest region they can think of. If they don't think of it, volunteer the idea of the Asia-Pacific region.
3. Prepare a transparency of the introduction. Discuss it with the class. Hand out a blank copy of the *yin-yang* diagram.
4. Assign each student in the class four of the following topics:

Climate	Culture
Sports and Cultural Events	Management of Resources

Foreign Aid Projects
Population
Architecture
Immigration
Literacy Rate
Travel and Language Education
Religion
Colonization
System of Government
Population Density
Border on the Pacific or
  Indian Oceans

Language
Size
Modern Communications
Military System
Standard of Living
Natural Disasters
Life Expectancy
Trade and Investment
Natural Resources
Urbanization

Explain that the four topics are either forces of *yin* (regional similarities) or forces of *yang* (regional differences). The students are to go to the library to investigate their four topics, decide if they are forces of *yin* or *yang* and place them on the blank diagrams. For each topic the student should try to find at least four examples of places within the Asia-Pacific region to illustrate why they have placed the topic in either the *yin* or the *yang* category.

Debriefing

1. In the second period, draw a large *yin-yang* diagram on the blackboard or prepare a transparency. Ask each student to explain where his or her topics should be placed on the diagram, and the reason for that choice.
2. Once the diagram is complete discuss the idea of *tao* in the Asia-Pacific region.

Concluding Activity

Have the students conduct further research into the Asia-Pacific Rim region. Students can find ideas in *The Asia-Pacific Rim Region: Student Projects*, BCTF Lesson Aid No. 2004, 1988 (BC Teachers' Federation Lesson Aids Service, 2235 Burrard Street, Vancouver, BC, Canada V6J 3H9, $5.00).

Charles Hou teaches social studies and senior history courses at Burnaby North Secondary School, 751 Hammarskjold Drive, Burnaby, BC, Canada V5B 4A1.

160 *Classroom Activities*

Appendix A: *YIN-YANG*
Blank Yin-Yang Diagram   FORCES WHICH DIVIDE AND UNITE THE NATIONS OF THE ASIA-PACIFIC REGION

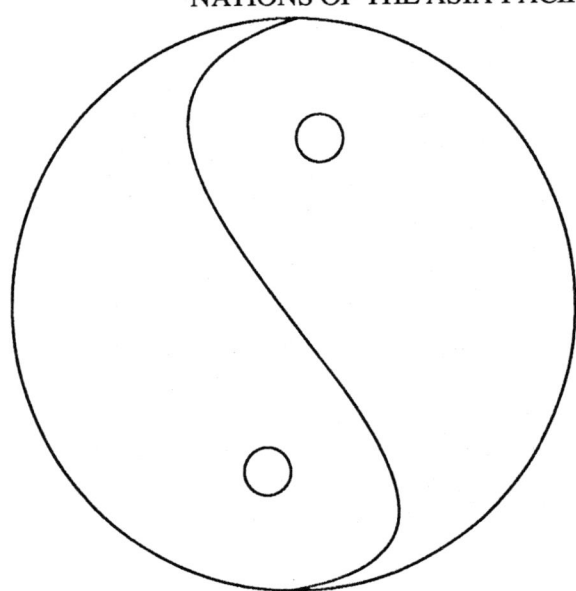

Appendix B: *Yin-Yang*
Completed Yin-Yang Diagram   FORCES WHICH DIVIDE AND UNITE THE NATIONS OF THE ASIA-PACIFIC REGION

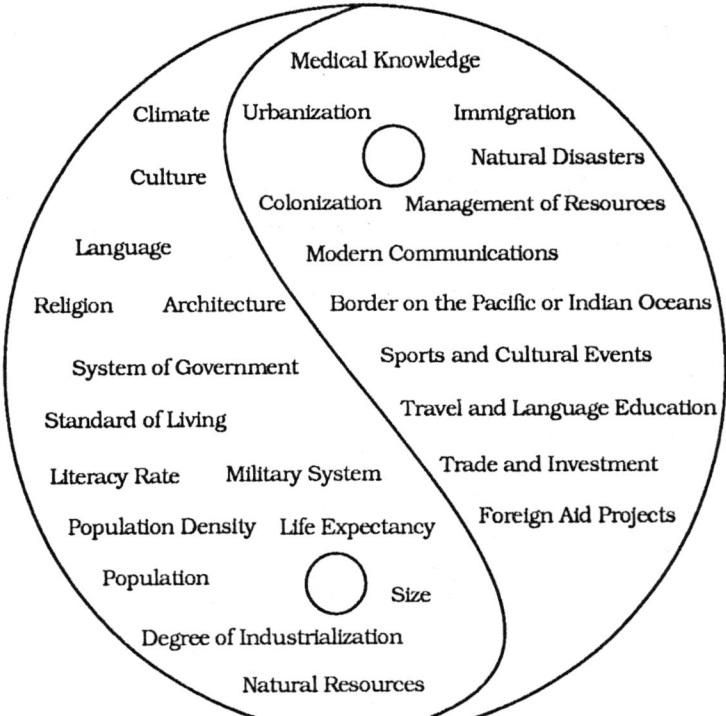

18

Teaching about Pacific Island Microstates

Margaret A. Laughlin and *I. Grace Bell*
University of Wisconsin – Green Bay, United States of America

Level: Middle school/secondary
Time: Several days

Introduction

The Pacific region covers more than one-third of the earth's surface and has more than 25,000 islands which range in size from small piles of rocks to larger land areas. The region covers thousands of square miles. This area is the last major region to be settled even though the first inhabitants, believed to have come from Southeast Asia, arrived thousands of years ago. Over time the most distant and isolated islands were settled by different groups and the inhabitants developed their own political, economic and cultural traditions and values. In recent years many of the islands have become independent nations while many are uninhabited.

Materials

One copy per student of the 'Pacific Island Area Retrieval Chart', a current student atlas or various classroom maps showing the Pacific Island area; individual student maps of Pacific Island areas, if available, otherwise students may work individually or in groups to make their own maps of the area; and other Pacific Island instructional materials which are available locally.

Objectives

- To gather basic data about selected Pacific Island areas.
- To complete the 'Pacific Island Area Retrieval Chart' concerning selected aspects of Pacific Island areas.
- To locate Pacific Island areas on a map using a textbook, atlas, other reference materials or databases; each island area should be labeled and color-coded; indicate which islands are included in the Melanesian,

Micronesian and Polynesian island groups.

To recognize that geography (location) influences the settlement, history, economic development, customs, traditions and values of Pacific Island area inhabitants.

Procedures

1. Ask students individually or in groups to identify any or all of the following island areas: American Samoa, Cook Islands, Coral Sea Islands, Fiji, French Polynesia, Guam, Kiribati, Marshall Islands, Federal States of Micronesia, Midway Islands, New Caledonia, Northern Mariana Islands, Papua New Guinea, Palau Islands, Pitcairn Islands, Solomon Islands, Tokelau, Tonga, Trust Territory of the Pacific Islands, Tuvalu, Vanuatu, Wake Island, Western Samoa and Yap on the Pacific Island map; label and color-code each area; indicate which islands are included in the Melanesian, Micronesian, and Polynesian island groups.
2. Using the same scale, superimpose a cut-out map of the United States including Alaska on the Pacific Island area map. Note the extent of area – the Pacific Island area is wider than the United States (Solomons to Marquesas) and northwest to southeast is longer than the area from Alaska to Florida (Northern Marianas to Easter Island). Note the vastness of distances between the islands. Ask the students what inferences (however tentative) they can suggest about Pacific Island areas on the basis of these map exercises.
3. Ask students individually or in groups to complete the retrieval chart for a particular Pacific Island area based on their research, prior knowledge, reading, viewing or films or videos, travel, or interviews with persons who have lived or travelled in the Pacific Island area. The completed charts should be posted for all to study. *Note:* Teachers may wish to add or delete information categories on the retrieval charts. A sample retrieval chart has been completed for the country of Vanuatu.
4. Ask students individually or in groups to study in some depth one or more island areas and report their findings to the class. In preparing their reports students should keep in mind that in Pacific cultures people relied on *oral* histories rather than written history.
5. After hearing the reports and concluding their own study of Pacific Island areas, ask students to prepare a brochure, poster, collage or other visual project to highlight some aspect of their study of Pacific Island areas.
6. Ask students to write several generalizations, however tentative, about Pacific Island areas. These generalizations should be saved for future discussion and elaboration or for comparisons when studying about other Pacific Rim areas.

Extending Activities beyond the Textbook and Classroom

1. Ask students to plan a journey to one of the Pacific Island areas. What would they expect to find? What would they do when they are in the island areas? What items would they need to bring with them? How is life in the Pacific Island areas similar to or different from life in their local community? How far are the various Pacific Island areas from the students' home town or capital city?
2. Many anthropologists believe that the Pacific Islands were first settled by migration from Southeast Asia. However, Norwegian Thor Heyerdahl formulated an alternative theory. He believed that the Pacific Islands were settled from South America. In 1947, in a small balsa-log raft with sails, Heyerdahl set out to prove his theory. Read about this theory and the voyage of the *Kon-Tiki*. Which theory is most likely to be accepted and why? What evidence is there to support one theory over the other? Debate the issue with several classmates.
3. Ask students to keep an eye on the news (print and TV) and report any information related to news about or from any of the Pacific Island areas. It is likely that topics such as the following may be reported: dependency; economic development; nuclear testing; environmental issues; education, regionalism; United Nations and the Pacific Trust Territories; transmission of information; elections; indigenous cultures, etc.

Selected References

Europa year book: A world survey (1988). 2 volumes. London: Europa Publications. (Provides detailed information on political, economic and commercial institutions of the world.)

International year book and statesmen's who's who (1988). East Grinstead, West Sussex: Thomas Skinner Directories. (Includes information highlighting basic country information.)

Ridgell, Reilly (1988). *Pacific nations and territories – The islands of Micronesia, Melanesia and Polynesia*. Honolulu, Hawaii: Bess Press.

Statesman's year-book, 1988-89 (1988). New York: St Martin's Press. (Found in most school and public libraries; provides statistical and historical information concerning the states of the world.)

Wesley, Smith (1988). Unity and diversity in the Pacific islands, *Social Education*, 54: 3, March.

World fact book (1988). Washington, D.C.: Central Intelligence Agency. (Includes information on geography, people, government, economy, communication and defense forces; also has current political maps of world areas.)

Maps

Pacific Rim Map (3 1/2 by 2 1/2) by World Eagle Publications, 1986, is useful.

United States Government Pacific Area Map (1:21,000,000) Document No. PREX 3.10/4: p 12/1986 is rather simplistic but also useful for these lessons.

United Nations Map of Pacific Area, Number 2295, April 1979, is also useful in teaching about this geographic region.

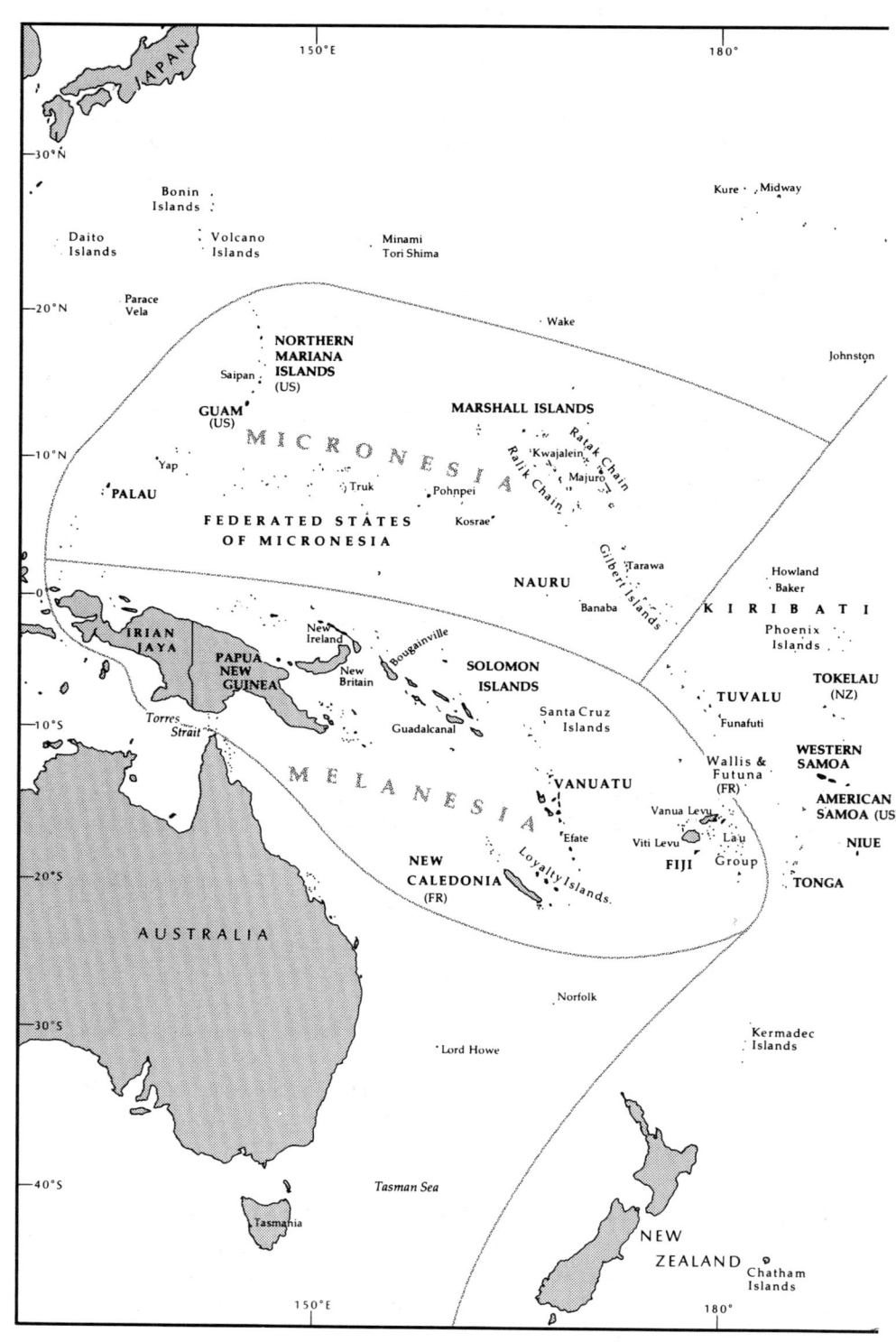

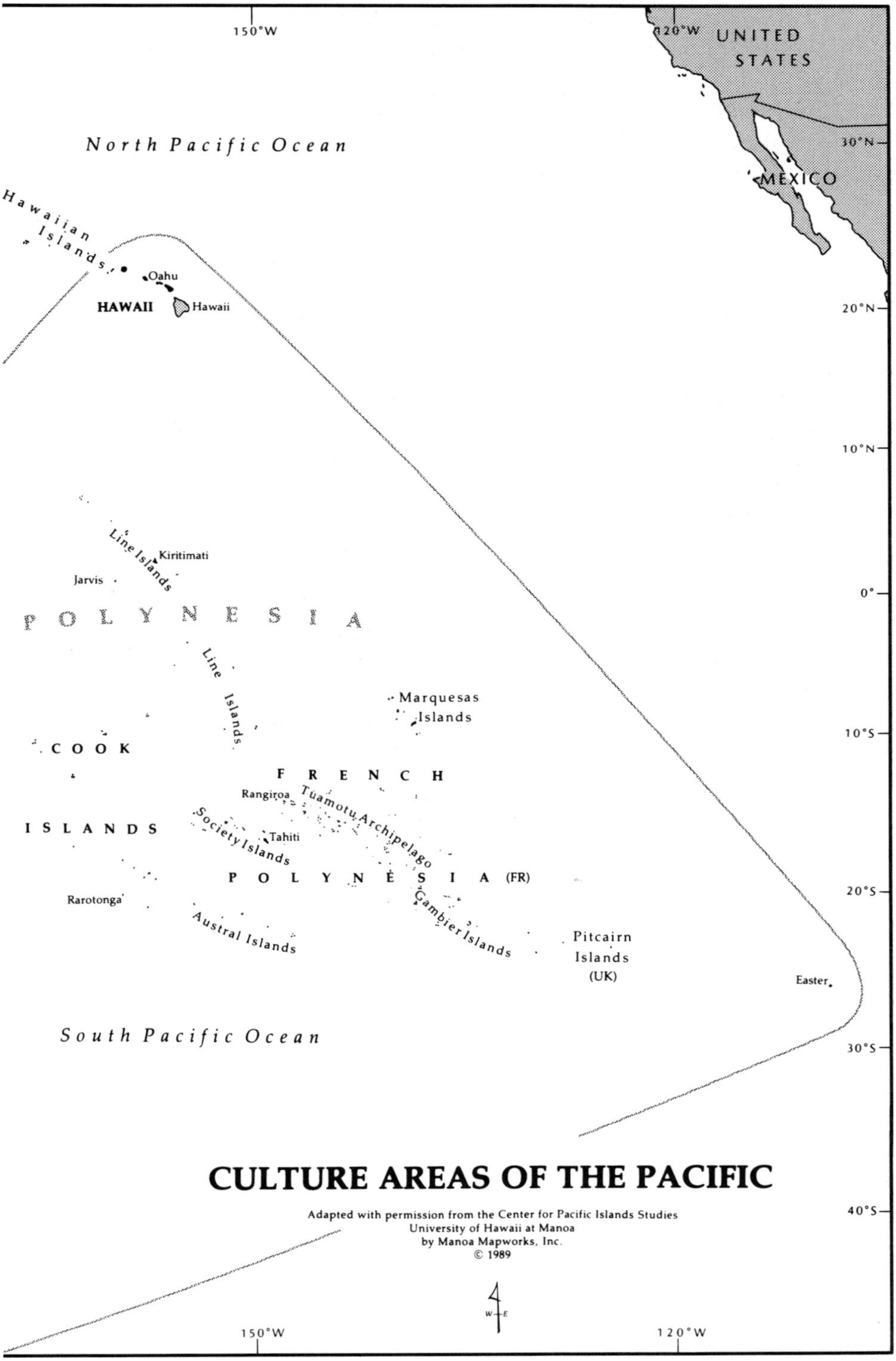

150°W

North Pacific Ocean

120°W UNITED
STATES

MEXICO

30°N

Hawaiian Islands
• Oahu
HAWAII ◊ Hawaii

20°N

10°N

Line Islands
• Kiritimati
Jarvis •

0°

P O L Y N E S I A

Line Islands

• Marquesas
  • Islands

10°S

•• COOK

•

ISLANDS

F R E N C H
Rangiroa • Tuamotu Archipelago
Society Islands
• Tahiti

P O L Y N E S I A (FR)

Rarotonga •

Gambier Islands

Austral Islands

• Pitcairn
  Islands
  (UK)

20°S

Easter •

South Pacific Ocean

30°S

CULTURE AREAS OF THE PACIFIC

Adapted with permission from the Center for Pacific Islands Studies
University of Hawaii at Manoa
by Manoa Mapworks, Inc.
© 1989

40°S

150°W

120°W

Appendix A: Pacific Island Area Retrieval Chart:
Island Area: ....(Name)

Complete the information requested in this chart as far as possible.

Geography	People
Land area	Population
Disputed territory/boundaries	Ethnic divisions
Climate	Religion
Terrain	Language(s)
Natural resources	Life expectancy
Land use	Literacy
Environment	Education
	Labor force
	Cultural group
Government	**Economy**
Type	Gross National Product or/
Capital	Gross Domestic Product
Independence	Agriculture
Legal system	Industry
Leaders	Exports
Suffrage	Imports
Elections	Trade partners
	Monetary system
Communications	**Defense Forces**
Highways	Military branches
Ports	Military power
Railroads	Military budget
Telecommunications	
Other interesting information about	....

Appendix B: Pacific Island Area Retrieval Chart: Island Area: *Vanuatu*

Complete the information requested in this chart as far as possible.

Geography	People
Land area: 14,760 km²	*Populations:* 155,000 approximately
Disputed territory/boundaries: NA	*Ethnic divisions:* 94% indigenous
Natural resources: Manganese; hardwood forests; fish	*Religion:* Mostly nominal Christians
Terrain: Volcanic mountains, narrow coastal plains	*Language(s):* English and French (official); pidgin (Bislama or Bichelama)
Land use: 1% arable; 5% crops; 2% pastures/meadows/ 1% forest; 91% other	*Life expectancy:* 55 years
	Literacy: Estimated 10-20%
Environment: Cyclones; volcanism causes minor earthquakes; over 80 islands	*Education:* Nearly 300 schools; 27,000 students
	Labor force: Primarily agriculture
Climate: Tropical; moderated by southeast tradewinds	*Culture group:* Melanesian
Government	**Economy**
Type: Republic	*Gross National Product or/*
Capital: Port Vila	*Gross Domestic Product:* $580 per capita
Independence: 30 July 1980; formerly New Hebrides	*Agriculture:* Export crops of copra, cocoa, coffee and fish; subsistence crops of copra, taro, yams, coconuts, fruits and vegetables
Legal system: Unified, created from dual French and British systems	
Leaders: Prime Minister Walter Hadye	
Suffrage: Universal adult suffrage	*Industry:* Food/fish-freezing; forestry processing; and meat canning
	Exports: Copra; cocoa; meat; fish; timber
	Imports: Machines; food/beverages; basic manufactures; raw materials/ fuels; chemicals
	Trade partners: Netherlands; France, Japan; Australia; New Zealand; Fiji; Belgium
	Monetary system: Vatu; 103 vatu = US$1 as of March 1988
Communications	**Defense forces**
Highways: 240 km	*Miliary branches:* No military forces
Ports: Port Vila	*Miltary power:* Paramilitary force for internal and external security
Railroads: NA	
Telecommunications: 2 AM radio stations; 3000 telephones; 1 satellite ground station	*Miltary budget:* NA
Other information about Vanuatu:	

Margaret A. Laughlin and I. Grace Bell are Associate Professor of Education and Graduate Student respectively at the University of Wisconsin – Green Bay, WIS 54305, USA.

19

Brainstorming about China: An Introductory Activity

Marilou Madden
Douglas, Alaska, United States of America

Level: Grades 10-12
Time: 40-50 minutes

Introduction

This lesson uses the technique of free and unstructured brainstorming to introduce students to the study of the People's Republic of China. The brainstorming is done from memory, providing for the recall and reinforcement of whatever knowledge the students may have about China. It is designed to bring out as many aspects of China as possible. While this lesson is focused on China, the technique could be employed in the introduction of any new culture.

Objectives

- Students should be able to list six to ten words or phrases associated with mainland China.
- Students should be able to group words or phrases related to China in some logical manner.
- From these terms and phrases, students should be able to make two or three general statements about the People's Republic of China.

Materials

Easel papers

Procedures

1. *Brainstorming:* Ask students to list everything they think of when they hear the term 'China'. Encourage a rapid-fire pace of student response and allow 4 to 5 minutes. List all student responses on the chalkboard.
2. *Questioning:* Brainstorm what questions students have about China; life there for students, their age, or about the relations between men and women in China. Record their questions on a large piece of easel paper and post it on the classroom wall to refer to throughout the units of study.
3. *Categorizing:* Once the students have listed several associated words or phrases, have them arrange them into categories. This can be done by asking, 'Which of these words or phrases go together?' or 'Which of these terms seem to have something in common?'.
4. *Labeling:* After students have grouped the terms, ask them to come up with a label for each group. For example, students may come up with something like the following:

Food	People	Physical
Rice	Chairman Mao	Great Wall
Tea	Confucius	Yangtze River
Stir Fry	Deng Xiaoping	Bamboo
Fortune Cookie	Marco Polo	Pandas
Government	**Culture**	**Sports**
Communist	Beijing Opera	Table tennis
Communes	Chopsticks	Gymnastics
People's Liberation Army	Kites	*Wu Shu* (martial arts)
	Silk	

5. From the data on the chalkboard, have the students each write a short paper, not to exceed a single page, describing China.
6. Have the students share their papers by reading them aloud in small groups. Have each group choose one to be read to the entire class.

Note: Record the responses to the brainstorming session for use in the China Quiz lesson.

Source: This lesson is extracted from *Half the sky: The changing roles of men and women in the People's Republic of China and Alaska.* Developed by Alaska State Department of Education; funded by Title IV Sex Desegregation Technical Assistance Grant.

Marilou Madden is a private consultant in the area of international affairs and business. Her residential address is Box 616, Douglas, Alaska 99824, USA.

20

What's in a Name?

Elaine Magnusson
Seattle, Washington, United States of America

Level: Grades 4-7
Time: 2 or 3 periods

Objectives

Students will:
- Read, for information, about Chinese naming patterns.
- Translate information onto a data retrieval chart.
- Hypothesize about changes in Chinese culture as reflected in naming patterns.
- Increase their sense of self-worth by creating their own name stamp.

Materials

1. Student reading: 'Chinese Name Their Babies'.
2. 'Chinese Naming Patterns' chart.
3. Stamp worksheet.
4. Materials for making stamps: rubber erasers, dull knives or nails, red printing ink.

Procedure

Optional: Teachers may wish to have students complete charts for American naming patterns, drawing from the students' knowledge of their families. This would develop the concepts that names reflect a culture and that patterns change with time. It also enables the teacher to start with who the students are and then explore other patterns. Good resources include dictionaries and books of baby names.

Day 1
1. Have the students read 'Chinese Name Their Babies'.
2. Have them complete the data retrieval chart.
3. Ask the class to share answers and develop hypotheses about reasons for changes by raising the following kinds of questions:
    (a) Is the family still important to contemporary Chinese: Support your answer.
    (b) Why do you think given names no longer describe political enthusiasm?
    (c) What can you tell about the status of women at various times?
    (d) Do you think the one-child family will affect naming patterns? How?
    (e) Titles often identify a person's status. What determines status in China in each time period?

Day 2
1. Explain that Chinese name stamps are used by individuals on important documents. This is in addition to the written signature and adds importance. Artists may own several stamps which are used to sign their work. One stamp may name the studio where the work is done and another may have the characters for the artist's professional name. The stamp is made of soapstone or other substances, including jade, wood and iron, and no two are exactly alike.
2. Have students experiment with designs for their names in empty spaces on the worksheet. Suggest initials, fancy scripts or pictographs.
3. When they have designs that please them, have them draw the design on the flat side of a rubber eraser. Remind them that the image will be reversed when it is printed.
4. Using a dull knife or nail, they should then cut away the area around the design so that the design stands out.
5. Then they should ink the stamps by pressing into stamp pads, and finally stamp the design on the paper.

Optional: An easier method of making stamps is to press the design into squares of styrofoam with a pencil.

Student Reading

Chinese Name Their Babies

The People's Republic of China, established in 1949, sought to eliminate many of the traditional ways in China in order to improve Chinese life. Not only government, but also housing, health and education changed. Even the choice of infants' names changed.

In traditional China, children's names were usually chosen by their grandparents or by taking the next name on the family list of names. The family name was written first and although the given name might be written with two characters, it was considered one name. If the child was a girl, the name might be *Jingxian*, which means Quiet and Virtuous. A boy might be named Courage. Often all children in one generation (brothers, cousins, sisters) were given names with one syllable in common, such as *Shushen, Shulin* and *Shugang*. *Shu* means tree in each name. *Shen* means forest, *lin* means grove, and *gang* means strong or tough.

When a woman married, she took her husband's name and was no longer called her childhood name. A girl whose family name was Lei who married a man named Gao, was called Gao Lei Shi which means wife of Gao Lei. Children were given their father's family name. Men were addressed as *xiansheng* (meaning elder born). Married women were addressed as *taitai* (great one) and unmarried women were addressed as *xiaojie* (little miss).

In the period immediately after the revolution, parents began to choose their child's name themselves. The family name was written first and two-syllable given names were still common. Names which honored the revolution were popular – *Hong* (red), *Weidong* (protect the party) or *Aimin* (love the people). It was no longer easy to separate girls' and boys' names by meaning. Generational names were less common as naming from family lists became less common. When a woman married, she kept her given name and her own family's name. Children usually were given their father's name. Both men and women were addressed as *tongzhi* (comrade). *Xiao* (little) was put before the surname of someone younger and *lao* (old) was added as a sign of respect to a senior.

Many of the changes mentioned in the previous paragraph are still true, but in the last decade some additional changes have occurred. Given names are now usually one syllable and revolutionary themes are not as popular. Names may reflect the place of birth, or the season, or the hopes of the parents. Every name may mean several things. The name *Ning* can be translated as frozen, staring, stable, smooth or winter. Born in winter, one baby Ning's name reflects both the season and the parents' desire for stability. *Hua*, meaning tree or China, was named after trees on the hillside behind his place of birth. Sometimes children may be given their mother's family name if there are no uncles with children to carry on the name.

Nowadays, colleagues and neighbors add *xiao* or *lao* to a person's family name. When they are being more formal, they use a full name, a job title and family name, or a family name followed by *tongzhi*.

Every culture has certain patterns concerning names and therefore the use of names and titles may differ. As changes occur in a culture, the naming patterns often change. Such is the situation in China. The practice of writing the family name first is one of the few traditional patterns still honored by contemporary parents in China.

Chinese Naming Patterns

Name _____

	Traditional (pre-1949)	Revolutionary (1949-1970s)	Contemporary (1980s)
1. Which name is written first?			
2. Who chooses a child's given name? Are there generational names?			
3. Give examples of what given names mean.			
4. Is it possible to tell if a person is male or female from the name alone?			
5. Whose family name does a child have?			
6. What family name does a child have?			
7. What forms of address are used?			

Elaine Magnusson is a global education consultant and a former elementary teacher. Her address is 11532 23rd NE, Seattle, Washington 98125, USA.

21
Comparing the Status of Women in Pacific Nations Today

Gayle Y. Thieman
Fairbanks North Star Borough School District,
Alaska, United States of America

Level: Middle school and senior high school
Time: 1-4 class periods (depending on student research and extension activities)

Introduction

As the United Nations Decade for Women draws to a close there is a need to assess the progress made by women in achieving equality. The focus of this lesson is on the political, economic and social status of women in Pacific nations.

Objectives

Students will use reference materials to research and compare the status of women in selected countries and develop a presentation of their findings.

Materials

Student Handout: 'Sample Statistics on Women's Status in Selected Pacific Nations'; reference materials such as encyclopedias and world atlas.

Procedures

1. Introduce the unit by asking students to define the Pacific region and to locate Pacific countries on a world map.
2. Use the Student Handout to teach students how to analyse statistics. Explain the source of these statistics and the fact that they will be *obsolete* within a few years, necessitating an updated chart.
   Compare the percentage of females in secondary school to the literacy

rate for men and women in each country. In Australia 88 percent of the females attend secondary school, and the literacy rate for men and women is the same (100 percent). Ask students to analyse the statistics for Canada, Japan, the USA and the USSR. (They will discover that equal literacy rates for men and women is associated with countries in which over 90 percent of males are in secondary school.)

Then ask students to analyse the statistics for China, Indonesia, Mexico and Peru. (They will discover that in countries with the lowest percentage of females in secondary schools (22 percent in Indonesia to 52 percent in Peru) the gap in literacy rates for men and women is much greater (e.g. Indonesia with 69 percent male literacy to 45 percent female literacy and Peru with 83 percent male literacy to 62 percent female literacy.)

3. Divide the class into five research groups. Each group will study the countries within a geographic area of the Pacific region to determine the status of women in those countries. Sample research groups: Canada and the United States; Mexico; Nicaragua and Peru; China and the Soviet Union; Japan and South Korea; Australia, Indonesia and the Philippines.
4. Ask students to rank countries according to the average number of children per mother, the percentage of women who use contraceptives, and the percentage of women in the labor force. Compare per capita GNP with the literacy rate and life expectancy for each country. Ask students to rank the countries according to population per square mile and consider the effect population density has on quality of life for families. Rank countries according to per capita GNP and consider the effect income has on quality of life for families.
5. Find out the historic significance of the date of women's suffrage for each country. Was women's suffrage the result of a change in the country's laws, such as a constitutional amendment, or associated with a national independence movement?

Debriefing

Student groups present their research findings to the entire class. Involve students in a discussion of the factors which affect the status of women, such as government policies regarding access to health care and educational and occupational opportunities; religious and cultural values; geographic location; and economic development of the country.

Extension Activities

1. Assign each group of students to additional research questions and sources of information. Allow time for research in the libraries and for writing letters. Help students develop telephone skills to assist them in telephoning for appointments or interviews with local resource people.
2. Suggest additional research topics such as these:

(a) Find out the percentage of women involved in national government positions in the administrative, legislative and judicial branches.
(b) Make a chart of the percentages of women involved in full- or part-time work, agriculture, child care, manufacturing, clerical, management, technical, artistic, and professional occupations in each country.
(c) Compare the income of males and females in each country.
(d) Compare the infant mortality rate and the maternal mortality rate of each country.
(e) From other data available on GNP, literacy, education, etc., suggest reasons for the health status of mothers and young children in each country.
3. Help students develop interview questions and invite community resource people to participate in a discussion of women's rights in different countries.
4. Assist students in investigating changes needed in the local community to improve the status of women, such as increased child care, protection against domestic violence, and education and job-training for the unemployed. Encourage students to develop their citizenship skills by sharing their research with local decision-makers.

Suggested References for Additional Research

1. Morgan, Robin (Ed.) (1984). *Sisterhood is global: The international women's movement anthology.* New York: Anchor Press.
2. United Nations Commission on the Status of Women. Reports on the UN Decade for Women.
3. Publications by the United Nations Economic and Social Commission for Asia and the Pacific, UNESCO, UNICEF, etc.
4. Shah, Nasra (1985). *Women of the world: Asia and the Pacific.* Washington, D.C.: US Department of Commerce, Bureau of the Census.
5. Chaney, Elsa (1984). *Women of the world: Latin America and the Caribbean.* Washington, D.C.: US Department of Commerce, Bureau of the Census.

Student Handout:
Sample Statistics on Women's Status in Selected Pacific Nations

Nation	Popul.[2] per sq. mi.	GNP per capita	Literacy[3] male	Literacy[3] female	Life[1] expectancy
Australia	6	11 900	100	100	76
Canada	7	14 100	100	100	76
China	288	300	86	63	66
Indonesia	238	500	69	45	58
Japan	851	12 850	99	99	77
Korea, S.	1 107	2 370	94	81	67
Mexico	108	1 850	88	80	67
Nicaragua	70	790	58	57	61
Philippines	531	570	84	81	65
Peru	42	1 130	83	62	60
USSR	32	7 400	99	99	69
USA	69	17 500	99	99	75

Nation	# children[3] per mother	% women[3] using contraception	% women[3] in labor force	% females[3] in sec. education	Year women's[3] suffrage granted
Australia	2.1	72	48	88	1902
Canada	1.8	68	56	90	1920
China	2.3	70	55	27	1947
Indonesia	4.8	26	39	22	1945
Japan	1.9	65	54	92	1945
Korea, S.	3.5	50	48	80	1946
Mexico	5.4	40	21	49	1953
Nicaragua	6.3	9	25	47	1955
Philippines	4.6	37	53	68	1937
Peru	5.4	31	26	52	1965
USSR	2.4	NA	58	121	1917
USA	1.8	79	56	95	1920

[1]*Junior Scholastic* (1988), vol. 91, no. 2, 23 September, pp. 19-24.
[2]Phillips, Douglas, and Levi, Steven (1988). *The Pacific Rim region: Emerging giant.* Hillside, N.J.: Enslow Publishers.
[3]Seager, Joni, and Olson, Ann (1986). *Women in the world atlas.* New York: Pluto Press Ltd, Touchstone Books, Simon and Schuster Inc.

Gale Y. Thieman is a social studies teacher in the Fairbanks North Star Borough School District, Fairbanks, Alaska 99707, USA.

22

Visual Images of the Pacific Rim

Virginia S. Wilson and *James A. Little*
North Carolina School of Science and Mathematics,
United States of America

Level: Middle school and senior high school
Time: 20 minutes in a series of class periods

Introduction

In this world of television, students have become passive viewers rather than critical observers. Exercises, such as the one described below, help to convey content and clear up misconceptions about the Pacific Rim. They also have the spill-over effect of teaching students to view visual images critically. Hopefully, the skills will be transferred to the observation of visual images in general.

Visual images of countries and peoples of the Pacific Rim can provide an excellent context for discussion of geography, agriculture, urbanization, industrialization, culture, dress, foods, recreation, the arts and ethnicity. If the images are grouped by time periods and/or by country, much about the history of a nation or the nations of the Pacific Rim will become evident to the viewer.

Objectives

Students will be able to:
- view visual images critically;
- make observations and explain them;
- make generalizations from visual information;
- form hypotheses about the nature of a given nation or nations;
- compare and contrast countries and peoples of the Pacific Rim.

Materials

Collect pictures from magazines, travel brochures, family trips and/or textbooks which portray some specific area of life in a nation of the Pacific Rim. If possible, slides should be made from the pictures; however, check for any copyright restrictions on the reproduction of pictures.

Procedure

Group the accumulated slides or pictures in categories. The following categories are suggested:

Coastal Geography	Interior Geography
River Scenes	Transportation Systems
Urban Street Scenes	Agricultural Sites
Industrial Sites	Faces/Groups of People
Art/Architecture	Housing Styles
Monuments/Historic Buildings	Sacred Edifices
Foods	Dress
Musical Instruments	Sports

Within each group re-sort the visual images into an order. Again, the following systems of order are offered as suggestions:

- Historical Periods/Chronological
- Given Countries or Sections of Countries
- Geographical Themes – such as location, place, human/environment interaction, movement, or region.

For example, in order to help students utilize a geographic approach, they could first be presented with five fundamental themes in geography outlined in *Guidelines for Geographic Education: Elementary and Secondary Schools* (Committee on Geographic Education, 1984):

1. *Location* (Absolute and Relative): Location answers the basic question: 'Where'?. Absolute and relative location are two ways of describing the Earth's physical and cultural resources.
2. *Place* (Physical and Human Characteristics): All places on Earth have special features that distinguish them from other places. Geographers usually describe places by their physical and human characteristics.
3. *Human/Environment Interaction* (Relationships within Places): Peoples interact with their environments and change them in different ways.
4. *Movement* (Mobility of People, Goods and Ideas): People everywhere interact. They travel from place to place, communicate, and depend upon other people in distant places for products, ideas and information.
5. *Regions* (How They Form and Change): Regions are areas on the surface of the Earth that are defined by certain unifying characteristics. These features may be physical or they may be human.

The students could then order the slides using these themes.

Prior to presenting any category or categories of visual images, students should be asked to record their preconceived notions of what they are about to see.

If the images are on slides, prepare a slide carousel to show the images in a sequence. Present the images to the class on the screen and have students write a caption or title for each visual image.

After screening the images, have groups of students compile their individual captions or titles and decide on one for each image. The group should be prepared to explain the reasons for this choice.

The class should then discuss each group's caption and/or title and make some generalizations about the images presented. Students could indicate what other images might have been helpful in preparing the generalizations.

This assignment can be repeated with another set of images focusing on a different category.

Alternative Procedure

If slides are not available and the images are in hard-copy form, the teacher should again arrange the images into categories. At that point each image should be numbered and placed in a folder clearly marked with the appropriate category name.

The folders should be passed from group to group with each group responsible for making its own list of captions and titles and then the same group and class procedures should be followed as with the slide presentation.

In this format, it may be possible to use an opaque projector to project the images on a larger screen for the entire class to view.

Debriefing

After the class has written a series of generalizations for one or several groups of images, the discussion of the class should focus on the validity of the generalizations. At this point, their post-viewing generalizations should be compared and contrasted with their pre-viewing ideas. The students should note which initial ideas were confirmed by the visual images and which ones appeared to be erroneous. In order to test the validity of their ideas, the students need to take both the pre- and post-viewing lists and check them against the information in available classroom and library resources.

Concluding Activity

At the end of a given unit on a Pacific Rim nation, students, after viewing different categories of visual images, should combine these generalizations into an overall statement. If over a period of time this is done for several Pacific Rim countries, students should be able to contrast and compare different aspects of the individual countries.

Enhancing Activity

Students who wish to examine the images further might be provided the opportunity to develop a slide-tape series on a particular group of images for use in another social studies class.

Students might also study the source of the images. Potential questions for consideration might be: What is the bias of the source? What is the intended audience? What is the projected impact of the image on the audience? In what ways could the image be more effective?

Uses of visual images are particularly valuable when studying Pacific Rim nations which are not only unfamiliar but also diverse. Here is an instance where a picture is truly worth a thousand words.

Virginia S. Wilson and James A. Little teach at the North Carolina School of Science and Mathematics, PO Box 2418, Durham, NC 27715, USA.

23

Creating a Product for the Pacific Rim Market

Tuckie Yirchott
Stanford University, United States of America

Level: Grades 4-12
Time: 2 or 3 class periods

Introduction

In this activity, groups will collect economic and geographic information on various Pacific Rim nations which will form the basis for developing a marketable product within the Pacific Rim. Each group will use an almanac or other general resource to validate sources of production materials needed, determine a production system, and design a marketing technique appropriate for their targeted export location.

Objectives

- Learn to use the *World Almanac and Book of Facts* for obtaining basic information;
- Develop an understanding of economic concepts by creating, producing and marketing a product;
- Demonstrate map skills by tracing international links of a product;
- Recognize the economic connections among Pacific Rim countries;
- Make a class presentation illustrating the group project.

Materials

World Almanac (1 copy per group)   Felt pens (2 colors)
Student handout (directions)   Newsprint per group
World map   Scissors
Colored paper   Gluestick
Transparent maps of 6 Pacific Rim countries (include countries from Asia, Pacific Islands, Latin America and North America)

Procedure

1. Divide the class into groups by using 8 1/2 by 11 color-coded maps of six countries *Cut into 6 pieces each.* Hand each student a piece as he or she enters the room. Students must match their piece with other pieces of the same country and form a group with those students, e.g. South Korea pieces are blue, China pieces are green, etc. Students will research this country for the remainder of the activity. Each group member should have a responsibility, such as facilitator, recorder, announcer, graphic artist, market analyst and researcher.
2. Before the group activity begins, the teacher will model the expected process, using a pencil as a sample product. Vocabulary of economic terms should be reviewed: *natural resources, labor, capital, market share, export and import.*
3. Distribute the student handout 'A Marketing Plan' and read it as a class to be sure instructions are understood.
4. At the conclusion of the activity, the students will have a visual reminder of the interconnectedness of Pacific nations through international trade.

Appendix: Student Handout

A MARKETING PLAN FOR .... (product) IN .... (country)

Our company has begun a new marketing strategy to develop closer ties with other Pacific Rim nations. You want to develop a marketable product within the Pacific Rim. Apart from using your own country's resources, you will need to *import at least one resource* from another Pacific Rim country. Then you will have to select the Pacific Rim countries to which you will market your product.

Use the *World Almanac* for information on: resources in your country, other nations from which you can acquire needed resources, nations where your product may be marketed, and educational level of the population.

PART 1 *Planning*

Assign individual responsibilities within your group

    Recorder   ....
    Announcer   ....
    Researcher(s)   ....
    Market Analyst ....
    Graphic Artist   ....

PART II *Market Research*

Answer all of the following questions:
- What is your product?
- What resources do you need, and where will you get them?
  – Capital
  – Natural

- Labor
- Technology
- What export market are you targeting?
- How will you advertise, market and distribute your product? Consider the language and customs of your target market.

What might be the impact of this product on your own country, and on the target country or countries?

PART III *Noting the Connections*

On your transparent map, illustrate the interconnectedness by tracing your import routes in *blue* and export routes in *red*.

PART IV *Product Design and Promotion*

Use any materials given to you to illustrate, construct or advertise your product. Create a two-minute 'commercial' which you present to the class.

PART V *Analysis*

Share with the class your decisions about resources, production and marketing. What factors determined your product choice and method of advertising? Did language or geography figure in your choice of countries to market your product?

Source: This lesson was developed by Toni Bowman, Mary Connestra, Jan Grodeon, Carol Lerner, Alice Lucas, Bev Maul, Kim McConnell, Jack Rauch and Doreen Schoenberg at the 1988 Bay Area Global Education Program Institute's 'Economics in an International Context' workshop. Editing was done by Lia Turk.

Tuckie Yirchott works at the Institute for International Studies, Stanford University, Stanford, California 94305, USA.

24

There's Someone at the Door!

Susan Soux
Canadian Red Cross Society, Canada

Level: This activity[1] is adaptable to almost any age group.
Time: Approximately one class period

Introduction

Why do we teach global education? Need we really concern ourselves with the lives and problems of people in distant parts of the world, such as the Asia-Pacific region?

The world today is very different from what it once was. Means of travel are rapid and efficient. People easily move from one hemisphere to another within a matter of hours. With international travel and trade many of us now lead transient lives. Few people today live and die in the same community into which they were born without exposure to the external world, as they did in the past. The time when we lived in small, virtually independent and self-sufficient communities has passed. Subsistence farmers and fishermen are rapidly decreasing in numbers as they become incorporated into the global economy. We have become an interdependent world – one wherein our lifestyles, our needs (as we interpret them) and desires affect the lives of people in far corners of the globe. One need only enter a grocery market to see that the items purchased on a weekly shopping list include sugar from the West Indies, coffee from South America, tea from China, spices from India, and fruit from New Zealand.

The problem that emerges from this global system is the inequality in access to, and control over, the world's resources. It is the few in the world that significantly direct the world's economy and benefit from the bounty of the planet. The majority of the people work to support the desires of the few, and often to the detriment of themselves.

But, how long can the planet survive when so many of its inhabitants are existing at, or below poverty level? How long can the environment withstand the abuse of those unwilling to forgo any of the comforts they have become accustomed to, and the overuse perpetrated by those trying to eke out a living on the only lands available to them – the marginal lands that are rapidly becoming deforested and desertified?

These are some of the issues facing us today, these are the issues that should no longer be ignored, these are the issues addressed under the rubric of global education. The following activity addresses the questions of 'Need we bother?' and 'If we do, what is the best way to help?'.

Objectives

- To examine concepts of charity, short-term relief and development aid, as they relate to attitudes of social responsibility, moral obligation and self-preservation.
- To examine concepts of dependence, independence and interdependence at a global level.

Procedure

– Divide participants into small groups, each group to represent a 'family'.
– Explain that they will be presented with specific scenarios that they must respond to as a family.
– Ask them to record their response to the scenarios and particularly the reasoning behind the decisions which are made. They will then be asked to report their decisions and reasons for the decisions to the group at large.
– Large-group discussion will follow the sequence of scenarios.

Scenarios to be presented

1. A starving man comes to your door and asks for some food. He's broke and wants to get back to his family. He only needs one meal to make it home.
   – What do you do?
2. A starving man, his wife and three children come to your door and ask for food and a place to stay for a few days.
   – What do you do?
3. The family has stayed much longer than they said they would, due to circumstances beyond anyone's control. They have to set up a sort of tent in the backyard. Your resources to provide for them, while not yet exhausted, are reaching a limit. Supporting the family costs $100 per week and you have only $300 left in the bank.
   – What do you do?
4. Two more families show up in much the same condition. They, too, are unable to care for themselves and request your help.
   – What do you do?

5. Your backyard is now full of tents, laundry and noisy children. The health inspector says there is danger of disease. Some of the people have dug up your lawn and planted a large garden, an indication that they expect to be around for harvest time at least. Your neighbors are complaining both to you and the authorities. No government assistance is available.

   It is clearly time to think about some solutions to this situation. Work up a plan to resolve these problems, and then go on to the last scenario.

6. Imagine that for a second that we could compress the world's population into a single village of 100 persons. In a very rough sense, only six of these 100 persons would be from North America. (By comparison nearly 60 would be from the Asia-Pacific region.) These six people would have about half of the town's material resources. In fact, of these six North Americans, the richest two would have nearly 25 percent of the village's total material resources. Would the non-North Americans in the village continue to allow this large a percentage of their resources to go to the six North Americans? How willing would the six be to share their resources with the other 94 residents of the village? How would the other 94 residents persuade the six to share these resources? Would they consider force?

Discussion

- Do we have a social responsibility or moral obligation to help others? (*Probe:* Does this mean 'all' others or just 'some' others?)
- Would it make a difference to the families of the needy people if they were (a) poor members of their community whose housing complex had burned down, (b) a refugee group newly arrived in their community, (c) cousins who were down and out?
- Some people refuse to help right from the beginning. What could happen if all help is refused to people without money or work? An outbreak of thievery, violence? Can helping those in need, in any way, secure your own future?
- What is the best way to help? Direct and continued charity can create dependence. Also one's ability to provide charity is usually exhaustible. Help to be self-sufficient will prevent depletion of your own resources and will assist people to become respected and contributing members of the community.

Notes for the Discussion

Discussion of these scenarios leads the teacher into a difficult and complex area of human behavior and understanding. There is much suffering in the world. Some people are born to relative wealth, and others are born to live in poverty. When confronted with such realities, we must make sense of these happenings. Social psychologists have hypothesized that people find the suffering of innocent people – those who have done nothing to bring about their own suffering – unacceptable. If we accept that innocent people can suffer, then we too can suffer without cause. To defend ourselves from this unattractive possibility, we often engage in defensive psychological acts. On the one hand, we may look for causality in actions by which the sufferers may have brought about their own suffering: 'As ye sow, so shall you reap'. On the other hand, if we cannot attribute the cause of others' suffering to their actions, we may very well attribute it to their character: they are just naturally lazy, no good. There is nothing you can do for them'. This is simply a way of coping with unpleasant, disturbing or threatening events we encounter.

By essentially blaming unpleasant events on the victim, either through the fault of their actions or their character, our belief in a 'just world', a world in which we, in essence, get our due, can be maintained. '. . . people will develop ways of coping with disturbing or threatening events, and, if these events are common experiences, then it is quite natural for people to develop a consensus, or shared solutions which are given the status of reality within the social unit. It follows also that if these social devices are at all functional, if they do the job of reducing or preventing the threat, then they will probably be retained and transmitted to succeeding generations'.[2]

In discussion of these scenarios which deal with the unpleasant realities of poverty and unequal distribution of resources, some, if not most, students (like adults) will undoubtedly tap into 'solutions' which reduce the threat of the situation by 'blaming the victim', so to speak. The reasons that lead people to view victims in a negative light are complex and not completely understood. But social psychologists report that the issue of 'identification' is the place to start: '. . . we would not react negatively toward victims if we identified with them. On the contrary, we would feel compassionate, and try to come to their aid. Conceivably, we might be somewhat indifferent with respect to the fate of someone with whom we felt no sense of identification whatsoever. As for condemning victims, such condemnation, if it ever did occur, would certainly reflect a failure to identify with them'.[3]

In encountering the type of pat explanations that focus on the victims of poverty as the causal agents of their suffering, the teacher may wish to alter this activity by utilizing role plays or simulations in which at least some students are asked to view the same scenarios from the perspective of the poverty-stricken family. This will complicate the 'identification' issue for the students and force them to examine their assumptions about the causes of poverty.

Concluding Activity

Now, extrapolate from these scenarios to a developing country in the Asia-Pacific region, perhaps one that is currently in the news because of a 'crisis'. For example, you could select a natural disaster such as flooding in Bangladesh, or human-generated crises, such as the resolution of the war in Cambodia. Is the resolution of these problems any different if they are on your doorstep, or if they are very distant from you? Can the issues facing your family and community be equated to issues of your country and a poor developing nation? How are they the same? How are they different? Would global solutions to such issues differ from local solutions?

Notes

[1] This activity has been adapted from 'There's a man at the door!' in David Pardoe, *Tomorrow's world*, Vancouver: Canadian Red Cross Society, 1982, pp. 12-13.

[2] Melvin J. Lerner. *The belief in a just world: A fundamental delusion.* New York: Plenam Press, 1980, p. viii.

[3] Lerner, p. 90.

Susan Soux is the Education Coordinator for the Canadian Red Cross Society, BC-Yukon Division, 4750 Oak Street, Vancouver, BC, Canada V6H 2N9.

Commentary on Section Three

Rick Beardsley
British Columbia Teachers' Federation, Canada

The Context of Practice: Asia and Pacific Studies

The ten lessons presented in this section, although written to stand alone, must be considered within a complex context of practice. Each lesson must be considered to be a small part of a much greater whole. A single lesson cannot hope to provide depth of understanding or breadth of knowledge of any subject matter. But what single lesson plans can provide are exemplars for direction: direction in pedagogy and direction in the organization of knowledge.

The lessons were selected to represent a range of approaches to the study of Asia and the Pacific. In terms of pedagogy all of the lessons have the potential, some more explicit than others, for cooperative learning techniques. Recognized as a powerful pedagogy, cooperative learning focuses learning as a group, gives a sense of group purpose, ensures a degree of mutual understanding within the group, and provides for mutual understanding between groups within a single class. Given the multicultural nature of our classrooms there is sure to be a variety of perspectives in many classes, some Asian and some Hispanic. Thus cooperative pedagogy allows teachers and students to come to terms with their own perspective and the perspectives of others, all of which may contribute to understanding Asia and the Pacific.

Another pedagogy found in most of the lessons is one which links students' everyday knowledge to the formal knowledge of the subject of inquiry. A common technique is to have students brainstorm collectively their knowledge, images and attitudes as a way of introducing a unit of study. This technique immediately brings personal meaning to the unit and allows for the organization of subsequent lessons to be based on students' everyday perceptions. As a process of validation students check their views against information and views somewhat different from their own. When confronted with the differences students are provided the opportunity to rethink and reconceptualize their view of the world, leading to greater understanding. Examples of this technique can be found in 'Living in Japan', 'Mental Maps', and 'Brainstorming about China'.

While there are common elements running through the pedagogy of the lessons there are significant differences in how the content is viewed and organized. Some lessons reflect the traditional disciplines, particularly geography and to some degree economics and business education. Often the goal is to have students become familiar with the concepts of the discipline and to apply them to knowledge about Asia and the Pacific. While traditional in their organization of knowledge it is not always safe to assume a traditional pedagogy. Innovative pedagogical techniques are used to lead students to knowledge found in the traditional disciplines. Examples are found in 'Mental Maps of the Pacific', 'The *Yin* and *Yang* of the Asia-Pacific Region', and 'Visual Images of the Pacific Rim'.

Issues are the focal points of other lessons. While perhaps relying on traditional sources of information these lessons call on students to view the world through a sense of social responsibility. In doing so such lessons also cause students to critically examine features of their own society. This is particularly true in two lessons: 'Comparing the Status of Women in Pacific Nations Today' and 'There's Someone at the Door!'.

Education Systems

Teachers create their lessons in a context much broader than what is suggested by the pedagogy and knowledge of the immediate unit of study. Teachers operate within education systems that respond to myriad pressures by offering an array of curricula. In a sense Asia and Pacific studies must compete for space within an already crowded agenda. Teachers may create Asia and Pacific studies programs in relative isolation but with the support of an empathetic school administrator, or, teachers working together may form a lobby group to pressure a school district to support such programs. Occasionally outside agencies, both public and private, fund curriculum projects in Asia and Pacific studies to act as catalysts in their jurisdictions. Less frequently a provincial, state or national government may mandate Asian and Pacific studies as instruments of government policy, usually to fulfil an economic mandate. Whatever the circumstance teachers mediate between various interests and pressures and teachers implement the programs in the classrooms. Asian and Pacific programs are found within the context of both centrally mandated and locally developed curricula with the underlying reasons ranging from economic instrumentality to social responsibility. Certainly this range is represented in the presentation of lessons in this book.

Values

It is also the case that teachers create lessons within the context of their own values and understandings. Most teachers in North America and Australia have been raised and educated in systems that reflect and, indeed, promote Eurocentric views of the world. Many are now reconceptualizing the world in different terms. They are in the process of recognizing and valuing views of the world that originate outside of the realm of their education and, for many, experience. Some have been engaged in this process longer than others and this is reflected in the sample lessons. Some lessons represent the beginning of the process and rely on traditional disciplines to give us knowledge about Asia and the Pacific in familiar terms. Other lessons take a step further to help us achieve a deeper level of cultural understanding and with a sense of social responsibility. In either case the lessons are authentic attempts to help students know about and understand areas of Asia and the Pacific.

The sample lessons in this book should be looked upon with generous spirit. They are not meant to be whole units or courses, but rather they are snapshots of practice, knowledge and pedagogy. Not to be followed by rote, these lessons should inspire teachers to conceptualize how they might implement similar studies. Readers can take their own hints and apply them to their own situations.

Rick Beardsley is with the Professional Development Division, British Columbia Teachers' Federation, 2235 Burrard Street, Vancouver, BC, Canada V6J 3H9. He has taught secondary social studies and economics in the Richmond School District. He was planning coordinator for the 1988 international social studies conference in Vancouver.

Final Commentary

Kerry J. Kennedy
Donald C. Wilson
David L. Grossman

This book seeks to set an agenda for social studies education. It accepts that connections with the past, important though they have been in bringing us to where we are today, will not suffice as we head towards the twenty-first century. The European mindset that influenced Asia and the Pacific throughout the nineteenth century and much of the twentieth century no longer serves the needs and interests of Pacific peoples. A reorientation focuses attention on the region itself and the kind of relationships needed at a time of increasing interdependence. Social studies education can play a significant role in preparing young people to meet the challenges of the future.

The reasons for focusing on Asia and the Pacific have been highlighted throughout the book. As a region it is large, diverse and powerful. Nations which formerly looked to Europe for their most important connections must now look to each other. New trade connections are becoming indicators of what the future holds. Newly industrialized countries have experienced rapid growth and are benefiting greatly from the increased trade among Pacific nations. For countries such as Canada, the United States and Australia it means a shift in trade patterns from Europe to the Pacific. So significant is this shift seen to be that in the late 1980s the Australian Prime Minister actively promoted a regional trading block, which some referred to as a 'Pacific OECD'.

There is no doubt that the changes under way are significant for all peoples of the Pacific. Of equal importance, however, is the fact that it is being promoted by governments who value education. Educational reform and nation-building go hand in hand. Education is essentially a cultural activity and the curriculum of schools is the means by which the most significant aspects of the culture are made available to young people. Many of the articles in this book demonstrate that curriculum development is not simply a mental activity. It can be the foundation for cultural survival as in the case of Fiji, or provide an impetus for economic transformation as in the case of Canada and Australia, or be one means of leading to greater social equality as in the case of the Philippines or Malaysia. However reform is seen, the curriculum of schools has a fundamental role to play in shaping the Asia-Pacific region.

Building agendas for change assumes a linkage between national policies, curriculum development and classroom teaching. These efforts must be genuinely interdependent. Just as there is little use in having grand educational policies that never see the light of day in classrooms, there is little value in promoting classroom practices that do not communicate significant knowledge, powerful ideas and important skills.

Teaching about Asia and the Pacific calls for a pedagogy that addresses the complex and dynamic nature of the region. Articles highlight a range of teaching considerations: the importance of being gender sensitive; the value of cooperative learning; the advantage of fostering new images of the Pacific; and the need to adopt multiple perspectives in addressing developments and issues of the Pacific.

To be successful in times of rapid changes, classroom efforts must be complemented by government policies that encourage a global society. In order to foster interdependence, national governments need to establish connections among nation-states as well as partnerships with their own educational constituencies and business corporations to ensure their place in a dynamic Pacific community. And the sense of connectedness that is so central to the existence of Asia and the Pacific can only be sustained by an appreciation and understanding of the politically powerful and the culturally rich landscape. While the framework of reform is increasingly becoming economic and political, the essence of change remains cultural.

If educators are to participate in setting an agenda of change for the twenty-first century, they need to acknowledge the cultural diversity and the range of economic interests that make up the Pacific community. They need to view the community as one linked by common concerns, yet having continuing tensions which will be dealt with in terms of understanding and tolerance. And it is a community in which educators are not alone in defining the content of schooling. Today, other constituencies want to contribute to educational change for pragmatic and ideological reasons. Such conditions provide opportunities for educators to address questions of change in schooling with new images and metaphors. A new vision of the role of social studies in education must seek to accommodate diversity and change rather than impose traditional solutions that assume a static world. Setting such an agenda is not beyond possibility.